A VIEW FROM THE MOON

A VIEW
FROM THE
MOON

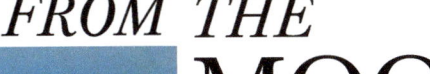

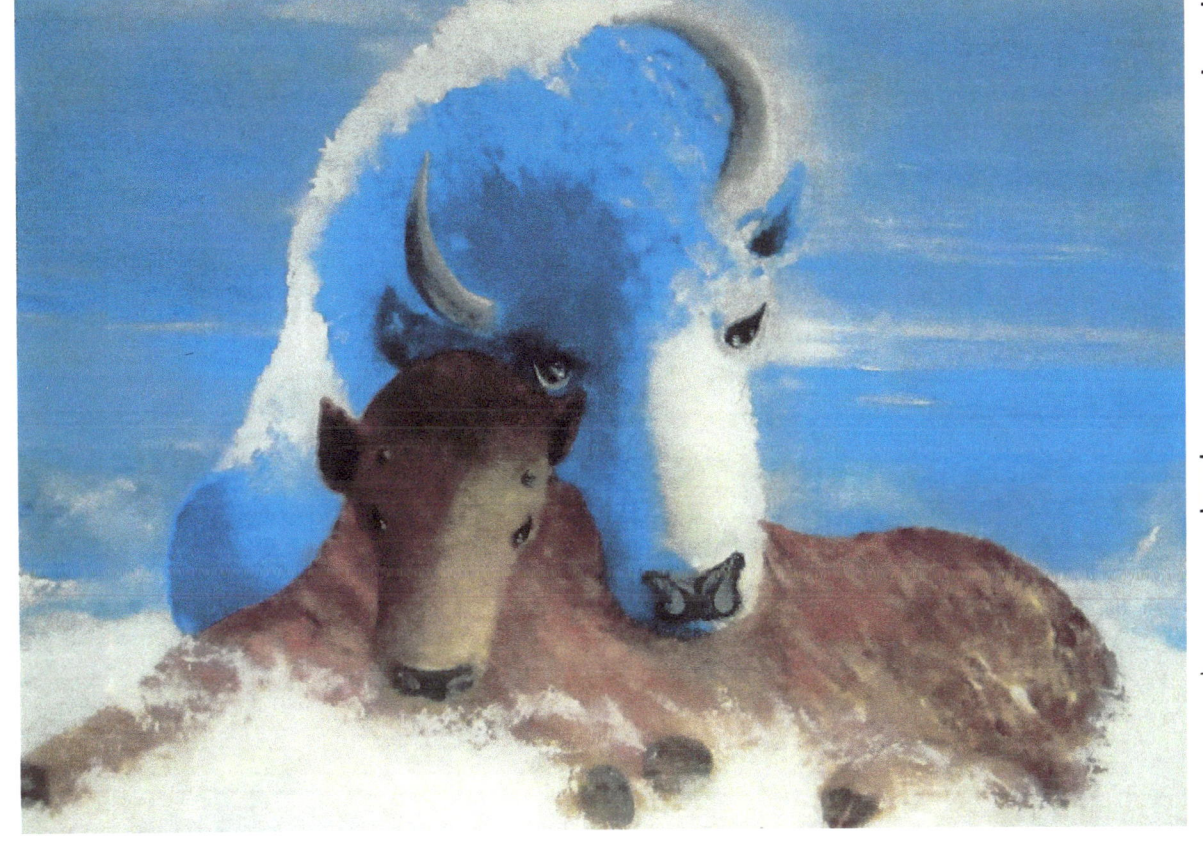

PAINTINGS
POETRY

PROSE

SHORT STORIES

TED C. LUNA

Sunstone books may be purchased for educational, business, or sales promotional use.
For information please write: Special Markets Department, Sunstone Press,
P.O. Box 2321, Santa Fe, New Mexico 87504-2321.
Printed on acid-free paper
∞

Library of Congress Cataloging-in-Publication Data

Names: Luna, Ted C., 1937- artist.
Title: The view from the moon / Ted C. Luna.
Description: Santa Fe, New Mexico : Sunstone Press, 2019.
Identifiers: LCCN 2019013293 | ISBN 9781632932631 (pbk. : alk. paper)
Subjects: LCSH: Luna, Ted C., 1937–Themes, motives.
Classification: LCC ND237.L864 A4 2019 | DDC 720.92–dc23
LC record available at https://lccn.loc.gov/2019013293

WWW.SUNSTONEPRESS.COM
SUNSTONE PRESS / POST OFFICE BOX 2321 / SANTA FE, NM 87504-2321 /USA
(505) 988-4418 / ORDERS ONLY (800) 243-5644 / FAX (505) 988-1025

PROLOGUE

THE TIME HAS COME THE WIZARD SAID "TO PRESENT SOME OF YOUR WORKS." HOW CAN I DO THIS I ASKED? PUBLISH IT IN A BOOK. THE WIZARD HAS ALWAYS BEEN RIGHT. THROUGH THE ANNALS OF MY RECORDED WORKS I TRIED TO CHOOSE THE BEST AS BY JUST DOING IT WILL IMPROVE MY EARLY LEARNING OF THE RELIGION OF ZEN. SO VERY MUCH A WALK DOWN MEMORY LANE. CUT, PASTE AND COLOR I LEARNED IN MISS IRELAND'S KINDERGARTEN. EVEN IN OUR CYBERSPACE WORLD I STILL USE THESE THREE BASIC WONDERFUL TOOLS.

IN MY WORLD TRAVELS AND WAY TOO MUCH UNIVERSITY ACADEMIC TRAINING I AM STILL A VICTIM OF LIFE'S CONTINUING EDUCATION (SOME TIMES DAILY). MASTER ARTISTS AND CRAFTSMEN IN CIDNA AND JAPAN ALWAYS INTRODUCE A FLAW IN THEIR MASTER PERFECTION WORKS TO ALLOW THE SPIRIT TO ESCAPE. YOU WILL NOTICE THAT I ALLOWED TYPOS AND WORD MISSPELLING FOR THIS REASON. OF COURSE, THERE ARE OTHER PLACES YOU WILL FIND WITH A DISCERNING EYE. MOST PROFESSAIONALS WOULD NEVER ALLOW THIS.

THERE ARE STILL PLACES TO SEE AND GET INSIRATION. I HAVE BEEN CLOSE TO NATURE AND ITS WONDERS ALL OF MY BREATHING DAYS. I HAVE ALWAYS TRIED TO DO MY WORK WITH PLACES THAT DON'T EXIST. FOR ME IT'S WONDERFUL TO CREATE A FANTASY IN WHATEVER MEDIUM I AM WORKING ON. IT IS VERY DIFFICULT AT TIMES TO MAKE SURE THAT THE MIND IS TURNED OFF. ON SOME WORKS I HAVE TO TURN IT BACK ON FOR DETAILS TO ENSURE THAT THE CONCEPT LEAVES NOTHING TO THE IMAGINATION. MY POETRY, PROSE, SHORT STORIES, SKETCHES AND ODES ARE AN EXCEPTION TO THIS SELF-MADE RULE.

THOUGHTS AND WORKS REMAIN UNSEEN AND UNSPOKEN UNTIL EXPRESSED. FOR ALL OF THE WONDERFUL PEOPLE IN THIS WORLD COME TRAVEL WITH ME. MY PRODUCTION OF THE PLAY IS FOR THE THEATRE OF YOUR MIND. THESE GENTLE WORKS ARE MY VEIW FROM THE MOON, FOR YOU TO ENJOY

TED C. LUNA

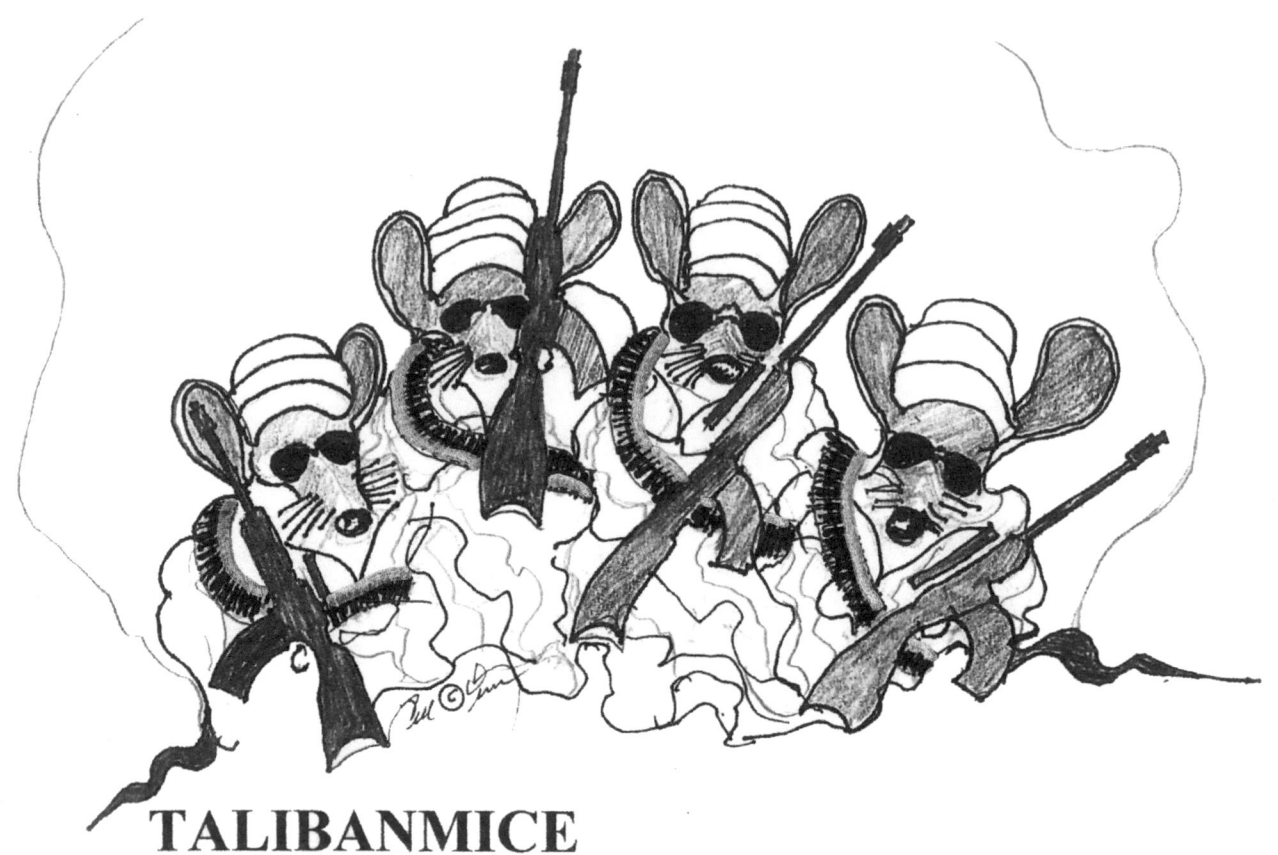

TALIBANMICE

Deep in the waste lands
In Afghanistan
Al-Qaeda and the Taliban
Joined forces in a training camp to be
We will create a weapon of mass destruction

Send our cells across the sea
Are only foe besides many the United States
We will set them free and concealed
By ship or 747 jet planes

Little did I know one cell
Would be sent to Albuquerque
With a plan directed at me
Soon it became apparent

Their plan was unfolding
Mass kitchen destruction
Then to the pantry
Where was CIA or FBI
Or Home Land Security

I knew then it was up to me
The trails were provided
Their paths I could see
I countered with human tactics
Of course it did not work

They were trained well
In desperation my intelligence
Said to me
Develop a old tried and true plan

Spring traps laced with peanut butter
Our internal war was on
The body count rose to 12
Soon I would have to clean my country

I had achieved victory
I did hold services to honor
Each departed one
End of the cell
The Talibanmice

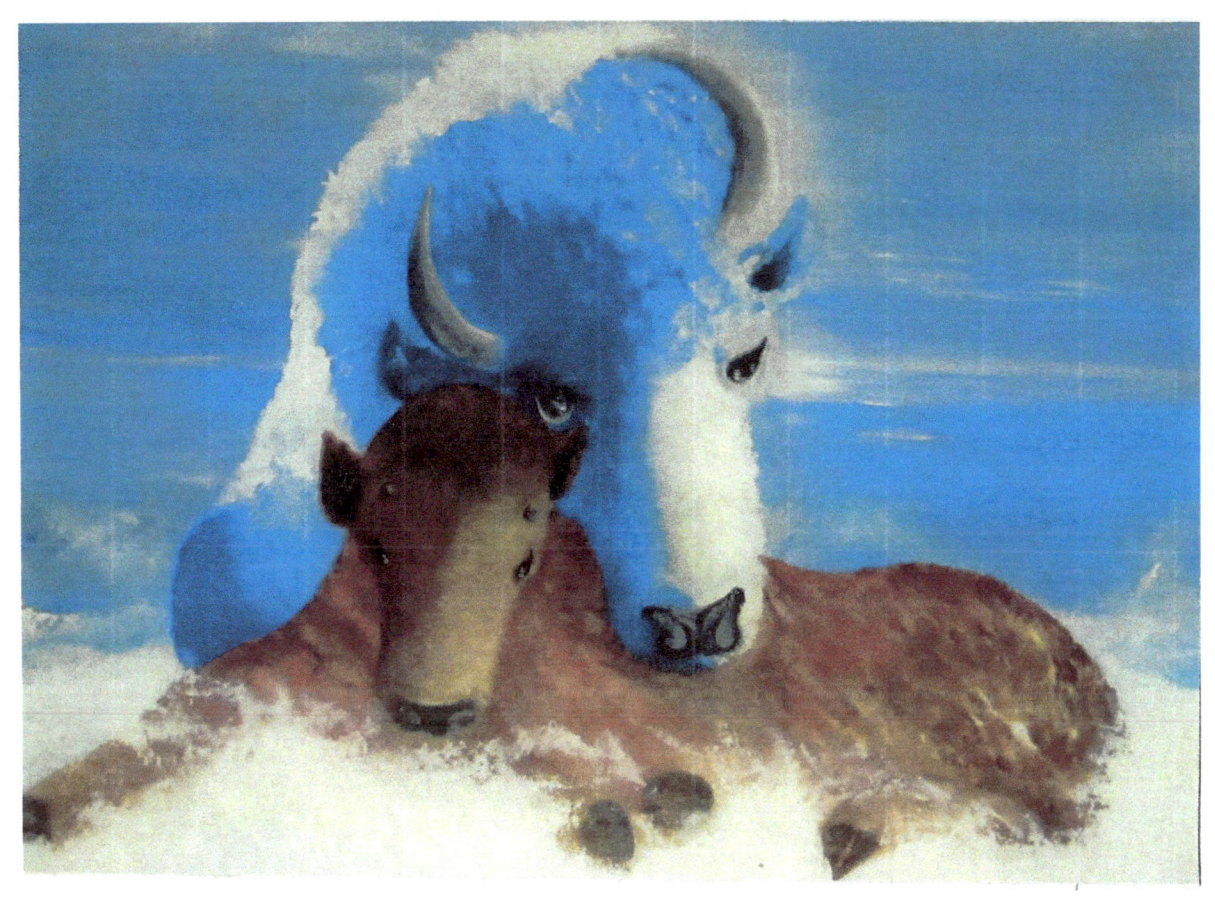

WHITE BUFFALO
IN FIRST SNOW.
BULLS ARE VERY PATERNAL TO THE SPRING CALFS.
THE YOUNG CALFS LOOSE THE FAWN COLOR AS THEY GROW.
OFTEN TIMES ONLY THE BEST BULLS WILL MATE.
THIS HELPS INSURE THAT THE HERD REMAINS STRONG.
THE FEMALES DO SELECT THE BULLS.

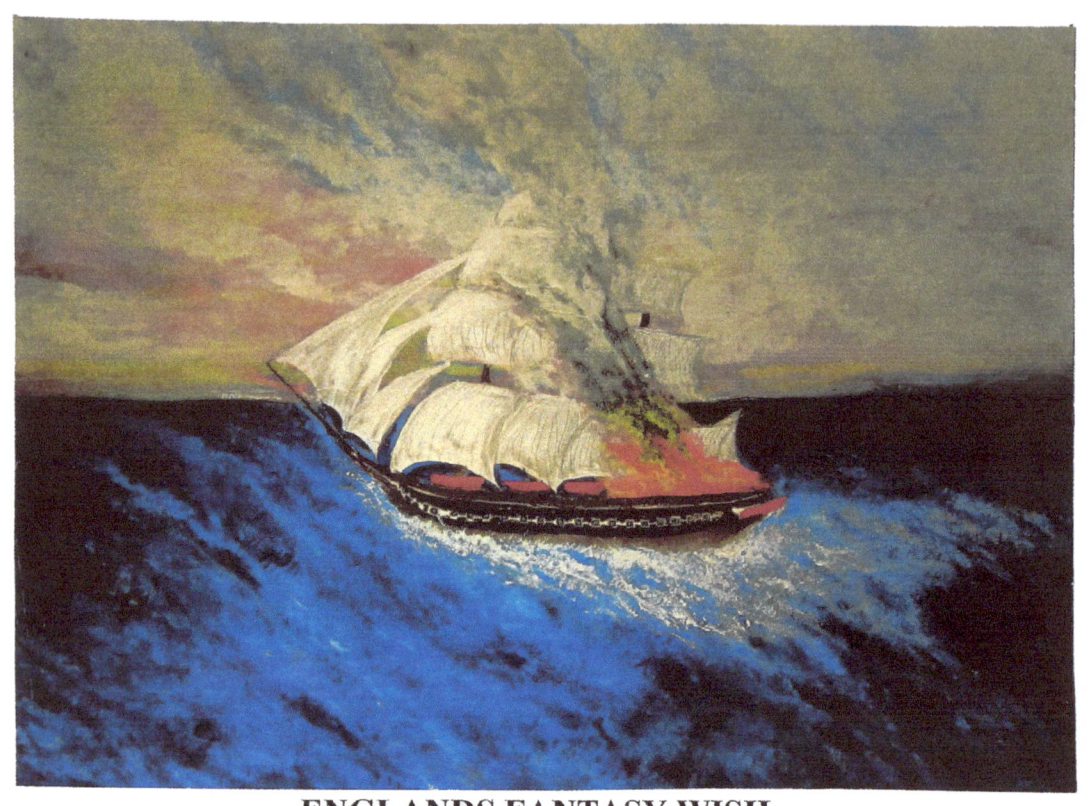

ENGLANDS FANTASY WISH
IN THE NAVAL WAR WITH ENGLAND IN 1812
THE USS CONSTITION SUNK THREE OF ENGLANDS MAN OF WAR SHIPS.
BECAUSE OF THIS ENGLAND SHORTEN THE WAR TO THREE YEARS.
THE USS CONSTITION WAS NEVER DECOMMSIONED.
IT WAS TOTALLY REFURBISHED BY 2017.
IT SAILS THE OCEAN TODAY.

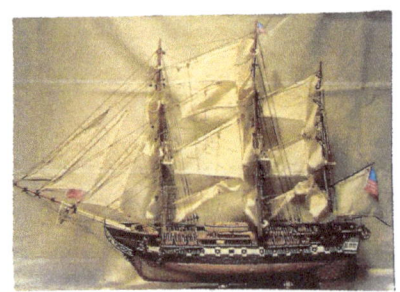

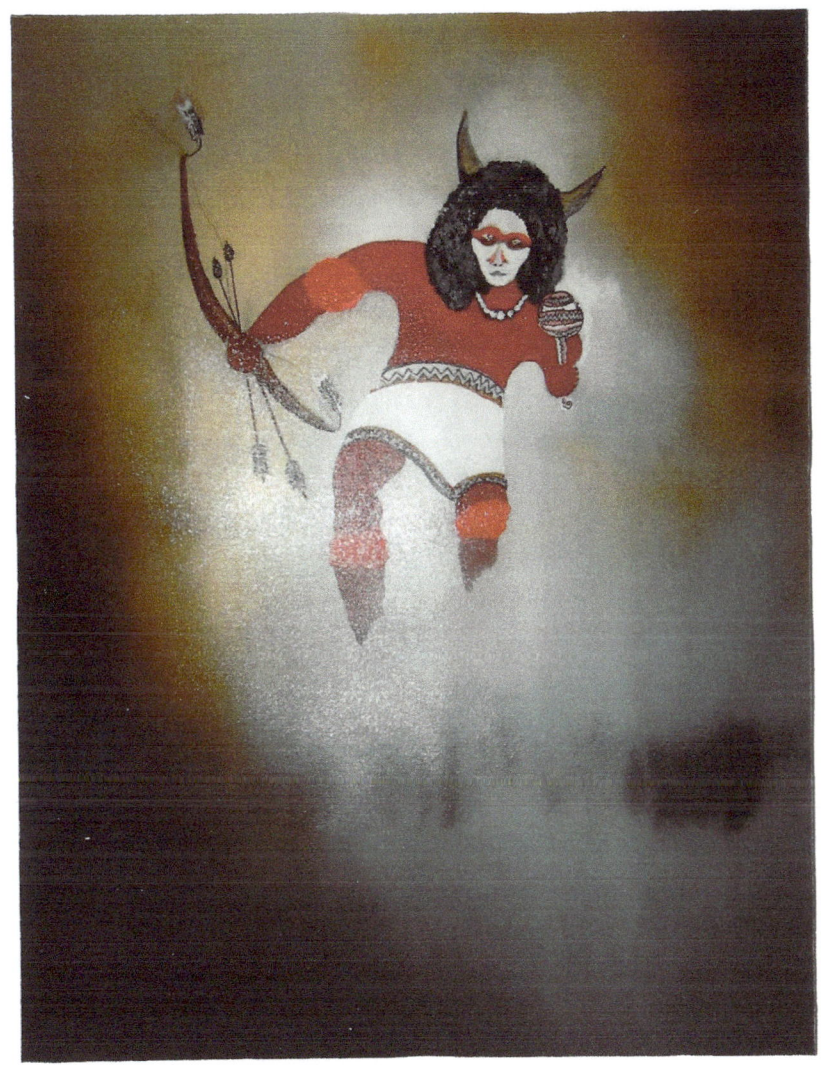

BUFFALO DANCER
THE BUFFALO WAS HIGHLY REVERED BY INDIANS OF
THE WESTERN NATIONS. FOR IT SUSTAINED THEIR LIVES.
TODAY NORTH OF SANTA FE, A RESORT CASINO
NAME SAKE IS CALLED BUFFALO THUNDER.
THE TURNER RANCH IN NORTHERN NEW MEXICO
HAS THE BIGGEST HERD IN THE USA

EAGLE DANCER
BEFORE IT BECAME OUR NATIONAL BIRD.
NATIVE AMERICANS LOVED THE EAGLE
MANY BELIEVED IT HAD MYSTICAL POWERS.
ONLY INDIANS CAN OWN ITS FEATHERS
A FEDERAL LAW

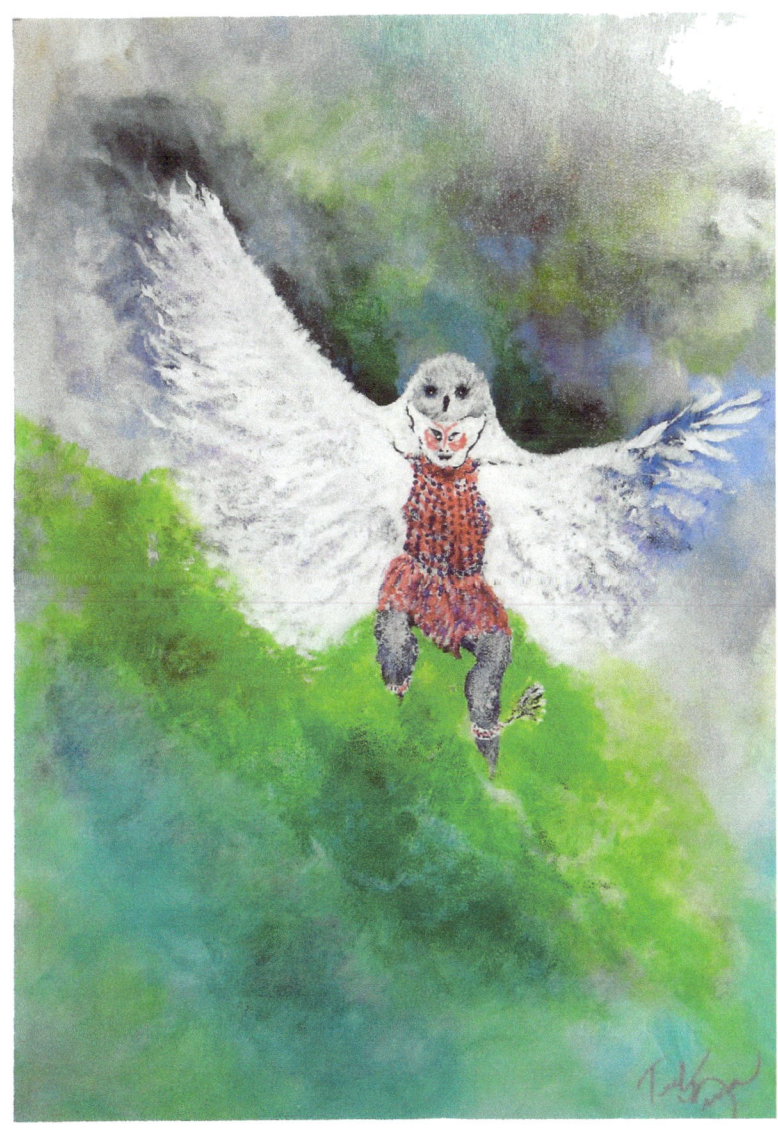

SAILING ON AUTO
NO ONE SAW THE BIG WAVE
CAPTAIN SHOUTED
AT LEAST WERE IN
THE RIGHT DIRECTION

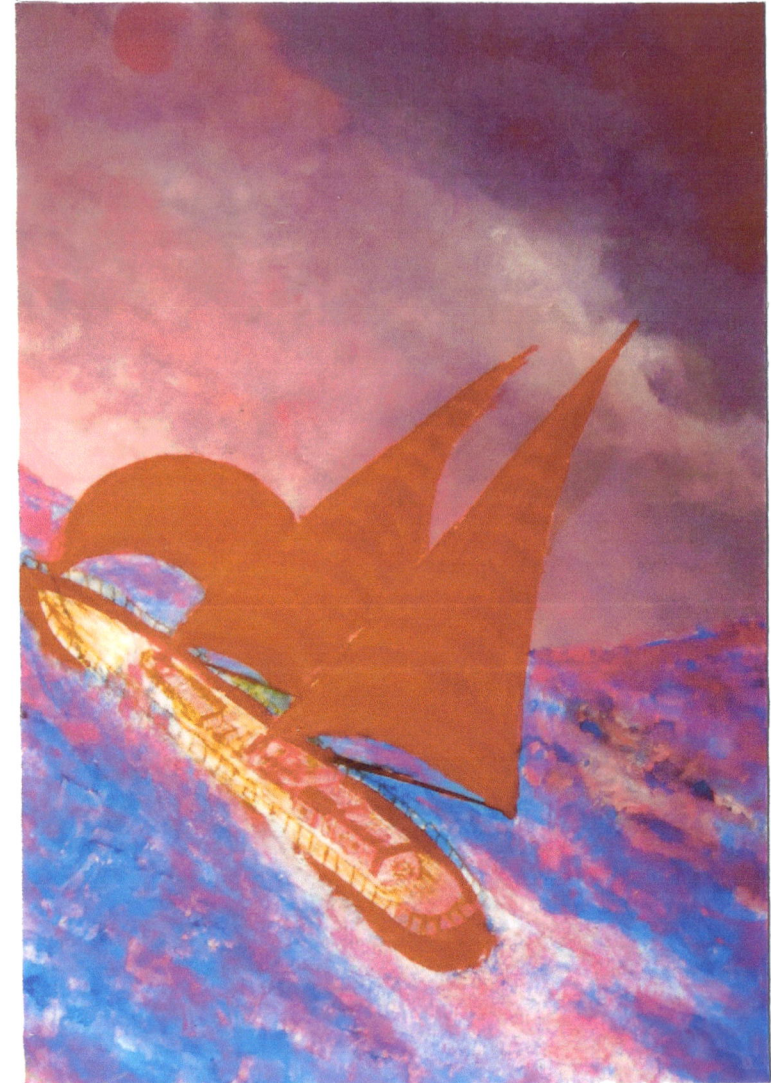

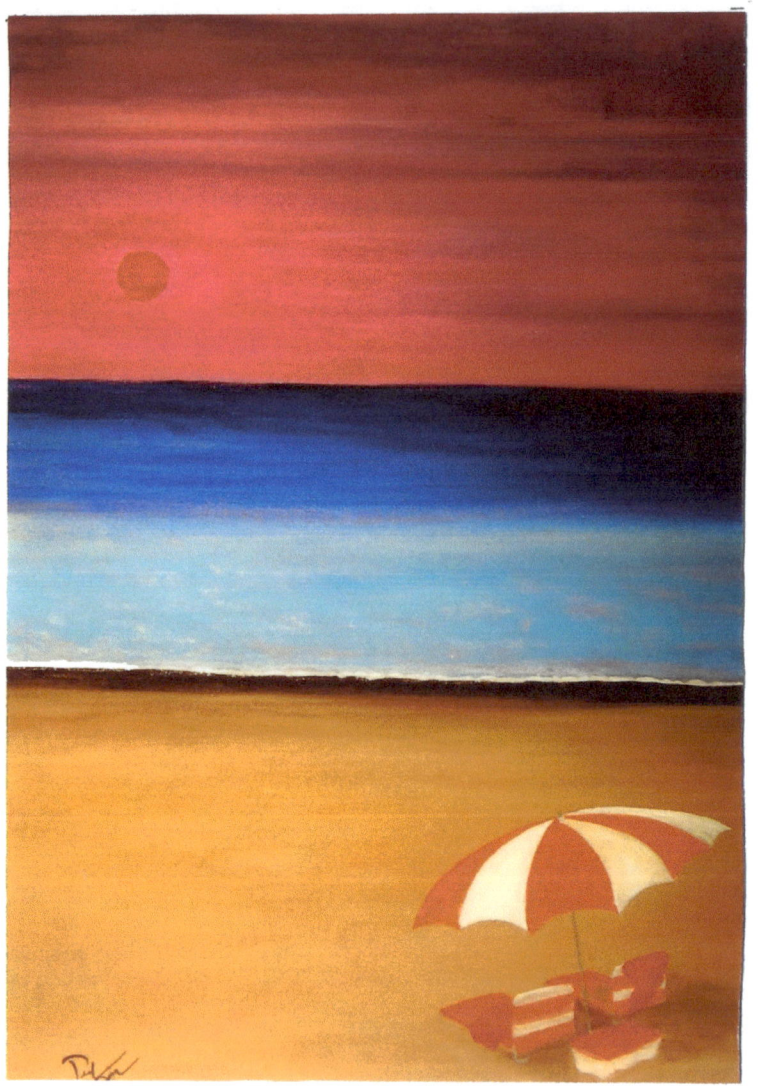

THE BEACH
ISLA MUJERES MEXICO
JOSE WHERE DID THEY GO
JUAN THEY WENT SWIMMING
LETS GO DOWN AND GET THE CORONA
THEY HAVE IN THE COOLER
VAMINOS

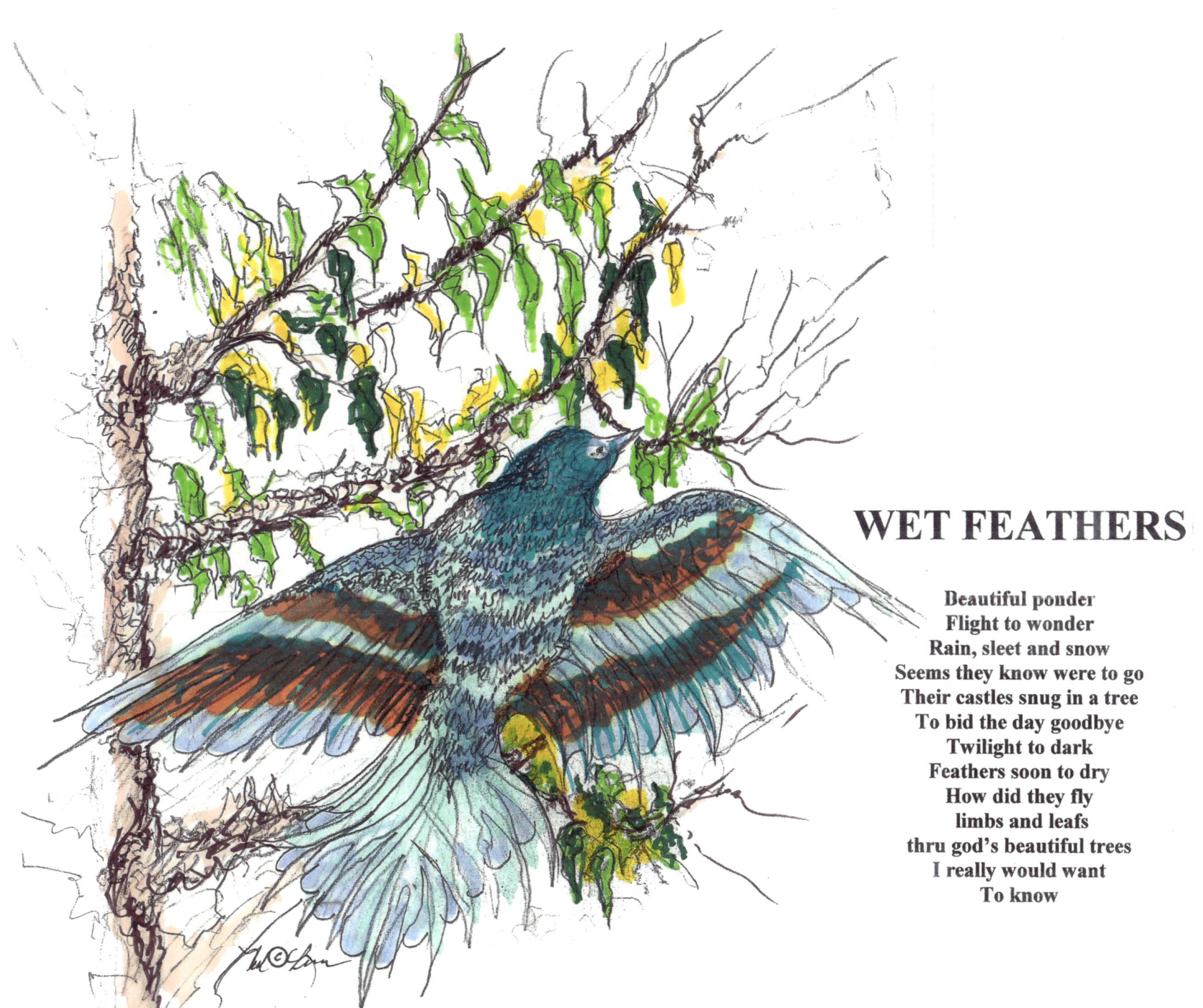

WET FEATHERS

Beautiful ponder
Flight to wonder
Rain, sleet and snow
Seems they know were to go
Their castles snug in a tree
To bid the day goodbye
Twilight to dark
Feathers soon to dry
How did they fly
limbs and leafs
thru god's beautiful trees
I really would want
To know

13

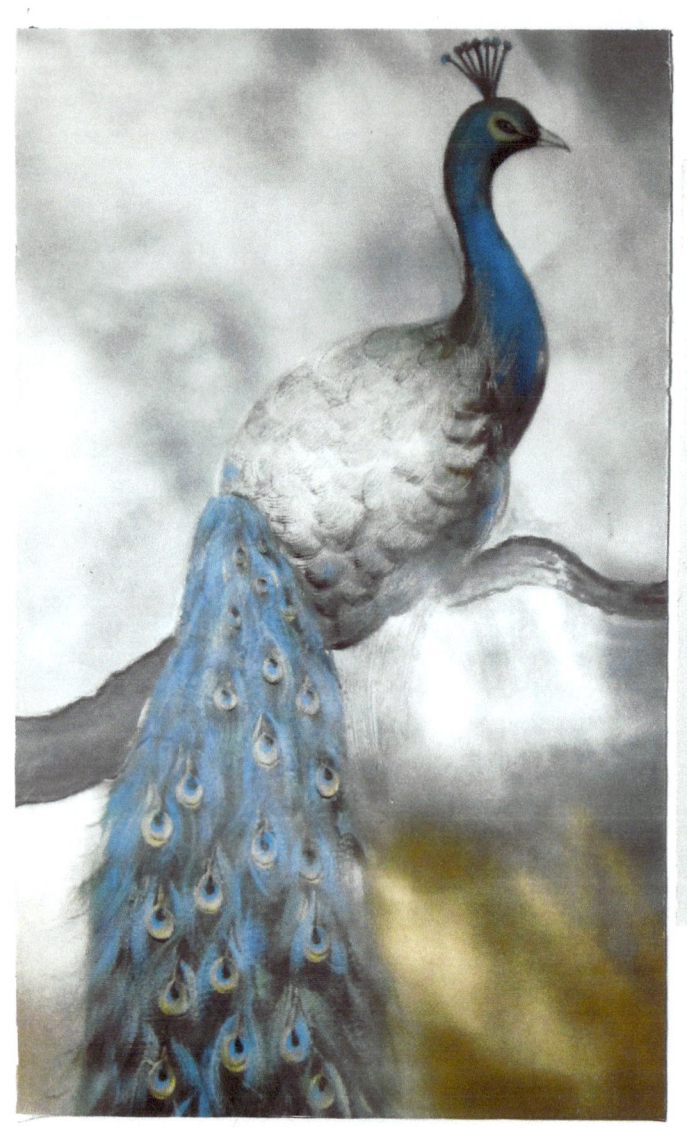

PEACOCK
OUT ON A LIMB
LOOKING FOR A MATE

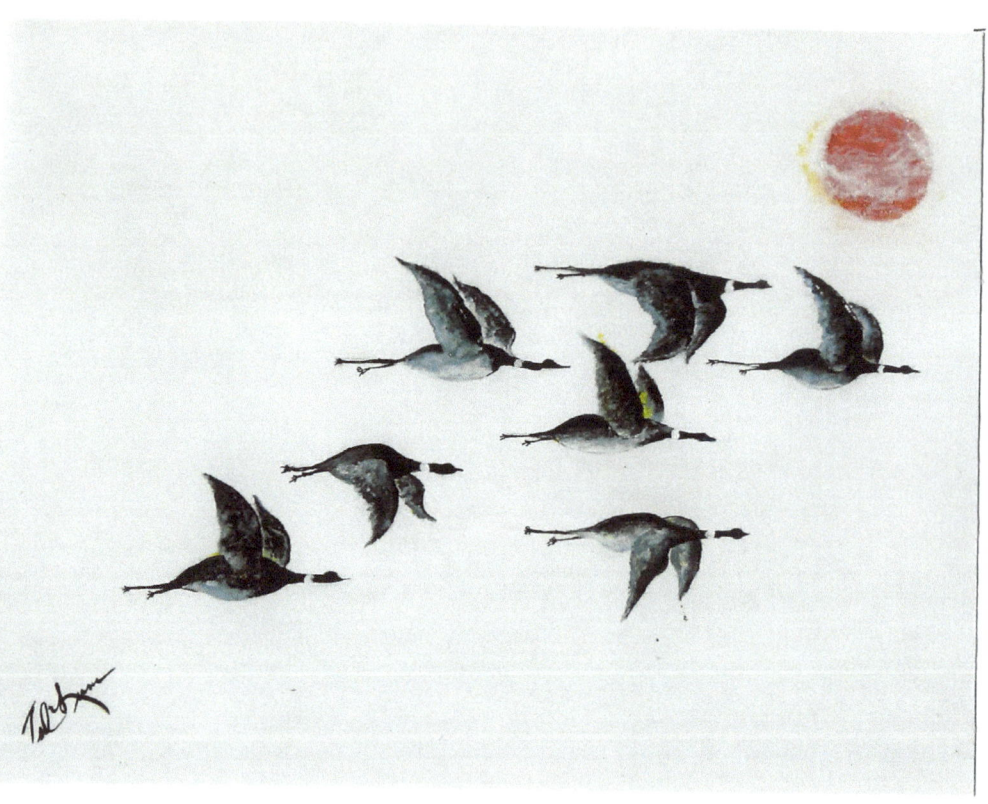

HOPE SHE KNOWS WHERE SOUTH IS
JUST FOLLOW HER
THE REST ARE BEHIND US

14

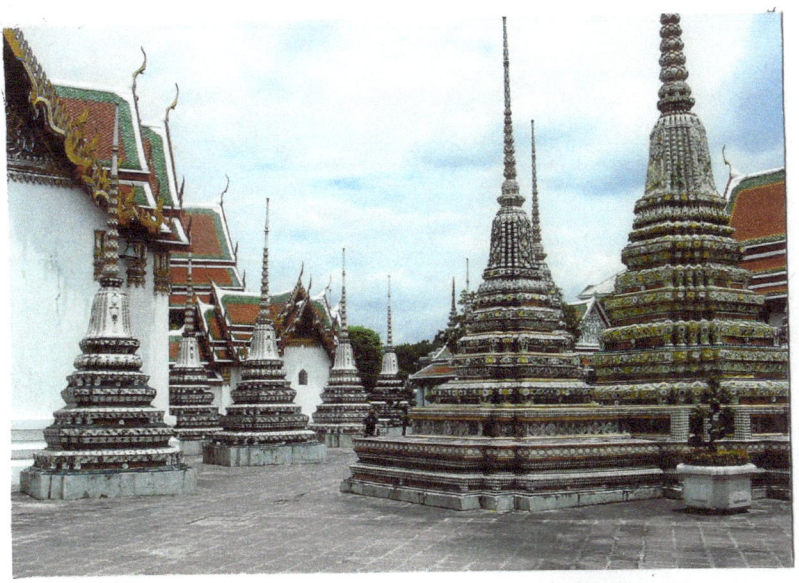

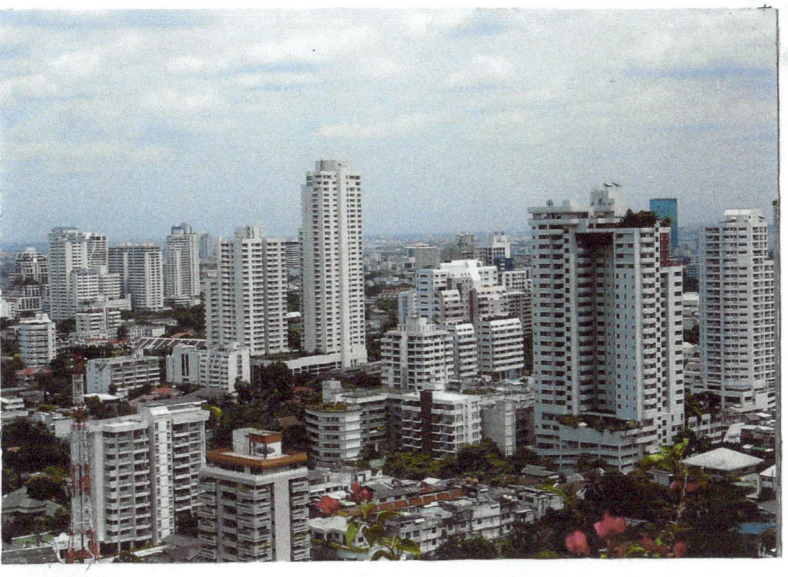

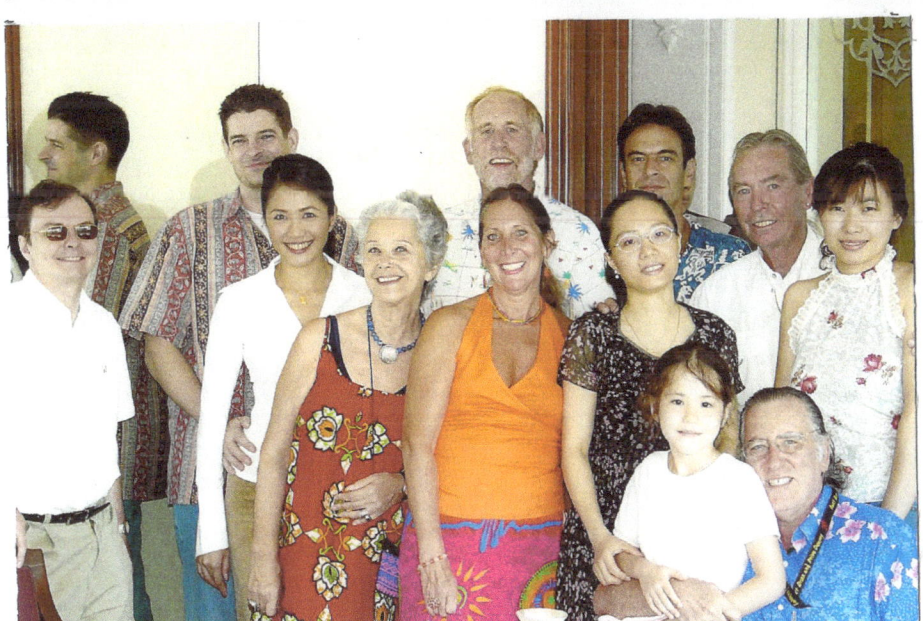

THE CLAN

BANGKOK

DAVA AND I WERE INVITED TO
ATTEND LARRY'S 60TH BIRTHDAY.
A VERY RICH CPA OUT OF
HONG KONG. HE PICK-UP THE
TAB FOR EVERYONE.
THE GUY IN THE BLUE SHIRT
HIS FRIENDS CAME FROM
EVERY WHERE AND ONE CIA
I NICK NAMED THEM THE CLAN
WE HAD PLUSH RESERVATIONS AT
5 STAR HOTEL DOWNTOWN
ON REQUEST YOU HAVE A
DRIVER AND CAR TO
TAKE YOU ANYWHERE
AND WAIT TO BRING YOU BACK
ON THE 12TH FLOOR WAS
THE VIP LOUNGE NEVER CLOSED
YOU COULD HAVE DRINKS FREE
BANGKOK IS TRAFFIC CONJESTED
CITY WITH 30 MINUTE WAITS
COMMON AT THE STOPLIGHTS
AND IN MANY WAYS A VERY

15

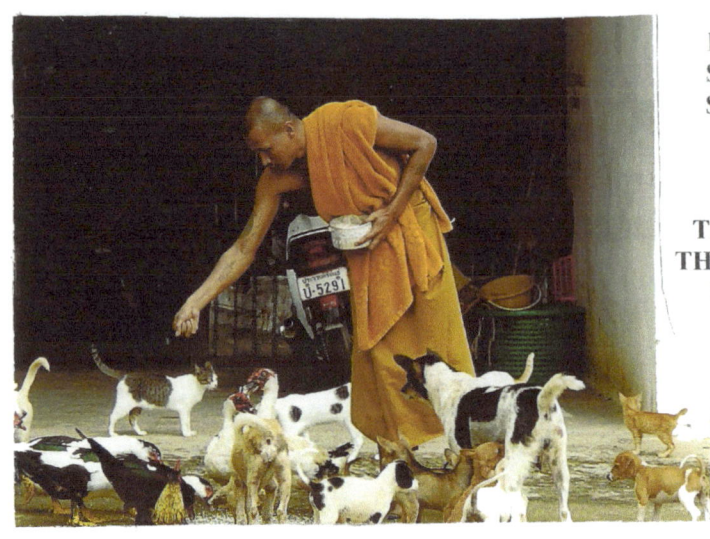

IN HER STORES IN NEW MEXICO
SHE SELECTED TO THE TUNE OF
$6,000.00 WHICH I LOANED HER
WE PURCHASED SUIT CASES
TO LOAD EVERYTHING
IT WAS CHEAPER THEN
THE COST TO SEND IT TO THE USA
THE CLOTHING PROVED TO BE A BIG
MISTAKE IT NEVER SOLD WELL
THOUGH THE YEARS I HAD
FINANCED HER TO THE
AMOUNT OF $30,000.00
WHEN WE PARTED COMPANY
SHE NEVER PAID ME

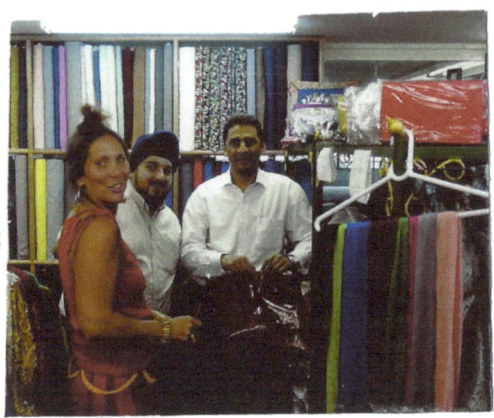

BEAUTIFUL CITY. WITH THEIR HISTORY
YOU CAN EXPERIENCE THE
OLD AND THE NEW
ALL MEMBERS OF THE CLAN
WERE DELIGHTFUL AND FUN
DAVA AND I SPENT 4 DAYS
AT A GULF RESORT SOUTH
OF BANGKOK JUST TO BE BY
WATER AND ENJOY LIFE
THEN BACK TO THE HOTEL
IT WAS BRITHDAY PARTY TIME
WHAT A PARTY, DINNER ,SINGING,
DANCING , CAKE AND CHAMPAGNE
DURING OUR STAY DAVA MADE
FRIENDS WITH THE OWNERS
DESIGN CLOTHING STORE
I HAD THEM MAKE ME
A WHITE SILK SUIT AND
A LOT OF CUSTOM SHIRTS
THAT I DESIGNED
DAVA WAS SURE THAT THE
OFF THE RACK CLOTHING
WOULD SELL WELL IN THE USA

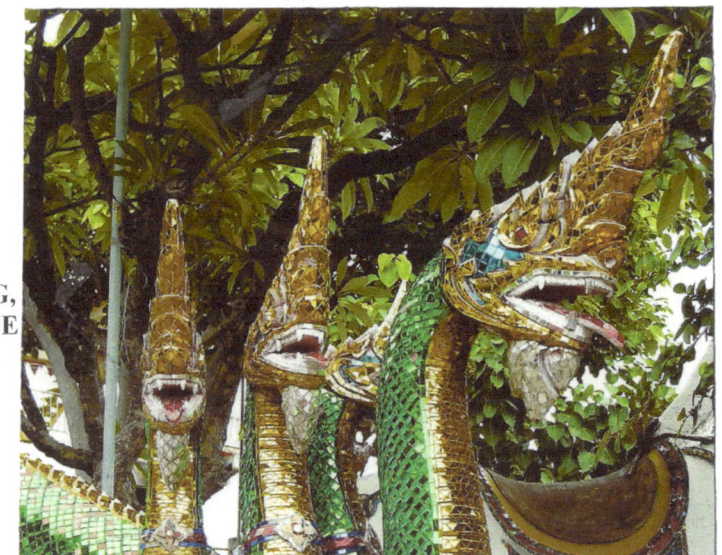

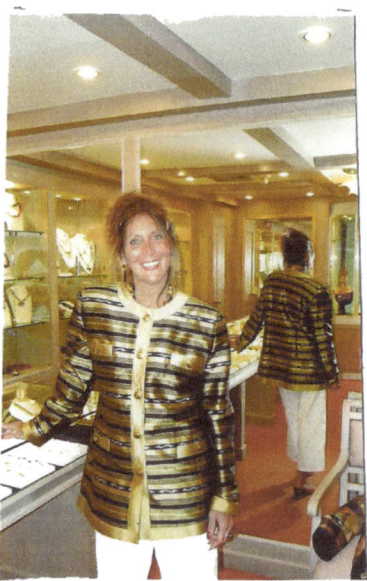

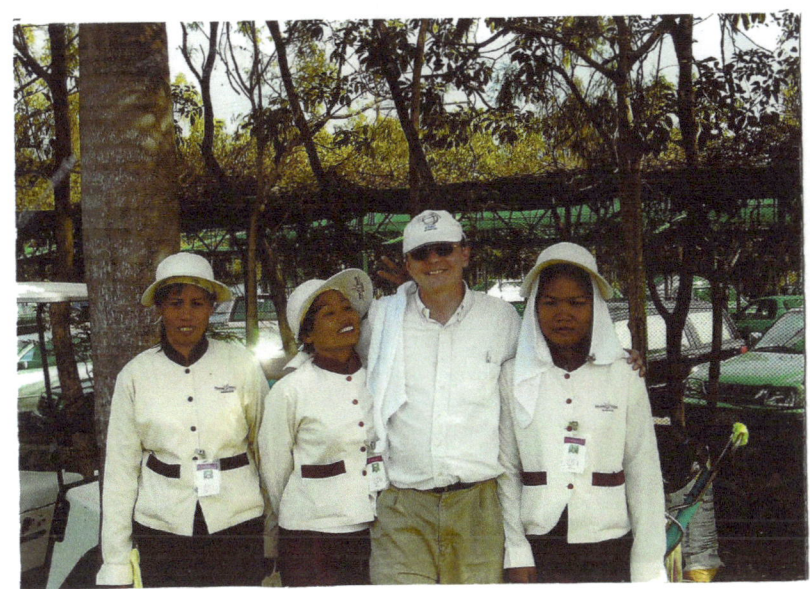 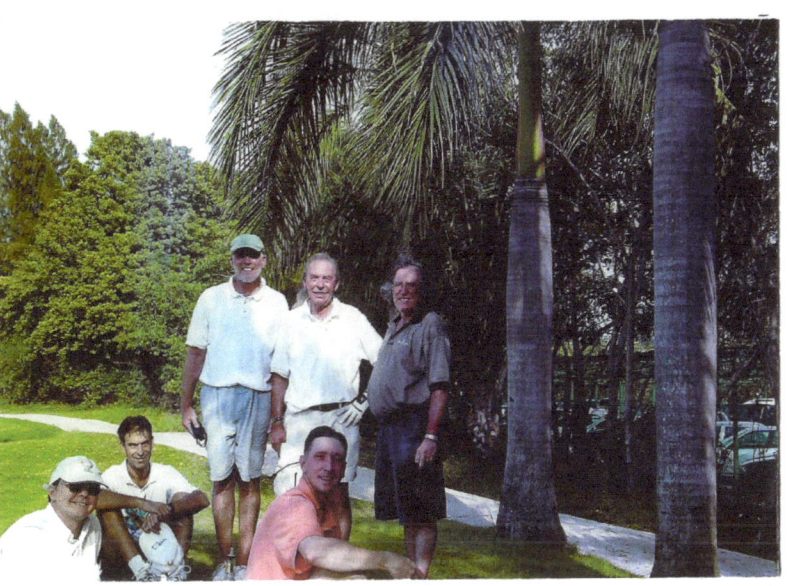

GOLF THAI STYLE, THE CLAN TOURNAMENT

AFTER BREAKFAST, WE LOADED IN VAN FOR THE HOUR AND A HALF TO THE GOLF COURSE. LARRY BROKE OUT THE JOINTS. I NEVER HAVE SMOKED THE WEED. IT DID NOT MATTER THE SECOND HAND SMOKE DID A JOB ON ME. WE RENTED THE CLUBS AND THE LADY CADDIES LINED UP AND ASSIGNED EACH ONE OF US A CADDIE. THERE WAS ONLY ONE REQUIREMENT FOR THE TOURNAMENT. WE WERE REQUIRED TO TAKE A SHOT OF JOSE CURVO (TEQUKILLYOU) ON EVERY TEE BOX. THE CADDIES WERE VERY WELL TRAINED. THEY WOULD HIT THE BALL FOR YOU OR TAKE IT OUT OF THE SAND TRAPS IF YOU LET THEM. WE PLAYED THREESOME AND THE CADDIES FILLED OUT THE SCORE CARD. IT WAS A LOT OF FUN AND BY THE 18 HOLE I BIRDED IT AND WON THE TOURNAMENT. (DID'T EVEN KNOW IT). GOLFS MOST FLEETING MOMENT IS WHEN YOU WIN OR COME IN LAST. THE PRIZE WAS A FULL BOTTLE OF JOSE. I AM SURPRIZED THAT ANY ONE COULD STAND FOR THE PHOTO.

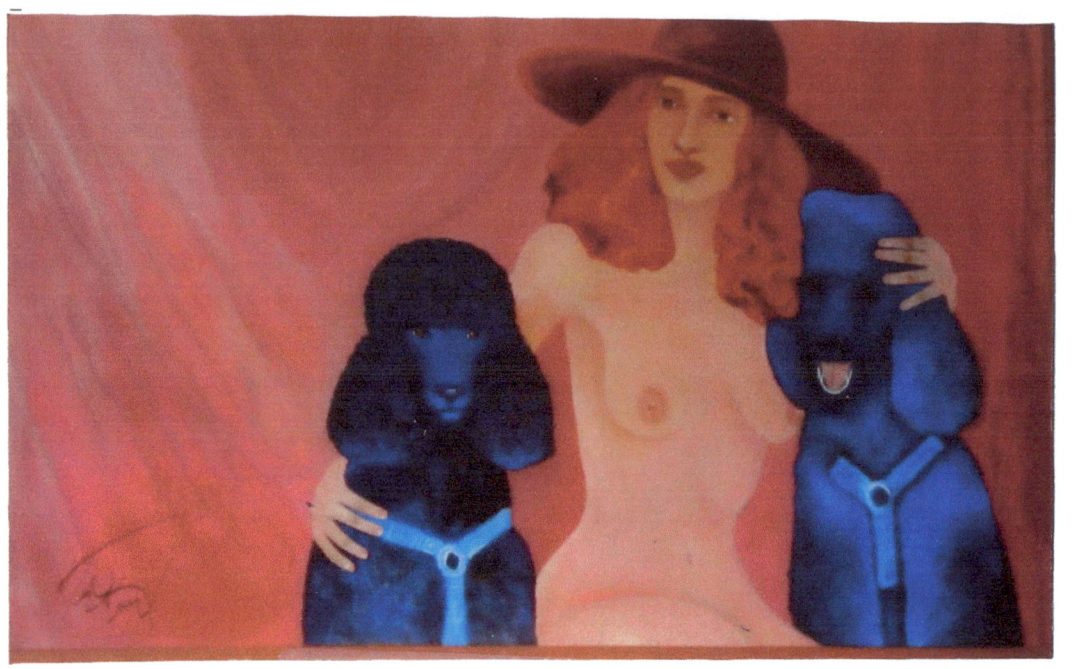

LADY OF TRAVEL
ENGLISH LADY A BREIF INCOUNTER
WITH CHAMPS AND TIFF

Traveleir she is
Places yet to ponder
Trains at night
Flying in the day

Buss's all the way
London town
They all drive by inches
On the wrong side of the road

Circles galore
No signals to explore
Elevated Eagles view
Hoping not to rain

Where to go
What to do
Where to stay
And not get blown away

Canyon road it was
When we first met
Time was short
In a dream you left

Santa Fe is waiting
For the grace of your presence
To enjoy evening rains
And late summer days

Early fall colors
First mountain snow
All of the above
Will make your heart glow

You can sleep at the Opera
Of course if its boring
Restful and peaceful
Unless you are snoring

What a place to be
When in beauty
you are wide awake
So goes the story

When the first act ends
Jolt is horrific
You Q up at the bar
Only to find you are awake

Time to measure
Things to come
Day to day
The only way

Romance first
Passion second
Feelings of flesh
Blooming to love

Fall to winter
Spring to summer
Seasons to be
Not together

Enjoy your travel
Yesterday you have gone
Tomorrow is my forever
Please stay away

CONCEPTION

They come by the thousands
To the furtile valley
With no sky
Fire in dad's eye
The long march to start
But only one will be
chosen
I really don't know why
The point it is called
Best of the best
He drives on with no rest
He finds his goal
With-in a mix
Of my mother to be
Soul and spirit
Both will intertwine
New generations
Hope for the coming years
Universal continuity
My room in my mother's womb
Very soon small to be
No interior designers
Can desecrate the space
What a wonderful place to be
I never wanted to leave
Soon I would exit
For the love of reality
To a new world of wonder
With concepts by me
All of the above
Created me

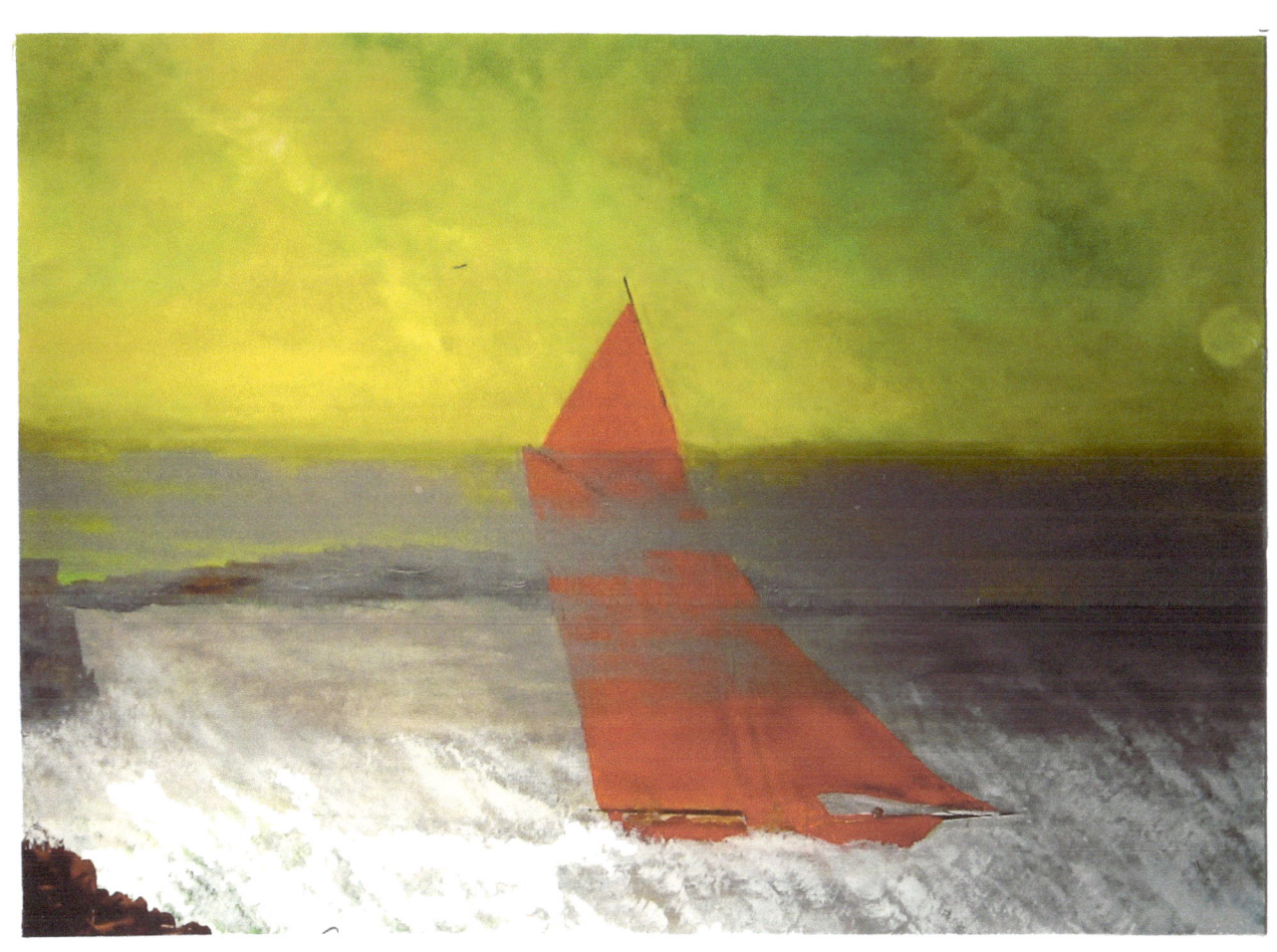

RED SAILING SHIP
THE FOG HAS STARTED TO ROLL IN THE BAY

EVERYTHING

PREFACE

They wondered and found
Flat fertile earth meadows
With a mountain fed
pure cold water river
Pitched their temporary shelters
Hunters still for wild game
They needed the meat,
Bone, sinews and skin
Gathers no more
For the found the secret
Of the seed
They built their new shelter
Which they could call home
Hand formed bricks
Out of mud and dried grass
Baked hard by the noon day sun
Very easy to handle
Stacked them one above the other
On a bed of mud in between
Cut the trunks of young pine
Out in the forest so green
Hauled on their shoulders
To span wall to wall
Set them in place
Letting the ends fly free
Crisscrossed small branches
And added a few more
Rows of earth bricks
Above the pine logs
Ready for the earth roof
Basket by basket \
Handed hand to hand
The shallow earthen roof
Grew grass
Mud plastered both sides
Of all walls

Packed the earthen floor
Until they could sweep
Clean the dirt and dust
In the corner
They left a small hole
In the earth roof
For the fire smoke to escape
They soon found out
The smoke was thick
And made their eyes water
And never went thru the hole
They cut the brick in half
And used the pieces too
Enclosing the corner
Little did they know
They just created the first funnel
And added more brick some to the
Corner walls
The kiva fireplace
Was born
And made its day view
GRANDFATHER, GRANDFATHER
ARE YOU HOME

JOURNEY ONE

Enter my grandson
Through open the blanket gate
Sitting in the corner
Warmed by the pinon fire
Wrapped in a blanket
White locks of white hair
Flowing down his shoulders
Aged but still very handsome was he
Your grandmother is hand weaving
Blanket she will give to you when its finished
Grandson what brings you here
Father send me so you could do
What you did for him
To take as many moons

It would take and not to hurry home
I now will call you my son
We must speak in the new tongue
The old tongue still remains
Among our people
I learned it well at the friar's school
A whip in his left hand
A black slate and white sticks
For us to draw on with dry rags to erase
Leaving white dust only when wet
Would wipe the black slate clean
He told us of a god so far away
If we did not follow his teachings
He would send us first to purgatory
Then on to hell
I knew my ancestors had better
Beliefs ague I could not do
Tell me grandfather
What must I do

JOURNEY TWO

Son go into our fields
No further than the river
And tell what you seen
Bring me back
Something of value
Out into the fields he went
Bright sonny day no clouds in sight
He marveled at the growth
From a single seed
He saw a few horses
With no place to go
A array of color lead the way
Corn in their husks
Pumpkins and squash lined the ground
Beans ready for the picking
Along side the earthen water troughs
Fed by the river

Other green leaf plants he did no know
He studied hard what should he bring
Back to grandfathers home he ran
With some thing in each hand
Grandfather I have told you
What I have seen
Some of value I hold in each hand
He gave him corn and beans
For they will feed us
Through the long winters white blanket

JOURNEY THREE

Son go to the river
Do not cross it
Then tell me what you have seen
And bring me back something of value
He made a small dance
Prancing like a prince
To the river
Set down on the grass covered
Bank this was his think tank
He now could see the little
Water falls formed by rock
And the white bubbles the water formed
And finally lay still in pools that were dark
That's were the fish would hide
He looked down stream
And heard the river singing
The tune would never change
Morning noon and night
For the fast flowing water
Was strumming the strings of rock
He looked further down
The pattern repeated its self
He then saw small flying creatures
Hatched and set free as by a fairy
He went to the bushy trees
And picked the red berries

They safe and good to eat
Washed them down
With hand cupped to hold
The wonderful fresh river water
He pondered what to bring back
For the water had value
But he had nothing to carry it back
Something of value
He waded the river and
With his hands
Captured one fish
Back to grandfather he ran
Grandfather I have told you
What I have seen
A fish I don't understand
O grandfather don't you see
We are all like the fishes
Swimming the river of life

JOURNEY FOUR

Go my son and cross the river
On to the dry land
No further then the small trees
And tell me what you see
Bring back to me
Something of value
He new where a fallen tree
Made a bridge bank to bank
A safe passage for he
His first sight was a land
Barren and dry
The sun so hot
He put his blanket over his head
He never new that with
Each step marked trail
Rocks upon rocks
Strange bushes galore
A rope like creature with no legs

Would coil and rattle its tail
He heard the cry of wild dogs
Calling the pack to form and eat
Birds too few strangers in the sky
Round green sculptures with needles
He dug a little and found
Water very bitter but it was wet
And pear shaped structures
With needles and red blooms at the end
He found a bush he kneeled and smelled
I know I have found something of value
Back he retreated with a small
Bundle in his hand
Grandfather I have told you what I have seen
He handed him the small bundle
Grandfather laughed
I now will show the true treasure
Of value you have brought to me
He dipped the bundled end
Into the pinon fire
The small smoke and the embers
Released a blessed scent
A gift from the gods
It cleared the stale air

JOURNEY FIVE

Go my son beyond the dry land
To the small trees and go no further
Tell me what you have seen
And bring back to me
Something of value
He new the trail well
It did not take long
The ground was gentle
Where the small trees were standing
He new of the pinon, juniper and thrushes
Small foreign flowers bloomed here and there

From there on the rocks grew as boulders
It was hard to pick my way
Little green plants few and very far between
Patches of grass here and there
No other living thing did I see
My quest to the top of the mountain
Took longer then I thought
He knew immediately the things of value
Gathered a few pinon pine cones bursting with nuts
Broke a branch from a dead pinon tree
Its pungent fragrant sap now hardened
Back to grandfather he flew
Not much to tell of what I have seen
And each hand were things of value
Handed them to him and with joy
And delight and uttered the words
The pinon branch that we cut and stack
Brings cooking and warmth to our back
As we sit by the fire
Often crackling sparkle the night
We gather the nuts when in season
Enjoying them raw or roasted
Often a treat thru the winters
White blanket

JOURNEY SIX

Go my son beyond the small trees
Up to the high lands and no further
Tell me what you will see
And bring back something of value
Of course the trail was like old friends
Bounded with boyhood energy
He made the journey quick
He entered the highland forest
And with a sudden chill
Embraced his blanket
This wonderland he had never seen
Dotted with grass meadows

Between the tall trees
Flowers in bloom spread their perfume
A grove of multi-colored leaves
Hanging from the branches
Dancing because of the wind
The trees all bunched together
A village of nature
Getting ready to undress for winter
The strong ever green tall pines and spruce
Bastions of the forest
Something value what should I bring
The earth under the trees was covered
By pine needles I know I will make
A bed for comfort through the night
He snuggled his blanket to await his dreams
The sun arose making fire in the sky
He new then he had found one
I must exam the multicolored trees
He set his knife free and scraped the bark
Decided to taste it and to his surprise
All aches and pain disappeared
I must take more another gift from the gods
With his two treasures back down
The trail he flew
Grandfather this what I have seen
The things of value are in each hand
He handed him first a fist full of pine needles
Proudly stated they make a comfortable bed
It will rest your weary head
Next came the wad of bark
Please taste this and see what its done for me
Its natural medicine to cure
Your aches and pains
Calming your being
Brings forth the spirit

JOURNEY SEVENTH

Go my son beyond the highland forest
All the way to the top of the mountain
Tell me what you see
Of course bring something back of value
The sun rose and fell times three
The blanket over the gate flew open
Grandfather Grandfather I am home
Son tell me what you have seen
It was easy to follow my moccasin trail
Up beyond the forest high land
I finally arrived when the sun said goodbye
It grew cold and colder that I have ever been
Glad for my blanket it covered me
Head to toe
Darkness came no fire could I light
I laid in crevasse between boulders
And wished I was home
I had seen the white lights in the sky before
But never like this for
Some twinkled some were still
The full moon slowly rose and
What I am about to tell you
You may not believe
The moon light cast shadows
In all the rocks and boulders
I new then by surprise
The spirits of my ancient ancestor
Were slowly dancing

I watched in awe the moon set go
I looked all around and then to the sky
Like bolt of lighting awaken in me
I new then that the ancient ones
Had take a liking to me
I have never felt
The peace, joy and happiness
Feelings I never new
That existed in me
My spirit and soul was set freé
It's a new life for me
Now you see my son
You have
EVERYTHING

Theodoro Carlton Luna
November 2012

Note:
These journeys were inspired
From the works of
Sir Earnest Thompson Seaton
for a few years I knew his wife Julia
And daughter Dee, who poured my first
Taste of red wine in Seaton's library
In Ole Santa Fe

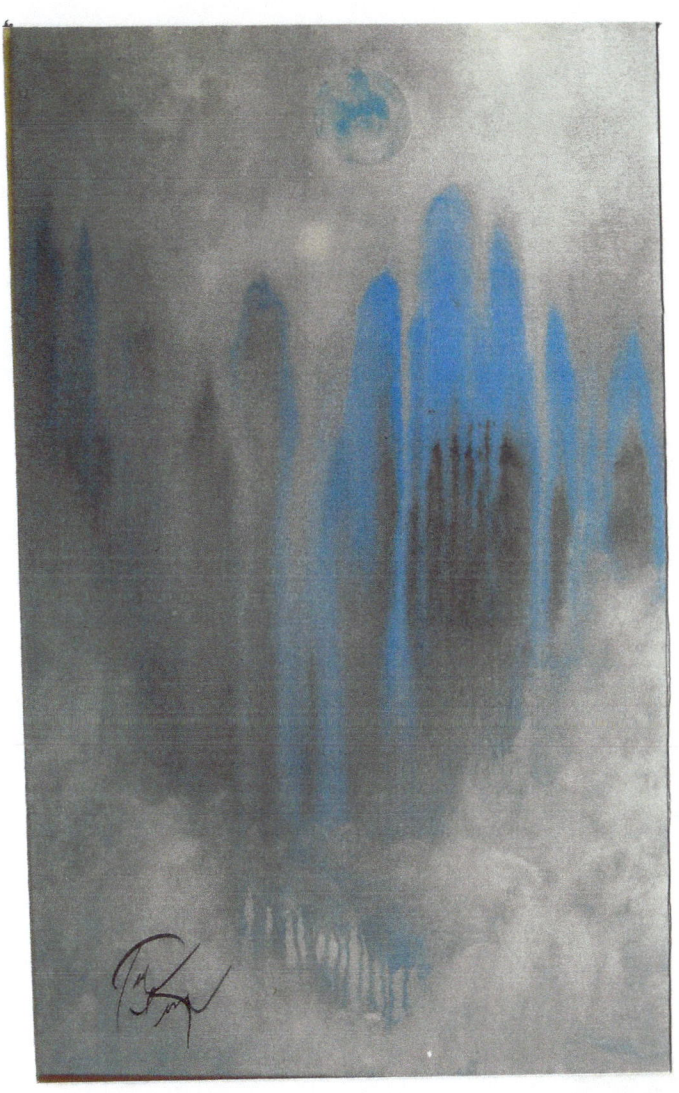

GATHERING OF THE SPIRITS

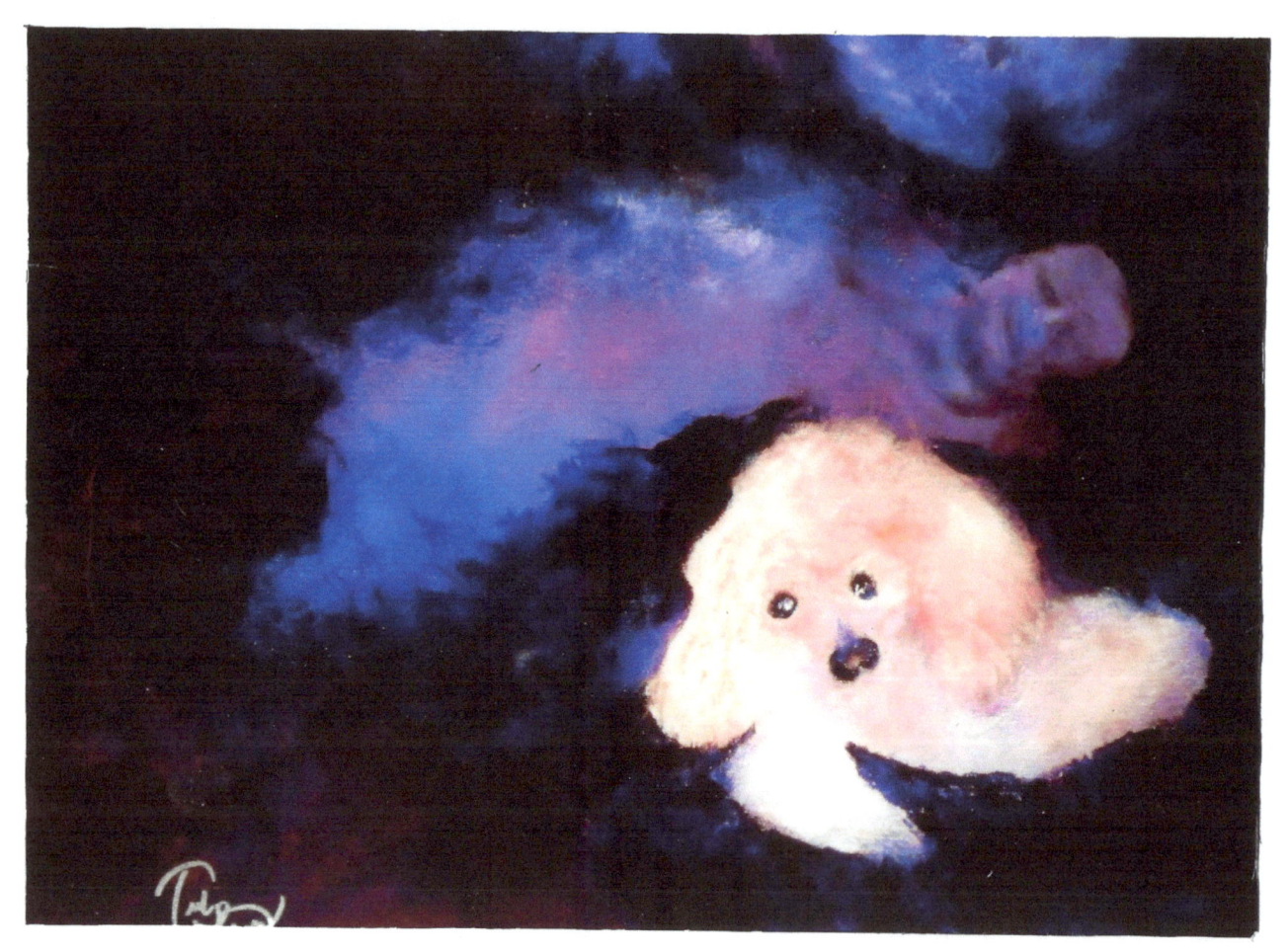

GUARDIAN ANGEL

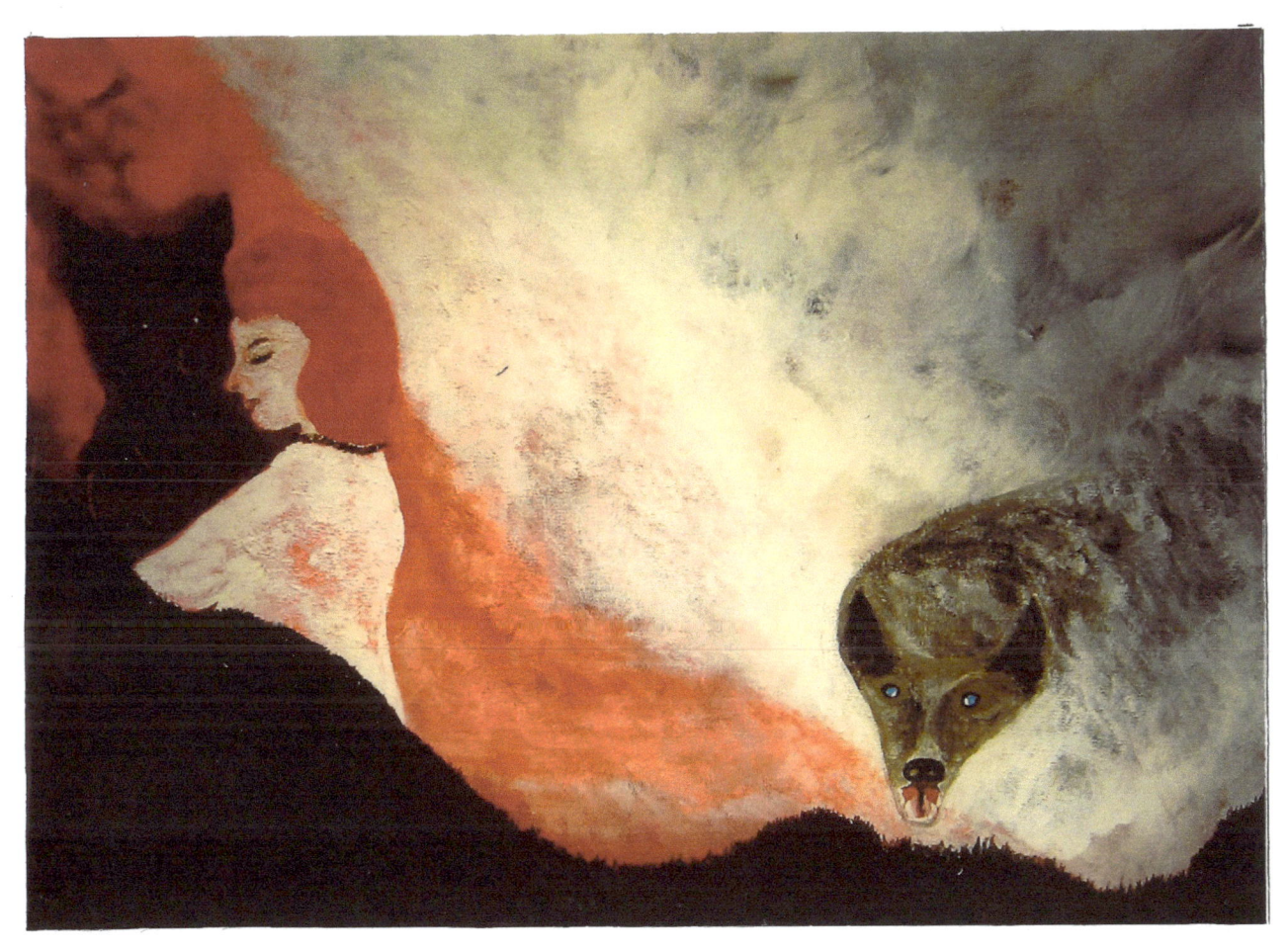

LADY OF THE BLACK FOREST

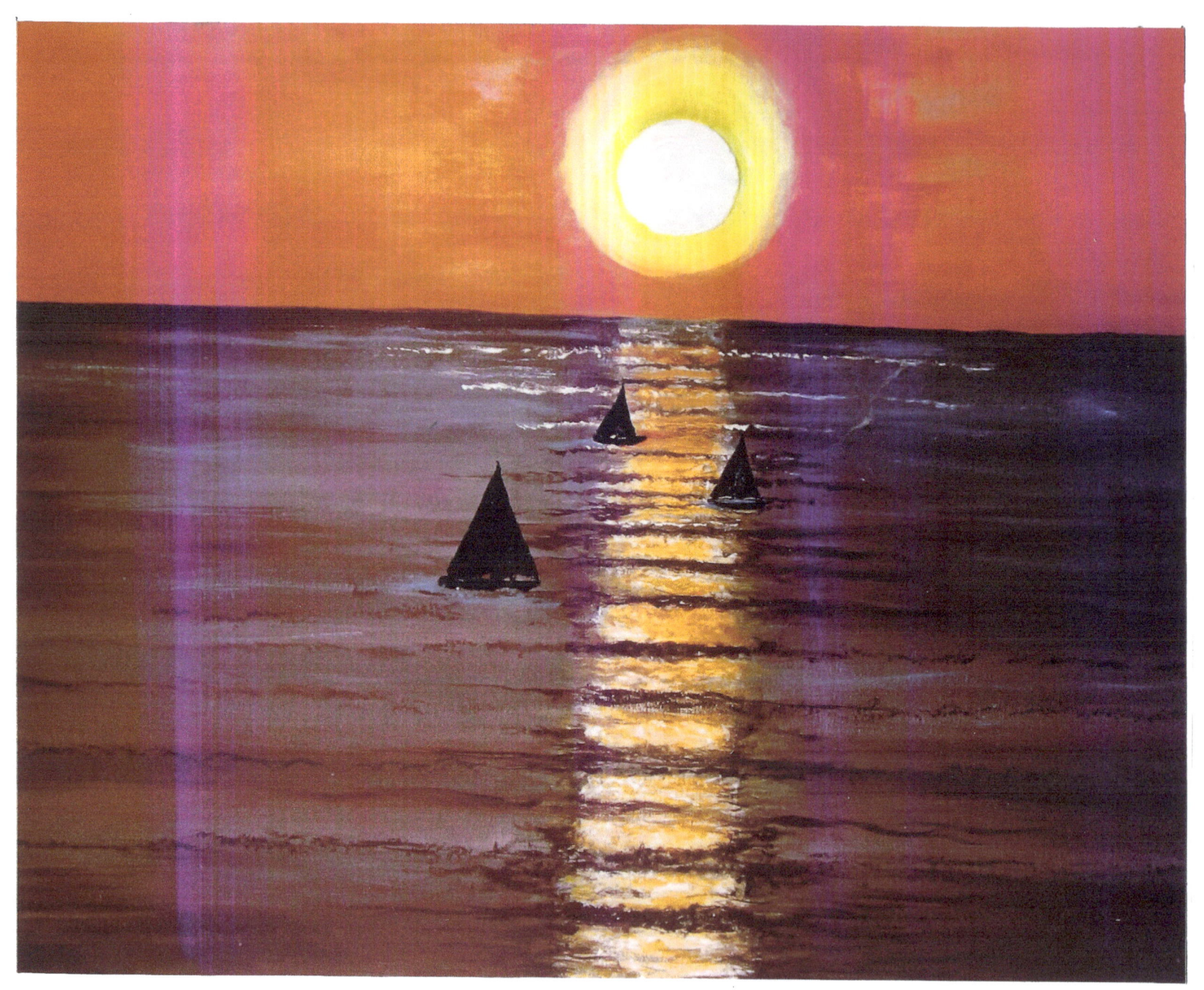

SUNSET AT EXTAPA MEXICO

Frozen Tears

Looking through my portal of glass
And seeing the world outside
Tacked to the tree
The gage said hello to me
A true forecast it was never wrong
As if it had a university degree
Numbers up or down
From zero and marked in red
Winter the time year
The season that tells the tale
Soon the white blanket
Will cover my earth
Dark and sultry demons
Spawned by oceans far from me
Gather and roll like
Bobsleds in the dreary sky
Soon to shed tears by and by
I would soon seek my shovel
To clear the way with no place to go
A book from the shelf
By the warm red fire bubbling
Lighting my pipe welcoming
My winters delight
In dream land were all that I love
Dawn stuffed blankets
Covered from head to toe
The fierce wind sent
The red mark down
I new then it would chill
Your bananas
From droplets to gentle flakes
Did it grow gathering
But soon melting it did not know
It gave us a white blanket
Transformed my world
Quite to peaceful
Setting my heart a glow
The dark blackened clouds
Had shed its
FROZEN TEARS

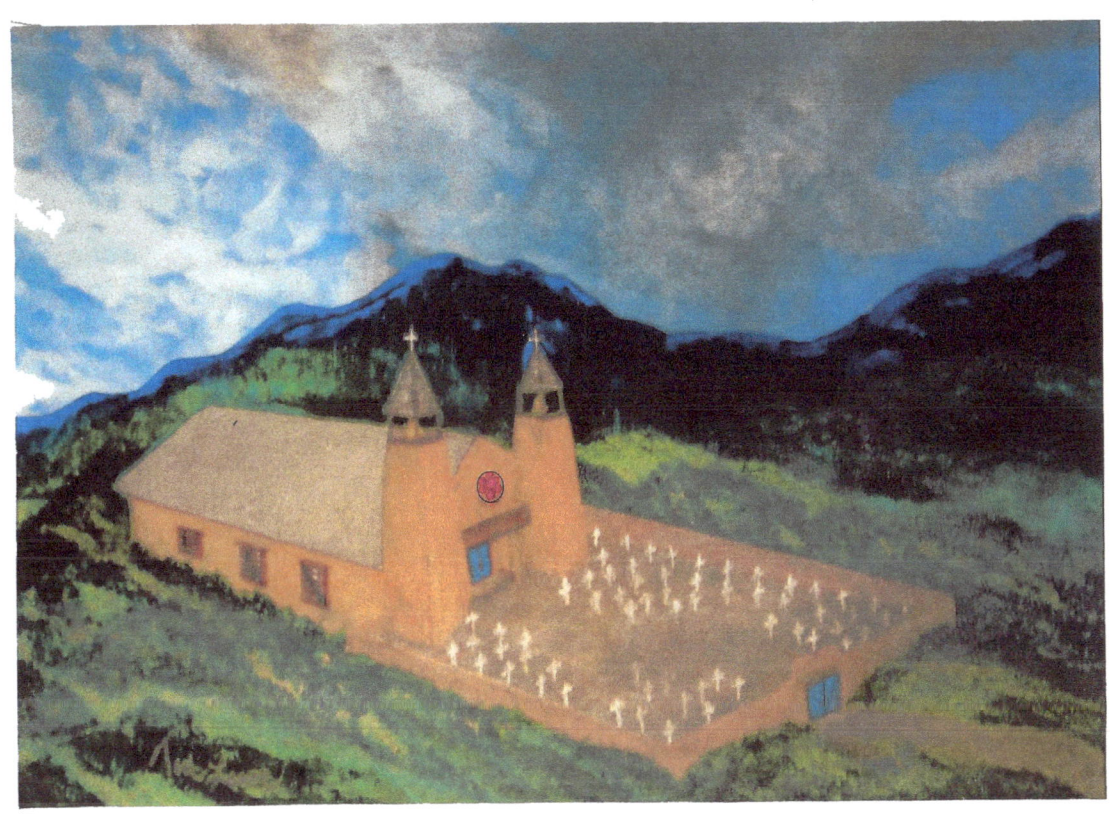

THE BELLS OF NORTHERN NEW MEXICO
THE PARISH PRIEST WENT TO THE VADICAN
TO BLESSED BY THE POPE
HE RETURNED AND DID
THE STAINLESS GLASS ROUND WINDOW

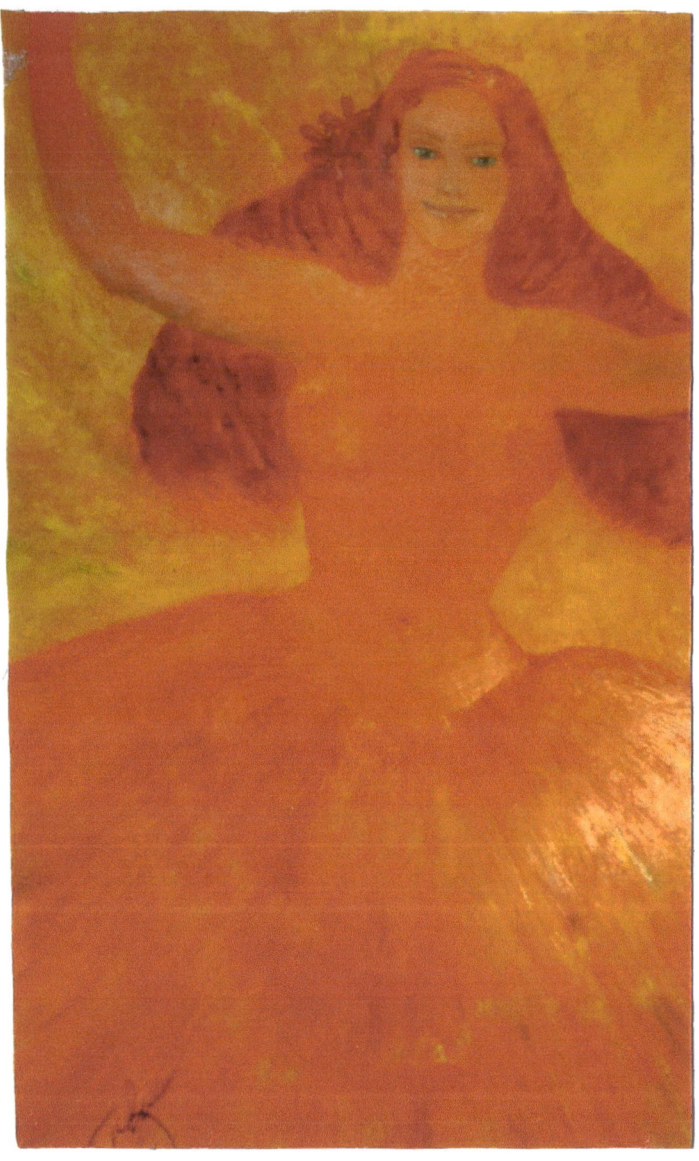

LOVELY HAILE HULA
IF YOUR NOT NATIVE HAWAIIAN
YOUR CALLED A HAILE

HAWAII AND MIDWAY ISLANDS

STATIONED AT BEEVILLE TEXAS (SANDRA FIRST DAUGHTER BORN THERE) I RECEIVED ORDERS TO GO TO AIRBARSON IN THE HAWAIIAN ISLAND OF OAHU TO BARBERS POINT NAVEL AIR STATION. WE DROVE TO SANFRANCISO IN 51 MERCURY. WE HAD A WEEKS STAY AT THE MARK HOPKINS TO WAIT THE SHIP TO SAIL TO HAWAII. JUST FOUR DAYS AT SEA. I WAS SEA SICK BEFORE WE CLEARED THE GOLDEN GATE BRIDGE. HAVING SERVED AS A PIO AND EDUCATION OFFICER I WOULD ASSUME THIS POST AT THE SQUADRON CALLED AIRBARSON. THIS WAS SHORT FOR AIRBORNE EARLY WARNING SYSTEM. WE SPENT A YEAR IN OAHU LIVING IN HOUSE WITH NO WINDOWS SCREENS ONLY A BLOCK TO THE OCEAN. IT WAS A WONDERFUL YEAR. TOOK UP ARCHERY MADE MY OWN ARROWS AND BOW. WENT HUNTING ON THE BIG ISLAND. OUR GROUP NEVER KILLED ANY OF THE WILD PIGS AND GOATS. GOT LOST IN THE LAVA BEDS MANY TIMES. MY ORDERS CAME AND SENT ME TO MIDWAY ISLAND THE HUB OF AND HEADQUARTERS OF THE SYSTEM. JANETTE AND SANDRA WENT HOME TO SANTA FE.

MIDWAY ISLAND IS BEAUTIFUL. SITE OF THE WW2 NAVEL BATTLE AGAINST THE JAPANESE NAVY AND ANNUALS OF NAVY HISTORY. WHITE SAND BEACHES, A FIVE MILE REEF ALL AROUND. GREAT SAILING AND SNOKELING.
SEA FOOD GREAT AND THE LOBSTERS DID NOT HAVE CLAWS. RED LABEL JOHNNY WALKER SCOTCH A $1.57 A BOTTLE. WE FLEW SUPER CONSTELLATIONS ON THE FULL FOURTEEN HOUR FLIGHT TO TURN AROUND AT THE ALEUTION ISLANDS THE CON'S HAD A ROUND BELLY ATTACHED TO HOUSE THE RADAR EQUIPTMENT FOR THE SEVEN TECHS WORKING IT. THE SYSTEM WAS DESIGNED TO DETECT ANY RUSSIAN FLIGHT AGGRESSION. OUR SYSTEM LASTED ONLY FOUR YEARS THEN HIGH TECH TOOK OVER. OUR NAVAGATION WAS BY THE STARS. OUR BIGGEST FOE WERE THE GOONEY BIRDS ON THE RUNWAYS OR IN FLIGHT. WHEN THEY MET THE PROPELLER NOT MUCH WAS LEFT. IT WAS JUST CLEAN UP. NO HARM DONE. IN GENERAL THE FLIGHTS WERE VERY BORING. WE USED THE BLACK BOX (AUTO PILOT) OFTEN. THE KOREAN WAR WAS WELL ON ITS WAY. MY YEAR WAS SOON OVER AND MY TIME IN NAVEL AIR WAS OVER. NO RE-INLISTMENT FOR ME. OFF TO SANFRANCIS TO LEAVE THE NAVY AND HOME TO SANTA FE.

Holiday gift

Time for the end of this year
The new peeks around the corner
Spend in it in good cheer
Thoughts of grace
This year to erase

Wishes of love
Given from below and above
Settling to earth
In blankets of white

Peace comes within
Making hearts glow
Renewal of spirit
Given to us all

Look in your heart
The gift has always
Been there

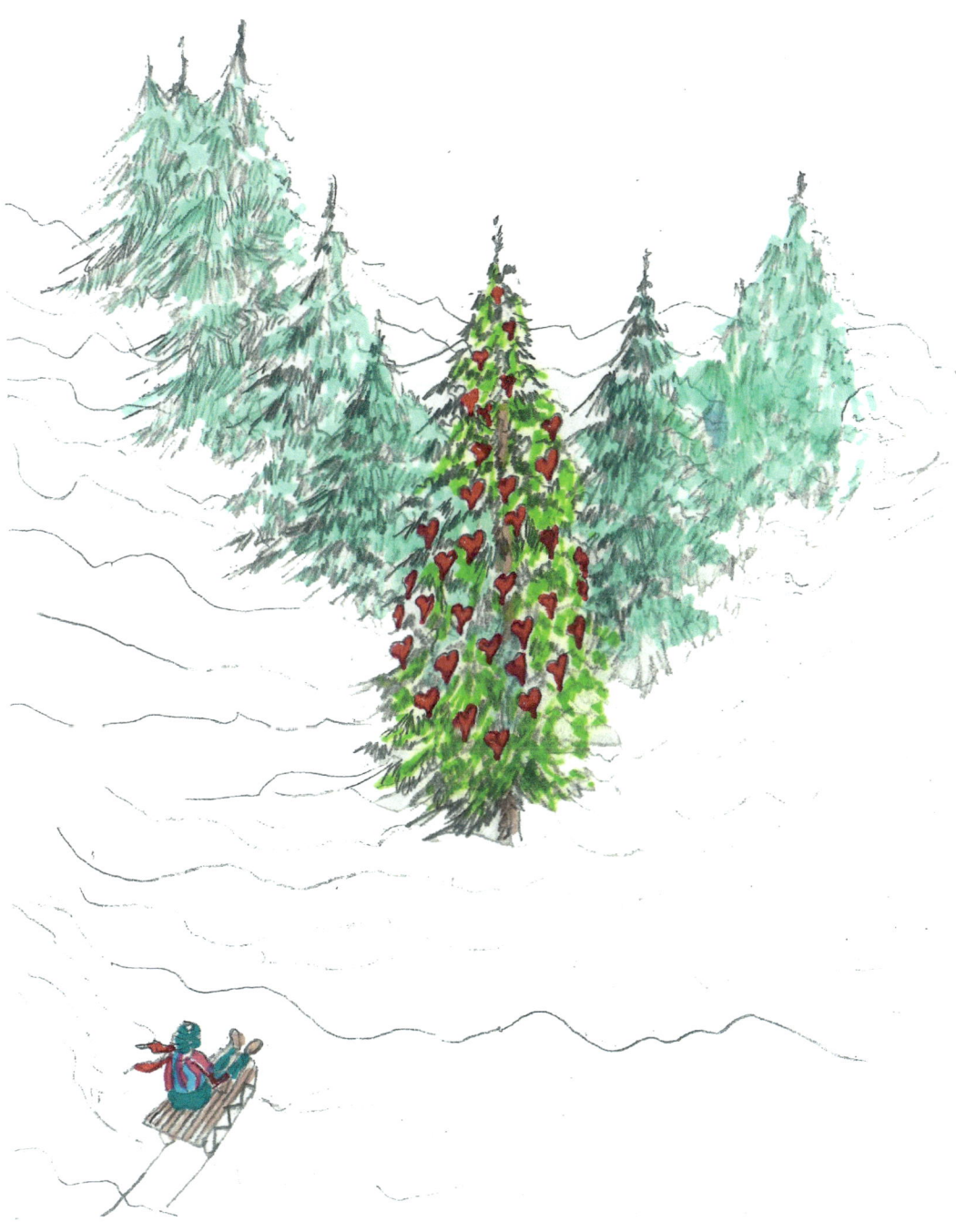

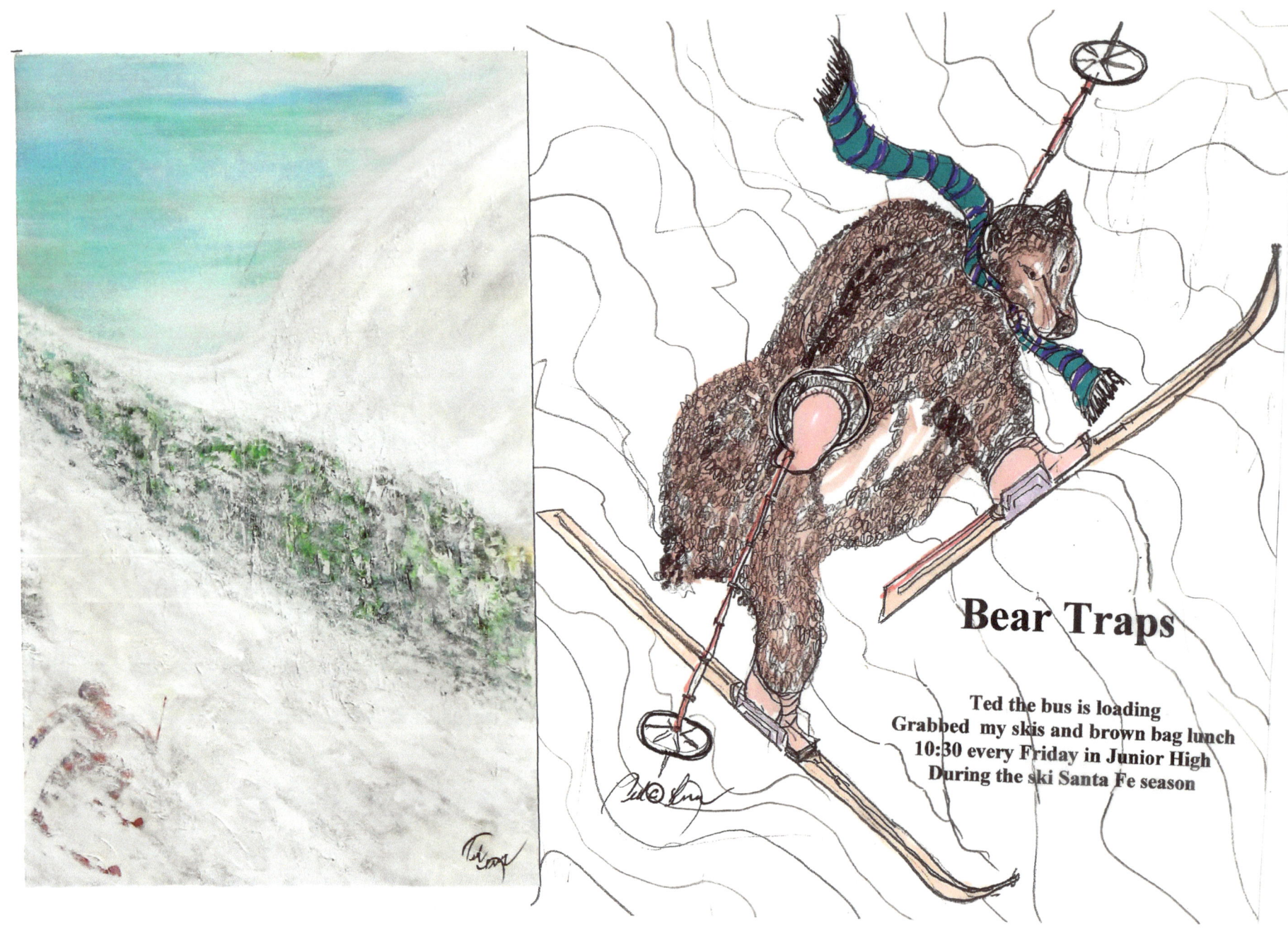

Bear Traps

Ted the bus is loading
Grabbed my skis and brown bag lunch
10:30 every Friday in Junior High
During the ski Santa Fe season

30

Thanks to the Ernie Blake family
The $1.59 tow rope fee was waived
Grades 7 through 9 accounted for
Only the one's wanting to ski

Hickory was the wood
Steel edges to come much later
Super long with points at the tips
Heavy to carry

Square toe leather ankle boots
To fit in the vise
Snuggly tied with strands of leather
Binding you forever
Bear Traps

Front cable throws
Coiled spring backs
Married you for life
Skis never to realize and let go
For Some broken limbs would follow

Bamboo long poles
Metal ring tied with leather
The loop for you to hold
Hands in canvas mittens

Two pair of jeans
A wool coat to heavy
No one new of goggles
You just simply blinked your eyes

Later to come
The new invention
A metal tow rope griper
Gone forever the strain
Of one hand forward
The other one behind

The machos game was simple
How many runs can you make
Before the bus loads
The trails were short not very wide
We always volunteered
To pack the new fallen snow

In a line tip to toe top guy is the leader
We side stepped from the bottom
Stomping up and down
Are reward at the top
Was to glide down on packed snow

Moments of joy
Was to ski in the powder
Thru the trees not a trail insight
The closest I have ever been
To earthly flying in natures white-out

As the years sped away
Thanks to Buzz Bainbridge
A new Red two chair lift was installed
A role model to me and
The best Boy Scout leader
Taught us how to drown a camp fire
With no water insight

Skiing in the zone
Through the years
Dancing the fall line
In perfect being
At One with the snow

Parallel skiing that added grace
Feet together skis acting as one
Planting poles for turns
Uplifting the weight

Traversing the slope
Or making short turns
A melody in the snow
The song in my soul
Groomed wide and long slopes
Some short some long
Not a sound to be heard
But the spirit of the skis
Cold rides on the lifts
Sometimes snow flying
Ski rests that lift
Seating now is four
No strain to your being

Spiced coffee with a drop or two
From unknown bottles
Tunes your faculties
To say hi to the
Devine-feminine

Hope in your heart
She take a run or two
Most always in front
And waiting for you

The kind childhood mountain
Has changed
High tech in everything
Engineering marvel

A life time of skiing
Enhancement of life
New areas abound
Waiting for you and me

Please go and enjoy the new science
Take a lot of plastic
For you see
Lift tickets are now
At fifty seventy five

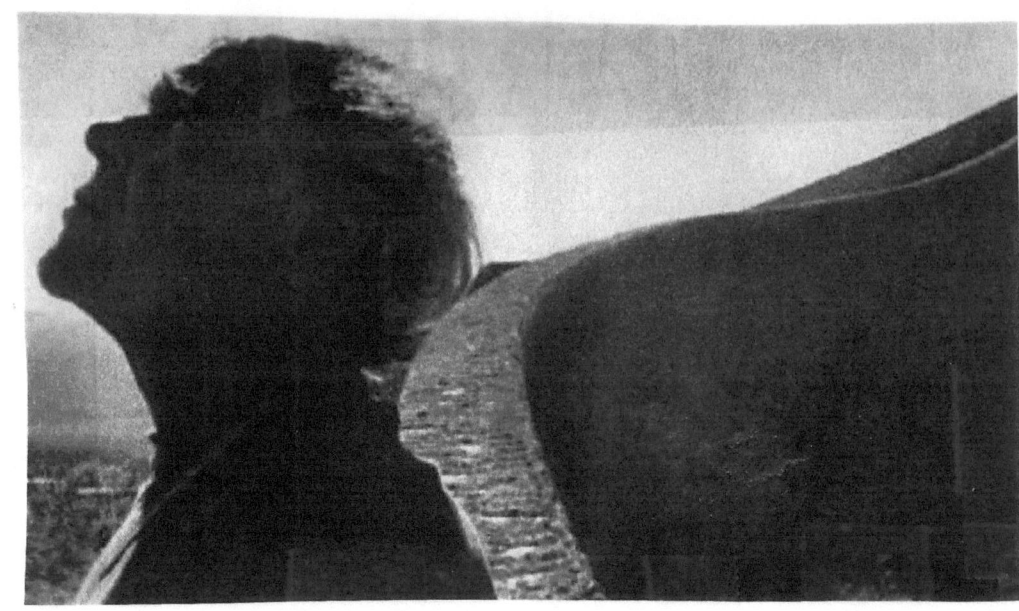

A FATHER'S HONOR

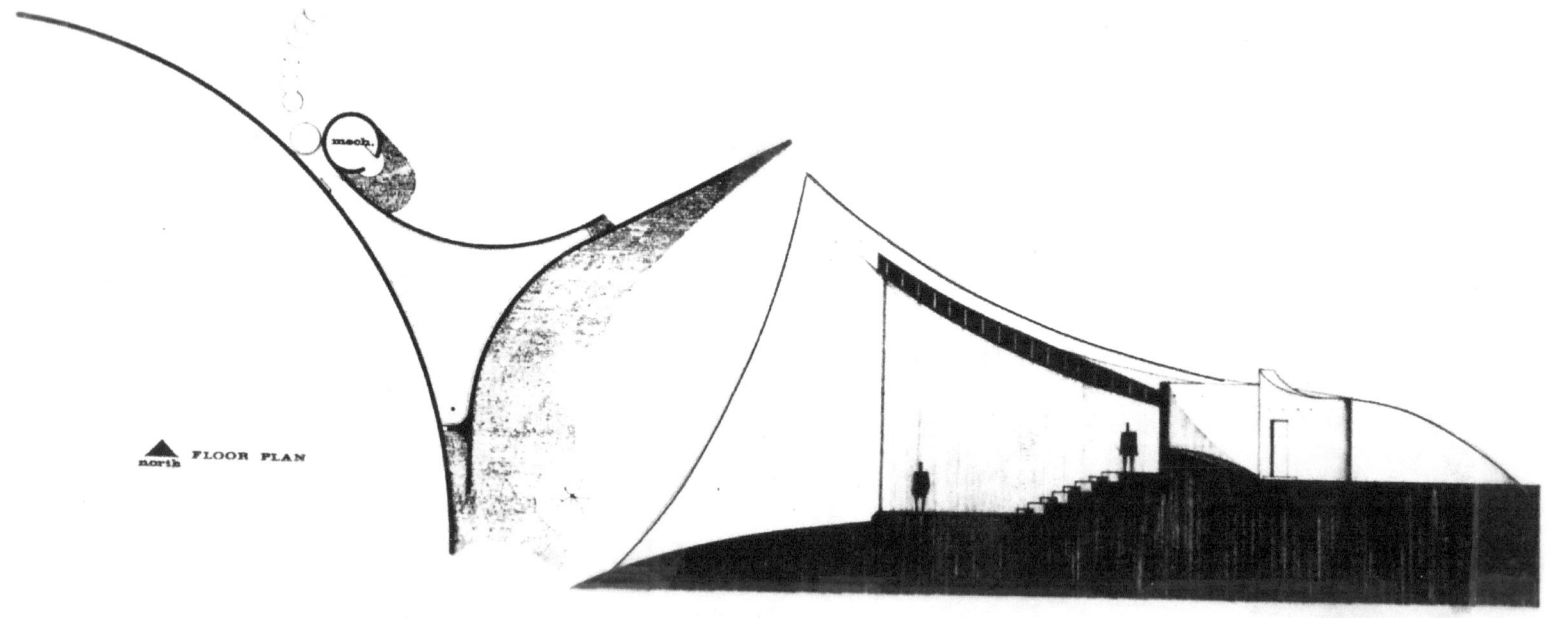

north FLOOR PLAN

SECTION

ARCHITECT'S PROLOGUE
HISTORICAL FACT

Tony and Enga Perry were ski instructors at Pararito Ski area at Los Alamos where we first met. The rope tow to the top of the small run was arm lurking. We became good friends with red hot wine at their home on Canyon road. And they spent their summers at Angel Fire in a double size trailer where Tony worked with Dr. Westphall helping him sell sites on his 800 acre Val Verde Ranch and golf course he single handed developed. Victor asked Tony if he new any Architects and Tony referred me to him. At that time Victor and Jeanne were in a quandary on what to do with the government insurance payment of $30,000 on the death of their son David killed in Vietnam.

Tony called me and I went to Angel Fire and met him at the sales shack on the main road to the development. He instructed me to just follow the development road to the golf course area where Victor was working. I did and on a neat par three I saw a man on a back hoe and stopped and asked him where I could find Dr. Westphall. He said that's me and I introduced myself. He then told me to go back to the end of main road and he would meet me at the house. Which I did, and the house not at all what I expected. It looked sinister and straight out of Grimm's fairy tales. He introduced me to Jeanne and we had coffee. They told me that they wanted something of sustenance to honor their son's death. Nothing to do with any transitory gifts or endowments to the many possibilities or universities.

We discussed many possibilities and the best is as follows in my Architect's Concept Statement.

Ted "c" Luna
Architect of the Memorial Chapel

33

CONCEPT STATEMENT:

Watching the rain start and the lighting at eye level, sitting on the brow of the hill Overlooking the beautiful Moreano valley surrounded by majestic mountains Forming the valley I was getting wet and cold. What I am getting into. I had met With my new clients earlier in the morning. They wanted something special to But did not now what. Their oldest son was killed in Vietnam they gave me the Budget from the insurance. After consideration I new what to do. My vision Became clear and they agreed We would do a chapel on the brow of the hill. I knew it wouldHave to be ecumenical in concept, peace, love, healing, and a retreat like (mecca) most of all timeless, my feelings were deep for veterans of all wars.

The site was overwhelming. I knew I had two choices, to build in sympathy with Nature or to build in contradiction (man made). In this isolated area, I could not Afford the traditional materials of stone,marble. My philosophy deep in Shibumi (understated eloquence) and Zen (Better by doing) soon found the answers by considering planes and sails,time less statements that have no PIT (point in time) And all of natures climatic seasons of the year, wind,snow, hail, temperture and rains.
I new never to build on the top of the hill. I new that in a design sense that Odds are better than Evens. This concept came together on a rainy Monday morning in my Santa Fe office in 20 minutes. I did the drawings but they could not convey my creation so I built a model and met with my clients. They were speechless for such a long time (I thought I missed the boat). First words were " we have never seen anything so beautiful." The legacy begins.

Little did we know that the impact on veterans of all wars, families, world wide Visitors would seek the memorial for 4 decades and find the emotional experience That each one would bring with them and leave with an enhancement of the human spirit . We are still creating veterans on a daily basis. The memorial is dedicated to current and future generations of all peoples in our world.

ARCHITECT'S CONSTRUCTION DOCUMENTS
HISTORICAL FACT PRE-GROUND BREAKING

We signed a standard AIA contract for 7% of $30,000 for my fee of $2,100.00 and no reimbursable which I donated. Little did I know that this would be the only compensation for more than 40 sum years. This did change when the state of New Mexico became the owners and wanted improvements.

I finished the construction documents to fit the budget and before I could find a contractor Victor called me and said that he had to make a payment on Val Verde Ranch that reduced the amount available to $15,000.00 and since my contract was for $2,100.00 that left only less than $12,900.00 for construction. I then knew we could not get a finished chapel for that amount. I had done some preliminary work with some Santa Fe contractors and under the adjusted circumstances they all declined. When I discussed the project with my good friend George Veddler both a civil engineer and good contractor he become very interested. His roots were from Norway and the Viking spirit was strong in him. Through the downsizing he knew he could do the foundations, concrete slab, three walls and mech. room for the budget of $12,890.00 no roof. Victor was ecstatic and signed Gorge's contract. We broke ground on late summer of 1968 he moved his crew to Angel Fire and they stayed at Victors house. As a young Architect this was my second commission in my new Practice. Little did I know that it would take 4 more years complete and be dedicated. George's worked went very fast. The following year Victor called me and said that the high West wall was moving 4 to 6 inches. Gorge was a very good pilot and we flew to Angel Fire with cables and anchors to be imbedded in concrete dead men either side of the west wall. I knew that the roof with transfer the wind loads to the east wall thru the roof that currently non existing. We stabilized the wall and the flight back it took us 4 circles to gain altitude to clear the pass to Santa Fe. I had a very good look at tree tops. Victor found a carpenter and had the roof installed for $1,200.00. No more moving walls due to the normal very high winds through the pass. Victor himself did all of the original hand dash stucco for the walls and interior.

ARCHITECT'S INTERIOR FOCUS
POINT AT THE APEX
HISTORICAL FACT

Early on Victor and I knew the importance of this special focus point of the chapel. We commissioned a Santa Fe sculptress to do design sketches of her interpretation of peace, ecumenical, brotherhood and a never ending tribute to Vietnam veterans, must be inspiring and thought provoking. She did this and Victor and I really liked her concepts. She wanted $2,500.00 to make it a reality. We did not have any funds available so we thanked her for her work. Shortly when the chapel was completed the local Baptist donated a Christian cross which is a religious endorsement and never in keeping with the original concept of the chapel. It's been truncated and modified through the years but it's still a cross.

One year before Victors death we met many times and discussed any solution that would remove the cross and be replaced with some symbol of the chapels basic concept. When the state became the owners and wanted improvements we held a nation wide competition and narrowed the field to 8 concepts. The selection committee declined all concepts. They asked me to come up with some and I did, they declined everyone I designed. In retrospect I think this was a blessing, so the cross remained.

Through the years I always have given this a lot of thought. I now think the perfect symbol in keeping with the chapel Concept of "PEACE" and brotherhood is an "Angel" in flight suspended or on a pedestal. I do believe this symbol transcends and is meaningful to all peoples and religions and most of all to war veterans. Archangels are still with us in many forms. Kind strangers that seem to appear out of nowhere to add a helping hand. Ask any war veteran in moments of crises who help save him or her a kind act by someone out of the blue. Thus a guardian angel.

Angels through history have been recorded both men and women with feathered wings. They are still around but with no wings. I think the best solution for the chapel would be a woman because all things considered humanity was nurtured by the female.

I would like to see this concept replace the cross in the chapel. Attached is more information and a photo of an angel only to amplify the concept.

Ted "C" Luna
Architect of the chapel

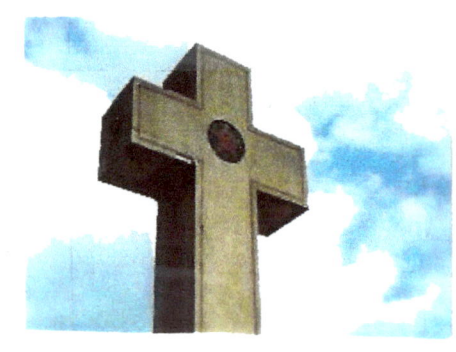
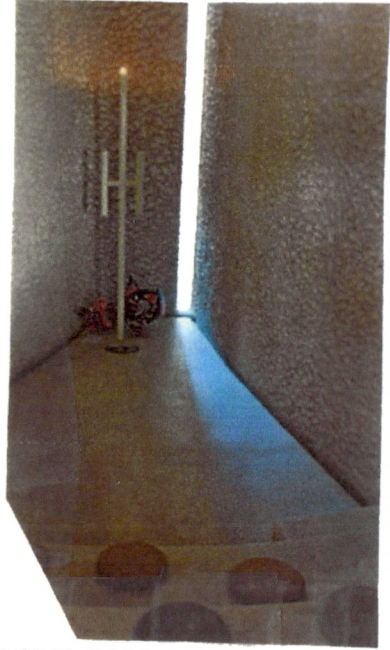

DANIEL MACH, DIRECTOR ACLU SAID A WAR MEMORIAL . THE GOVERNMENT HAS NO BUSINESS HONORING SERVICE MEMBERS OF ONE FAITH.

JASON TORPY , AN ARMY CAPTAIN SAID NON-CHRISTIANS FEEL LIKE A SECOND-CLASS CITIZEN WHOSE SERVICE IN LIFE AND DEATH DOESN'T MATTER.

MONICA MILLER, LEADER OF A WASHINGTON BASED GROUP SAID. THE CROSS GIVES THE IMPRESSION THAT ONLY CHRISTIANS ARE BEING HONORED.

When it was dedicated I was never invited
and the Washington power, John Kerry, Jan Scruggs wanted
to duplicate the chapel in Washington, Victor declined on the
basis there were no hills there. Victor being a Machiavellian
really did not want the chapel duplicated. I was never informed
to inter the competition for the memorial in Washington.
To me it's depressing. One veteran said it best "Washington
has the wall, Angel Fire has it all".

Ted "C" luna
Architect of the Chapel

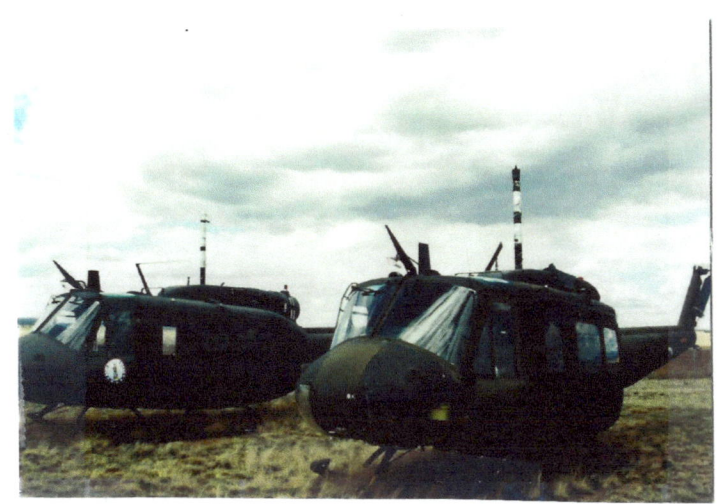

ARCHITECT'S HU-1 "HUEY"
HISTORICAL FACT

Victor asked Dava "director of the chapel for 4 years" they had just
received notice that the New Mexico National Guard located in Santa Fe
wanted to donate a helicopter "a Huey" to the memorial. Since it was
the work horse and an angel in the Vietnam war. She called me and
and asked if I would to the New Mexico National Guard site and select
one Huey out of many on the site to be refurbished and delivered and
installed at the memorial. I agreed and saw the Huey grave yard. I
took time and inspected all of the Hueys and took pictures for future
information needed to mount the Huey at the memorial. I selected
one and little did I know that this one was a Viking class and its only
pilot still lived. I guess the universe was at work! The odds of this
revelation are beyond believe. According to the article in the
Albquerque Journal dated November 6, 2016. His name is
Jack Swickaard he new the serial number on the tail of the
Huey. The Huey was removed from the memorial and transported
to Roswell to be refurbished and re-installed at the memorial
spring of 2017 with a ceremony. Of course I would like to meet
him. I saved his Huey for prosperity and a new re-born life.
Enclosed are some historical facts of interest.

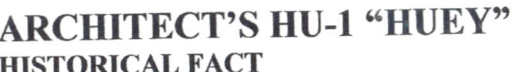

Ted "C" Luna
Architect of the Chapel

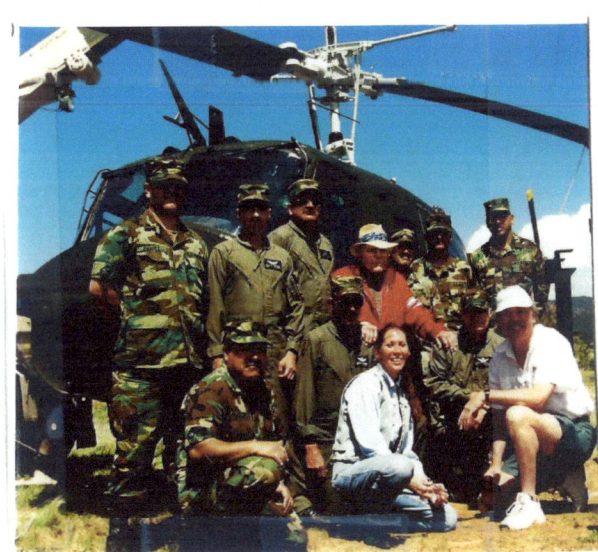

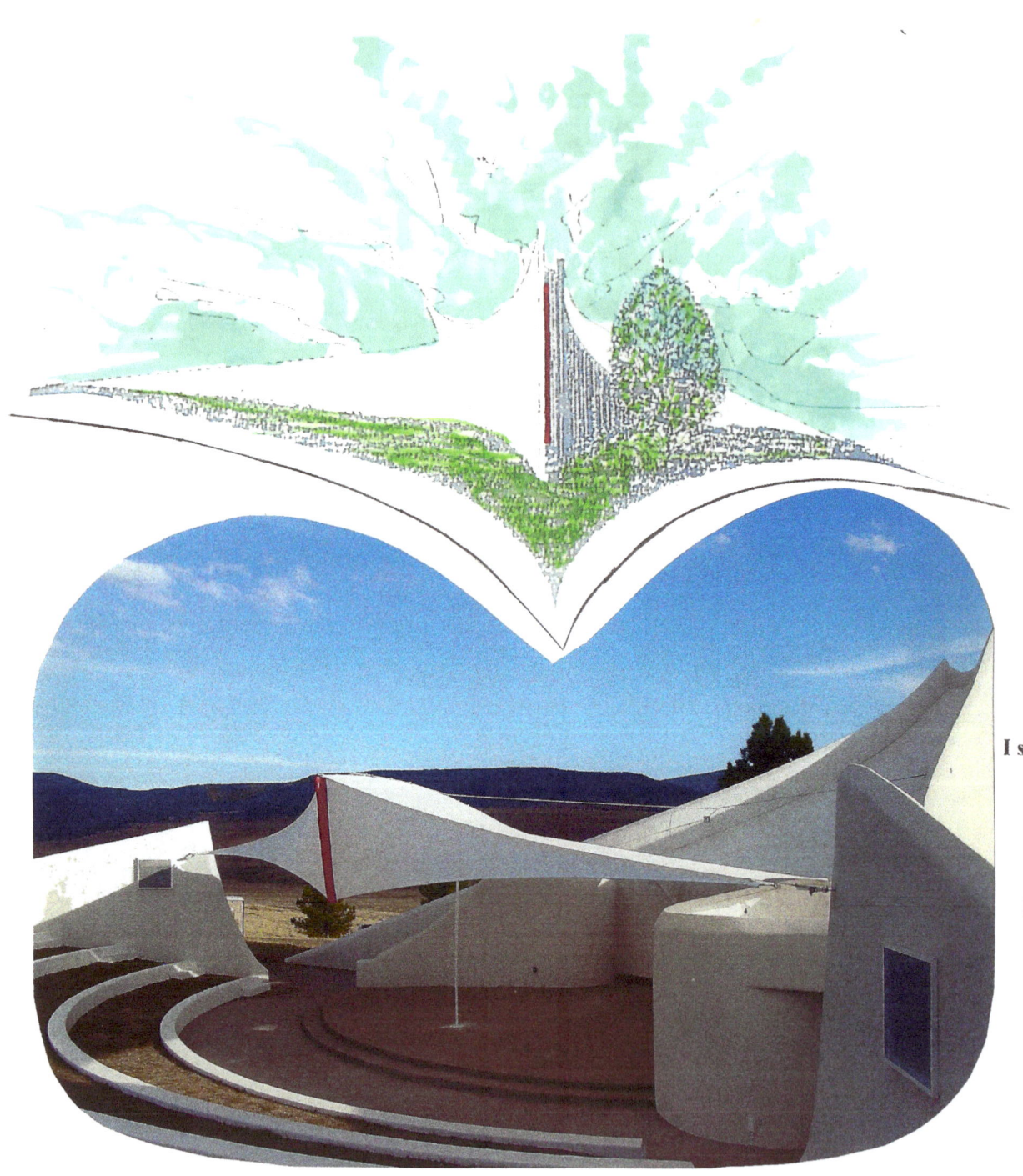

ODE TO
DAVID WESTPHALL

Where are you son
Why are there
A place called Nam
Feeling the pain
Who can you trust
No one I can see
Why can't you see
Tears cloud my eyes

Comrades in arms
New found friends
Blown in rice paddies
Huey to retrieve
Body bags galore
Some in hammocks
Dangling from the sky
I shy away from the replacements
Close I don't want to be
Yet I love him
The mirror in him is me
Dad I just want to live
Just so I can be
I guess I was not meant to be

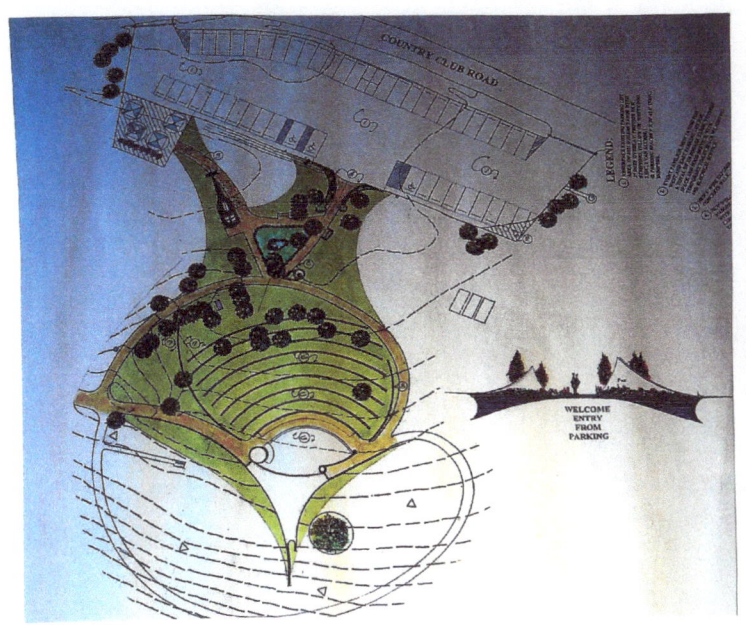

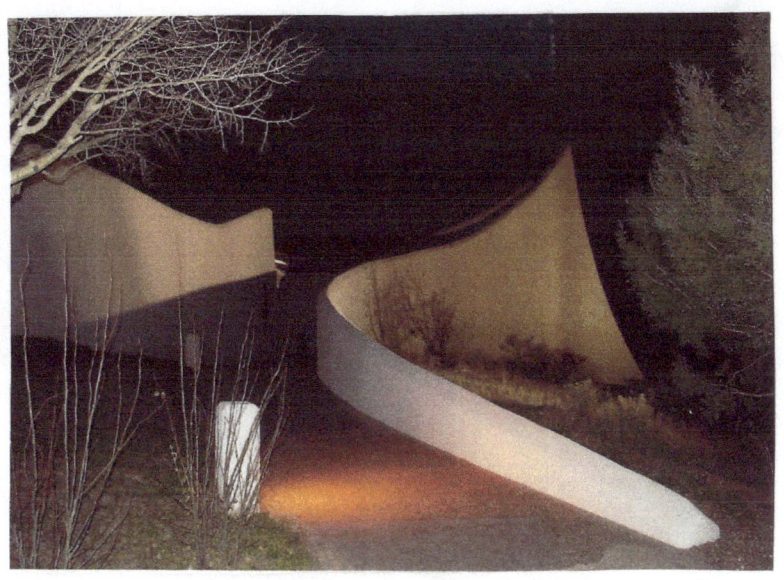

I HAVE TAKEN THE NATIONAL MEMORIAL INTO THE FUTURE

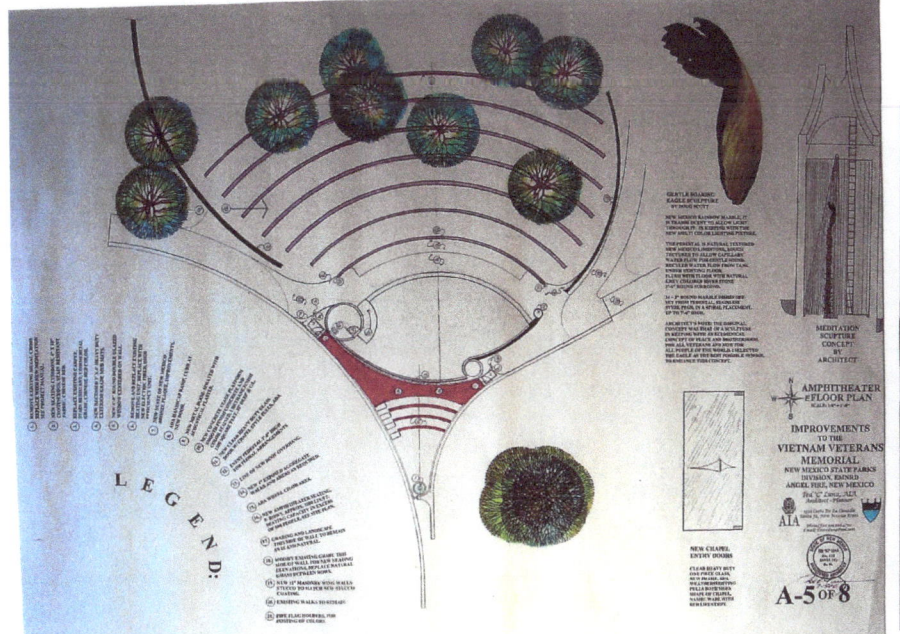

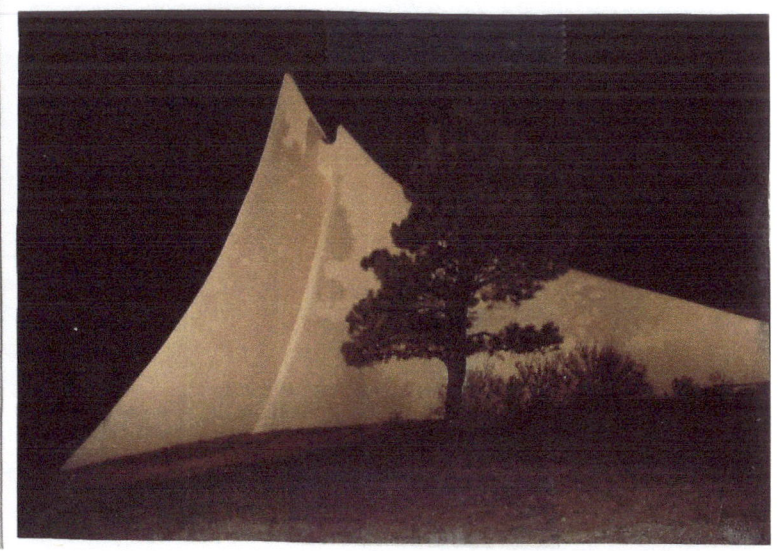

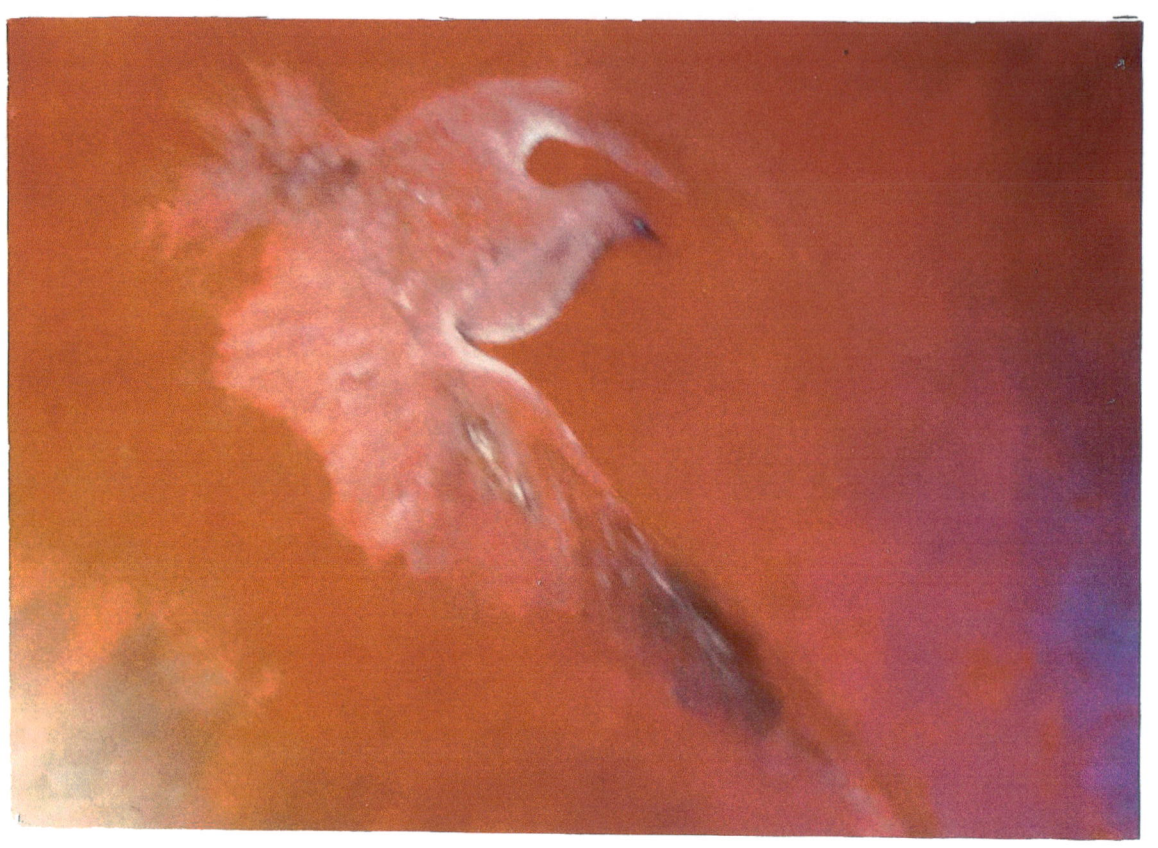

SAYINGS RE-VISTED

Dam the torpedoes
Full speed a stern
We have to outrun the Dam things
In harms way
I drive it every day

I left my heart in San Francisco
And my American Depressed card too
Out in the West Texas Town of El Paso
I had an affair

How many arms have held you
I'm glad they let you go

DANCING WITH THE WIND

America the beautiful
Remains
Global Warming
Drink cold beer

Give me Liberty or Death
Death is Liberty
O say can you see by the dawns early light
Sorry I lost my glasses

The only fear is fear itself
Unless your in a foxhole
Up you go to San Juan's hill
Sorry I lost my way

Old Chinese Proverb
May you live in interesting times
Make your life interesting

Our president ran on change
He meant the sheets in the White House
For whom the bell tolls
Quisimotto doing his job

Ask not what your country can do for you
But what you can do for your country
Don't send Lawyers to congress

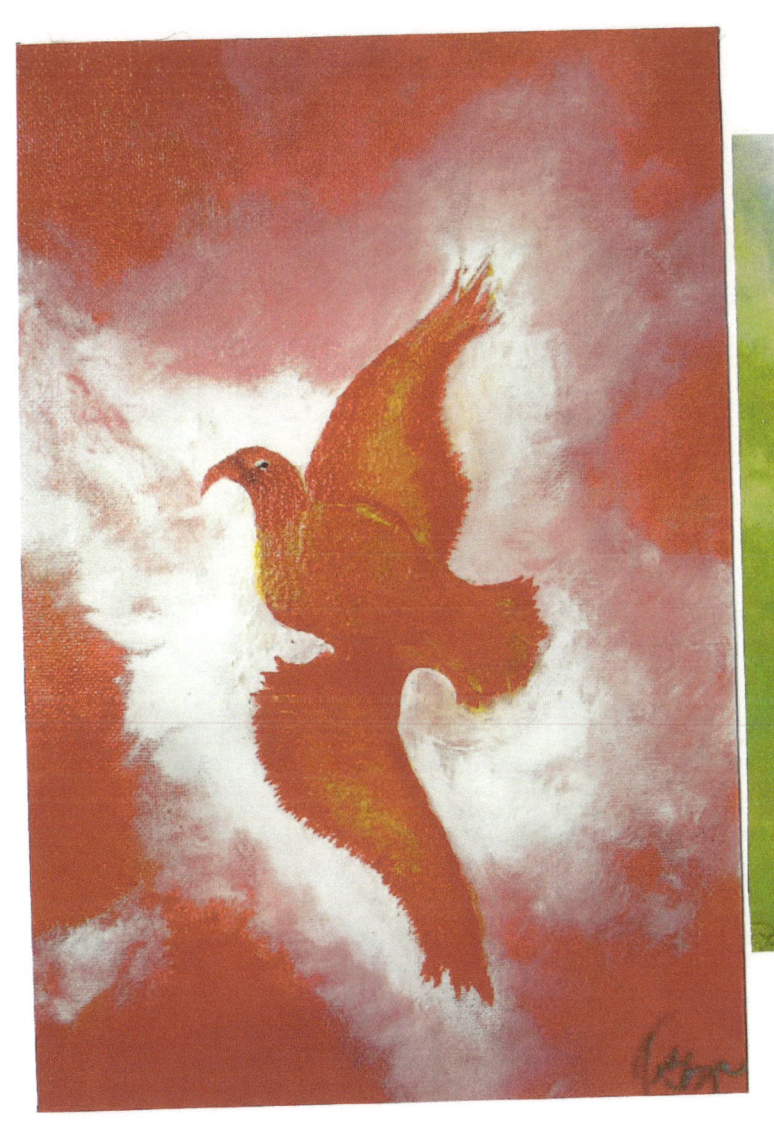

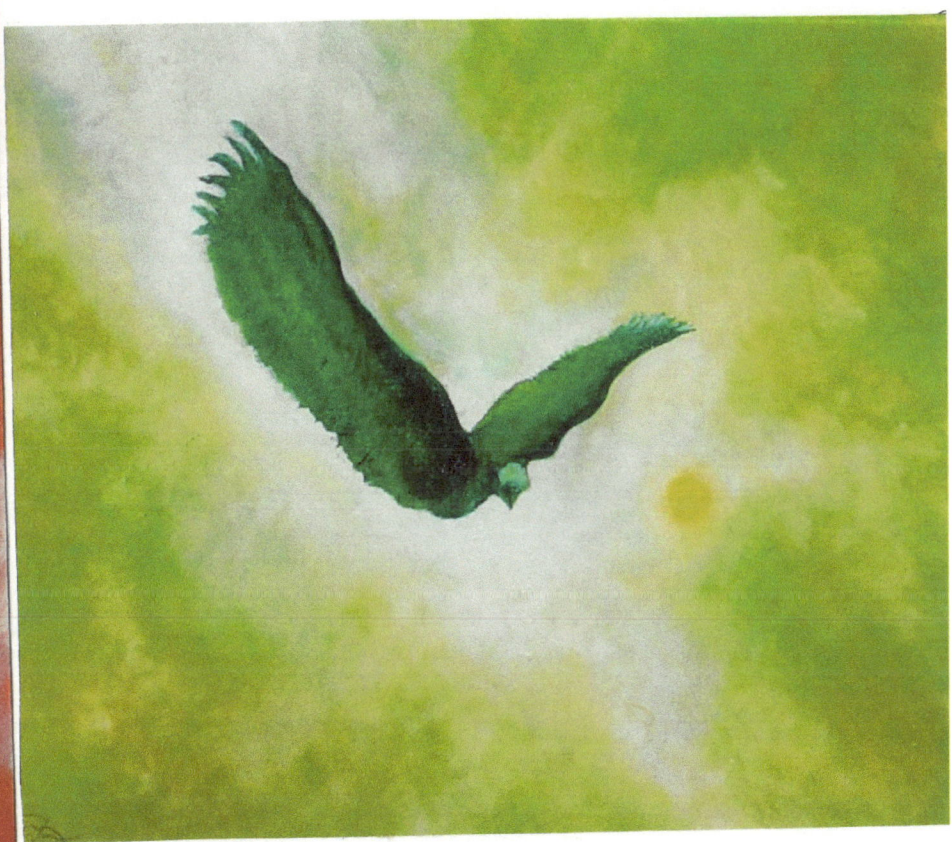

BIRDS OF A FEATHER

SOMETIMES DON'T STICK TOGETHER

AUTUMN BLAZE

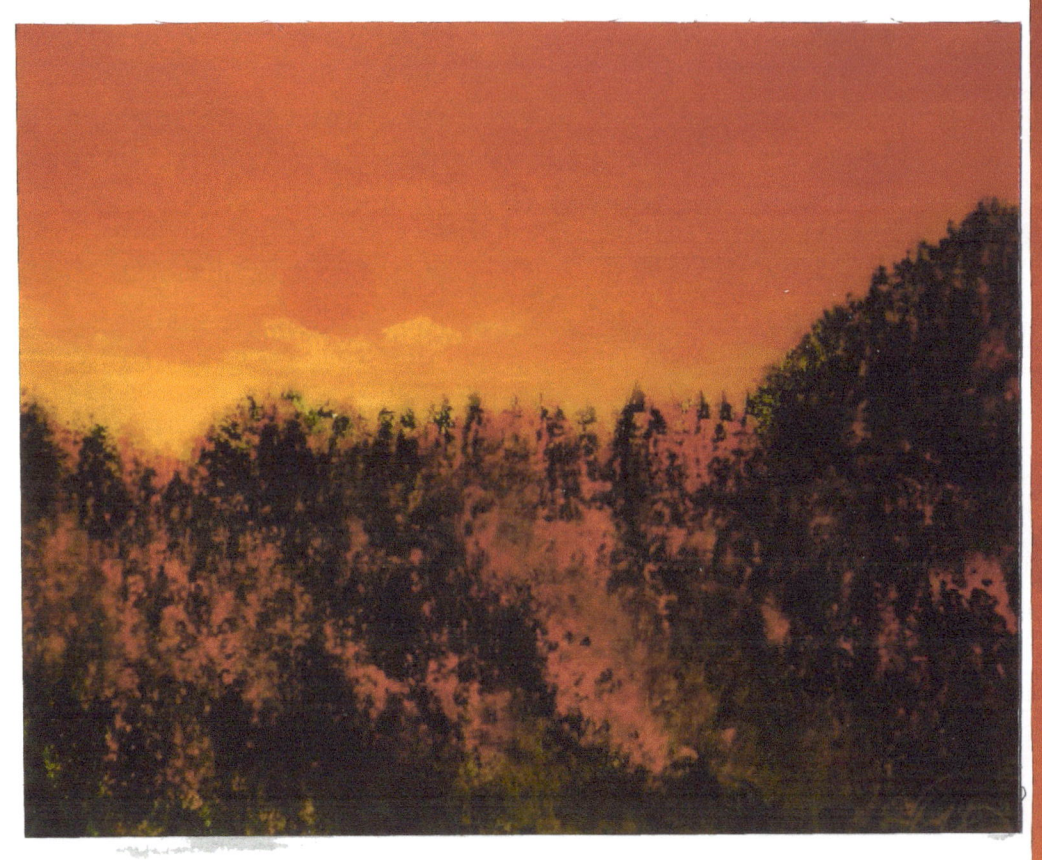

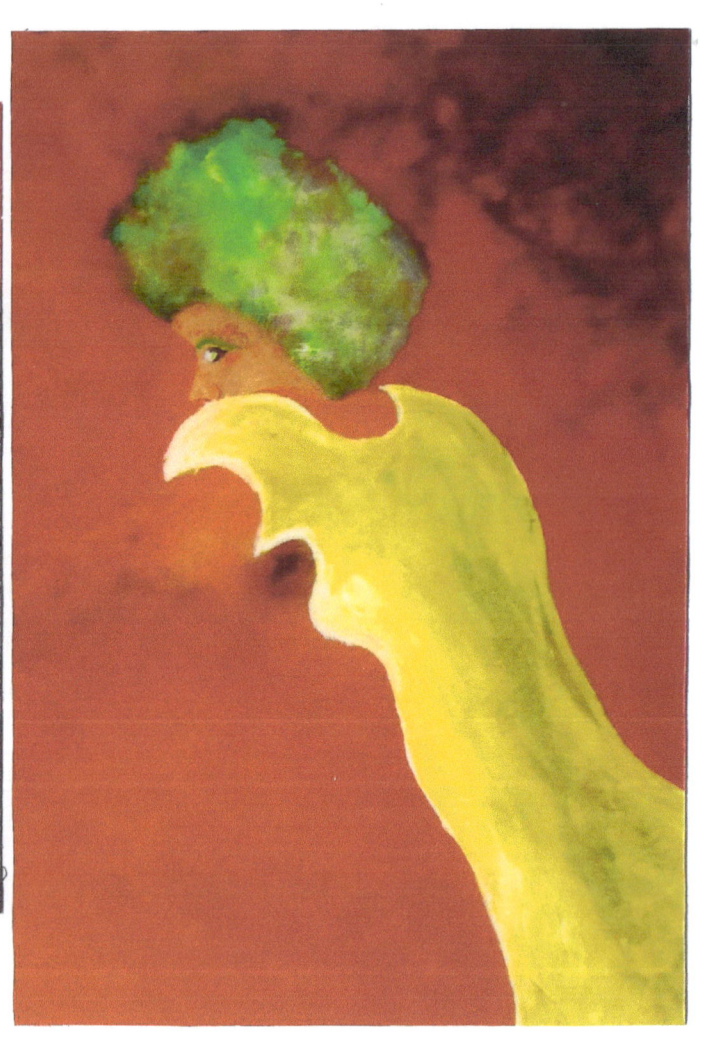

PRETTY LADY

THE FLOOR

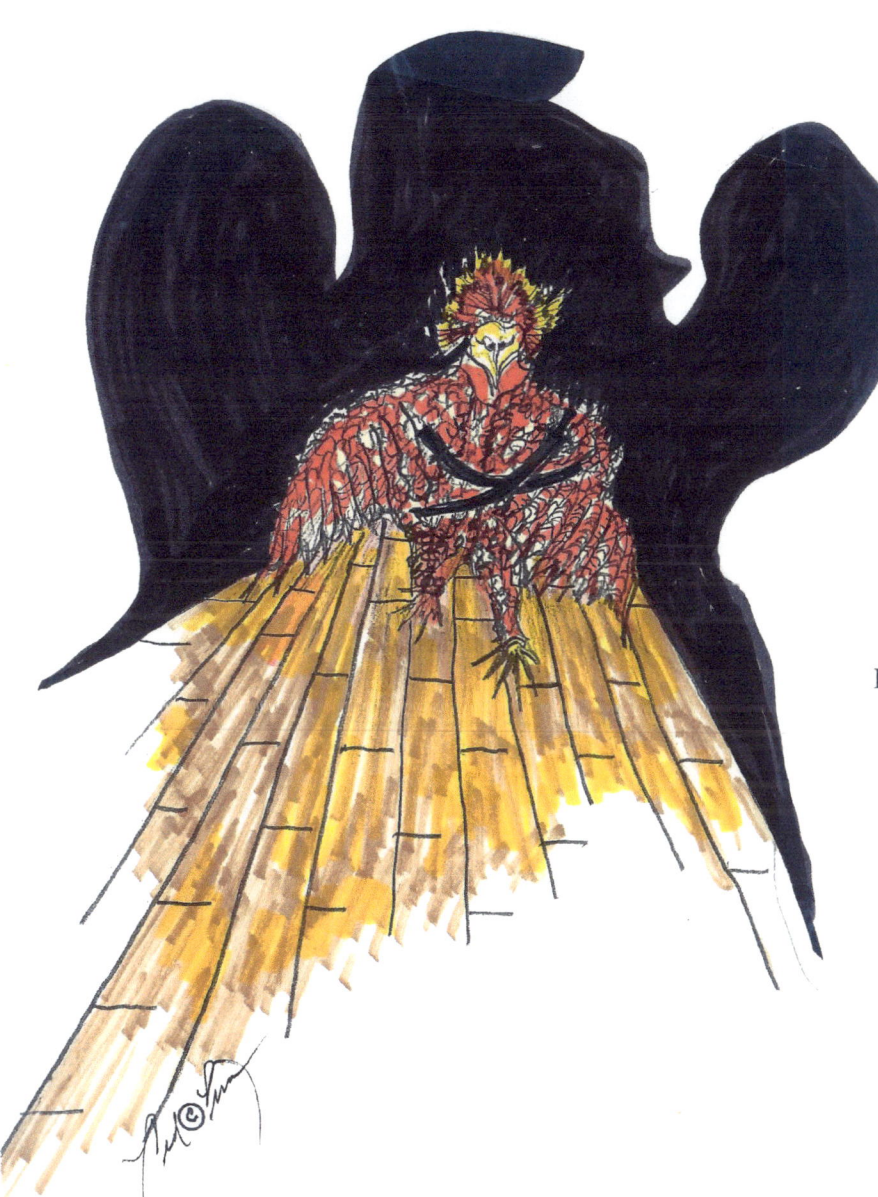

In ancient Japan
A dire need arose
How to protect
Lord , ladies
Concubines in repose

Samurai guards
To insure that the realm
Would remain
Under one lord

The conquerors would come
In the dark of night
With far more numbers
They had considered their plight

Laying the samurai guards in gore
What can we do
To insure a warning
The lord did cry

He summoned his
Masters of the wood
Build a floor that sings
When one walks in its way

But what song will it sing
Squeaky in tones
Clear to the ear
Night and day

A nightingale floor
It's the only way
The floor will sing
Like the rising sun
Clearing the dawn

Nightingale's song
Bolted all awake
With time to draw
Each samurai sword
Fighting the foes

Reserve guards in the wings
Will join the melee
The feudal lord
And all would live
All treasurers he will
Never have to give

The nightingale
Had sung its song
Saving the night
National treasure

It still sings to this day
In most all of Japan
The floor remains
In a land ever so far away

**THE NIGHTINGGALE
FLOOR**

43

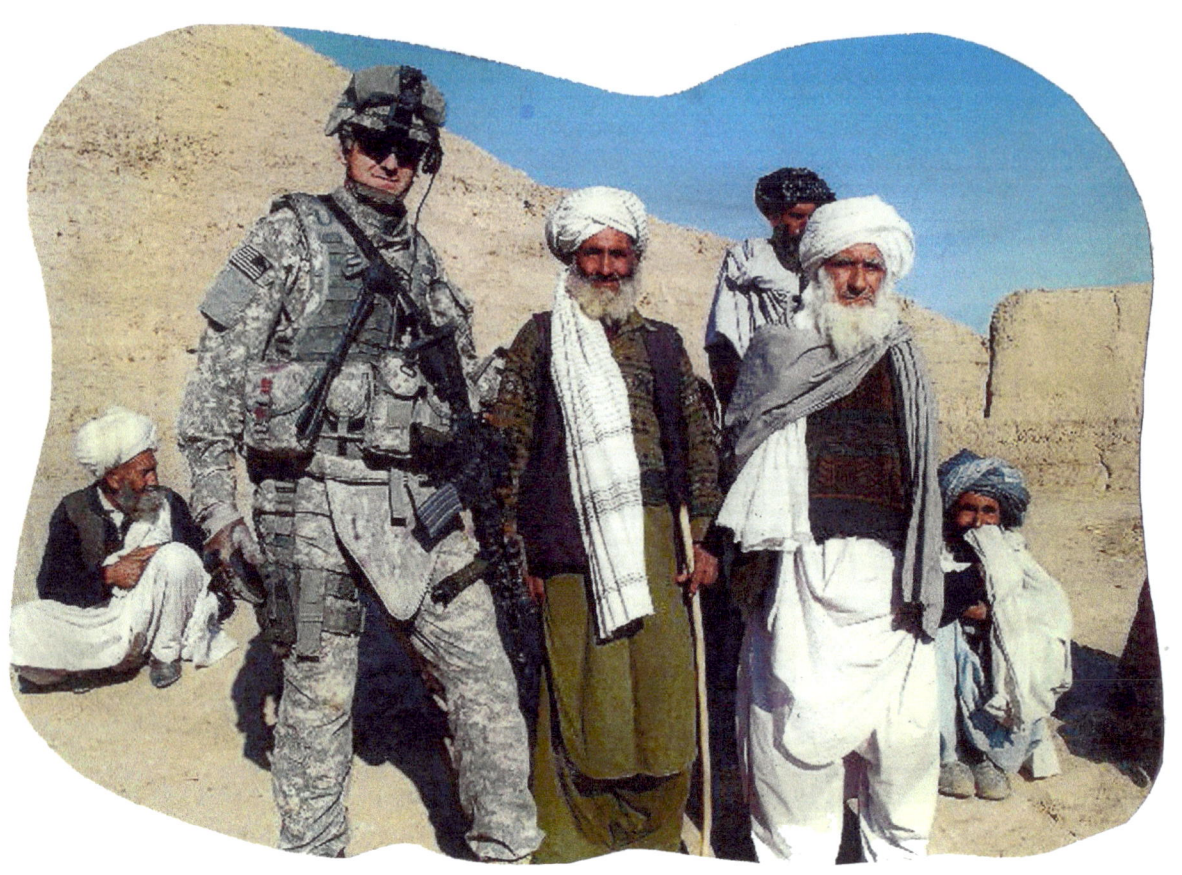

Rich's Odyssey

365 The Number Rings
Gone To A Land Less Known
In A War Without Ending
Noble Deeds Never To Tell
A Star Of Bronze
Reward For Living
Humane Treatment
You Gave To All
Hope For Change
Under Your Command

Your Time Spent
Sleeping
Like A Can Of Beans
Metal Was All Around
Unlike Armour
Foot Hills Valleys
And A River Too
Children In Huddles
Some Games To Play
But Now Dressed
In A Contempory Way
Gifts To Them
Because Of You
From All Of Us Here
Four Weeks Of Travel
No Parcel Lost Their Way

Black Hawks Landing
Sweeping The Parking Lot Clean
Hat Less Soldiers
All Eyes With A Gleam
Joy And Love
Soon To Receive
Smiles, Hugs And Kisses
You Are Home
RICH IS MY STEPSON
I HAVE AWAYS
CONSIDERED HIM
AS THE SON I
ALWAYS WANTED

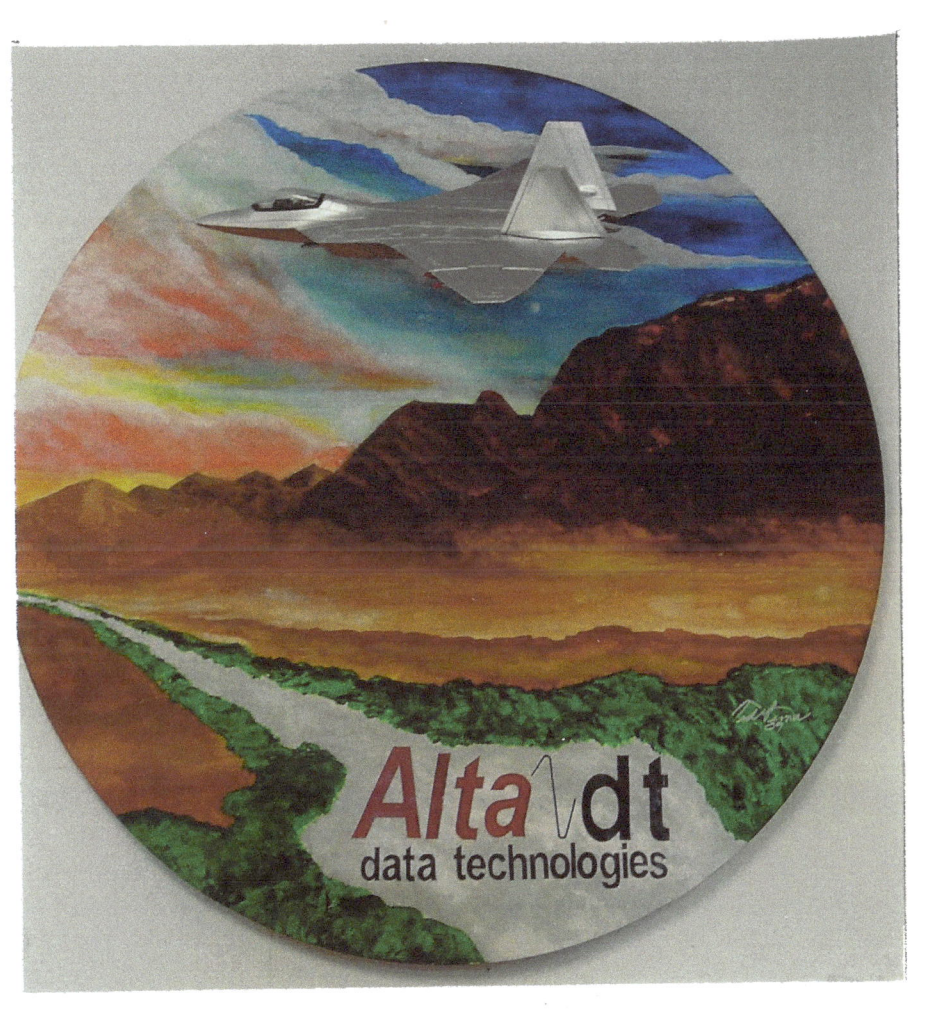

ALTA

IS THE NAME OF THE AVIONICS
COMPANY THAT RICHARD AND STEPHANIE
HELP ESTABLISH IN RIO RANCHO
THEY ASKED ME TO DO A PAINTING
FOR THEIR RECEPTION ROOM
FOR THEIR NEW OFFICE
THEY WANTED THE SANDIA
MOUNTAINS AND THE RIO GRANDE
MY GRANDSON ERIC AT NMMI

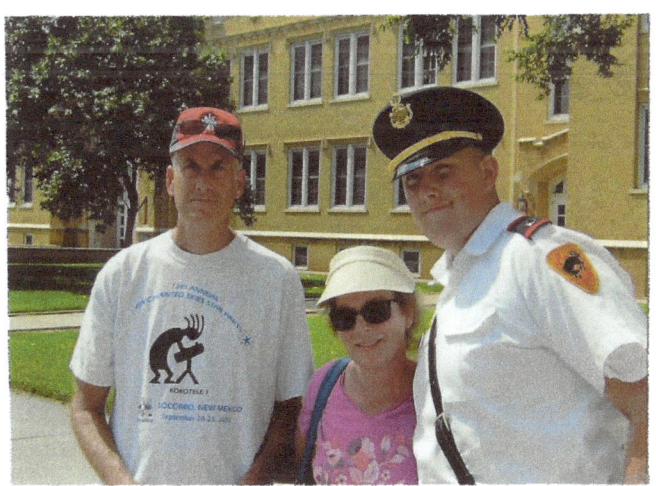

Sailor

Feelings with in
Hard to define
Wayward winds
Blowing the seas

Gentle and harsh
Tugging at the helm
Safe port to come
far far away

Guiding by waves
Tassels white
Sailor I am
In the ocean of life

Boundaries do not exist
Overwhelming with in the sea
Ponder the stars
Lacing diamonds in the night
An ocean wake in making

Experience this with me
Close you eyes then to see
The beauty of the universe
That lives with in you and me

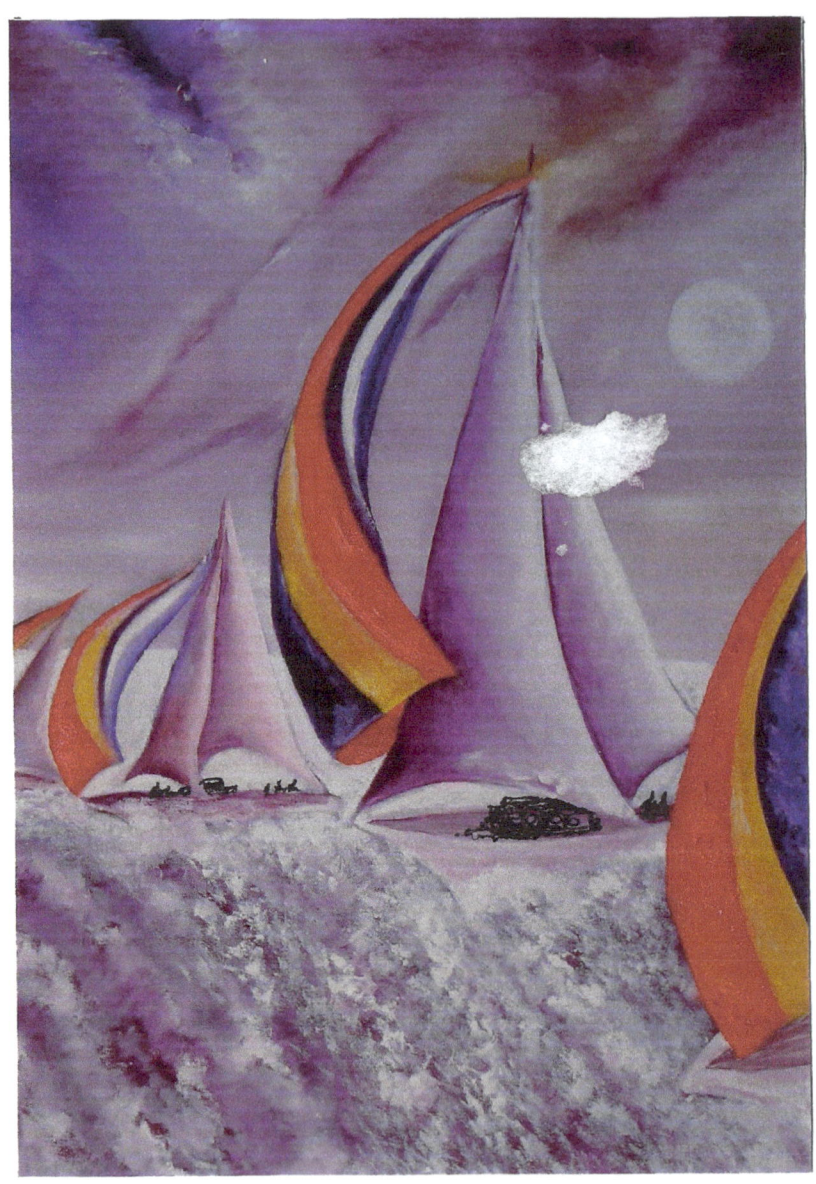

"REGATTA"
AROUND THE LAST MARK
HEADING TO THE FINISH LINE

WISDOM

Behold wisdom spoke
Time to drop the yoke
To cast you straight to prison
Or refresh your brow
With early morning dew
It will tell you
Where to fine the other shoe
Tails of woe they bring you
Set their hearts a glow
It will melt like frozen snow
It may remain I hope you know
Age will grant you

A late realize of toil
The house you built
And reside within
Windows to the world
Doors to open paths
Where are you my lass
Gone with the breeze
A gentle northern wind
But there come in droves
Humanity in plight
Some with joy
Others with delight
Fear not you troubled ones
Wisdom lights the way

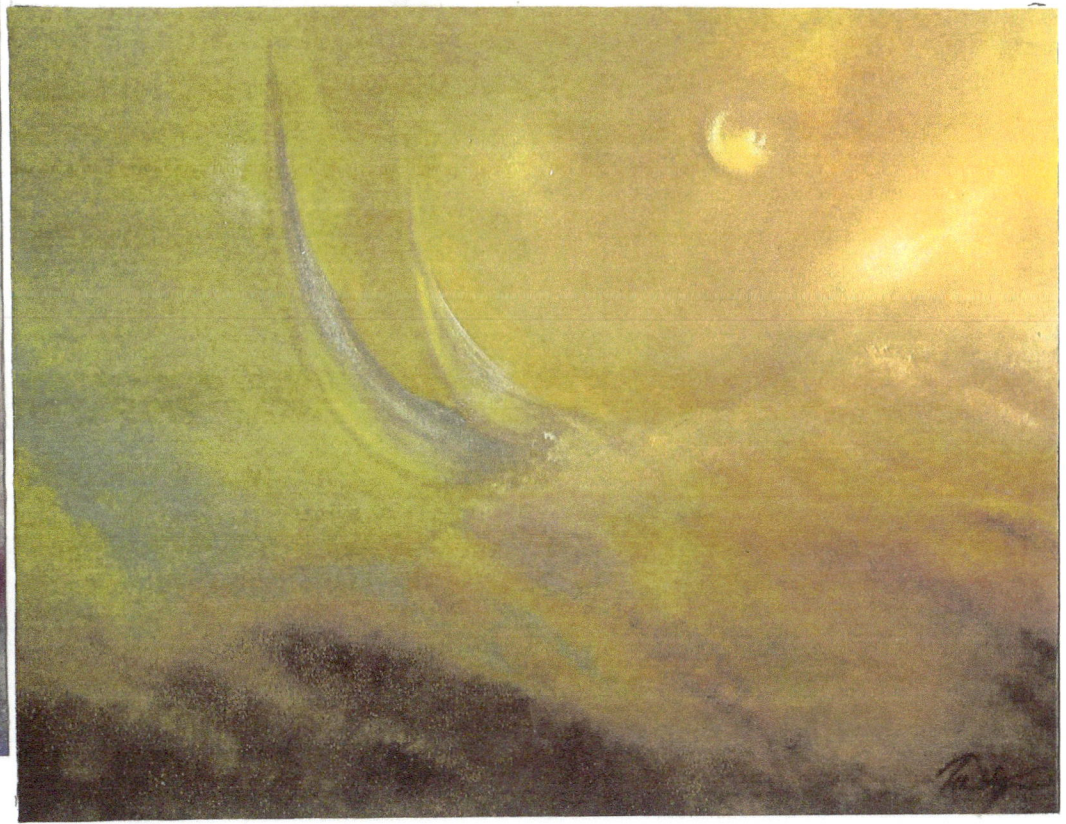

SAILING IN MY DREAMS
IN WILD SEAS AND SKIES

COLUMBINE

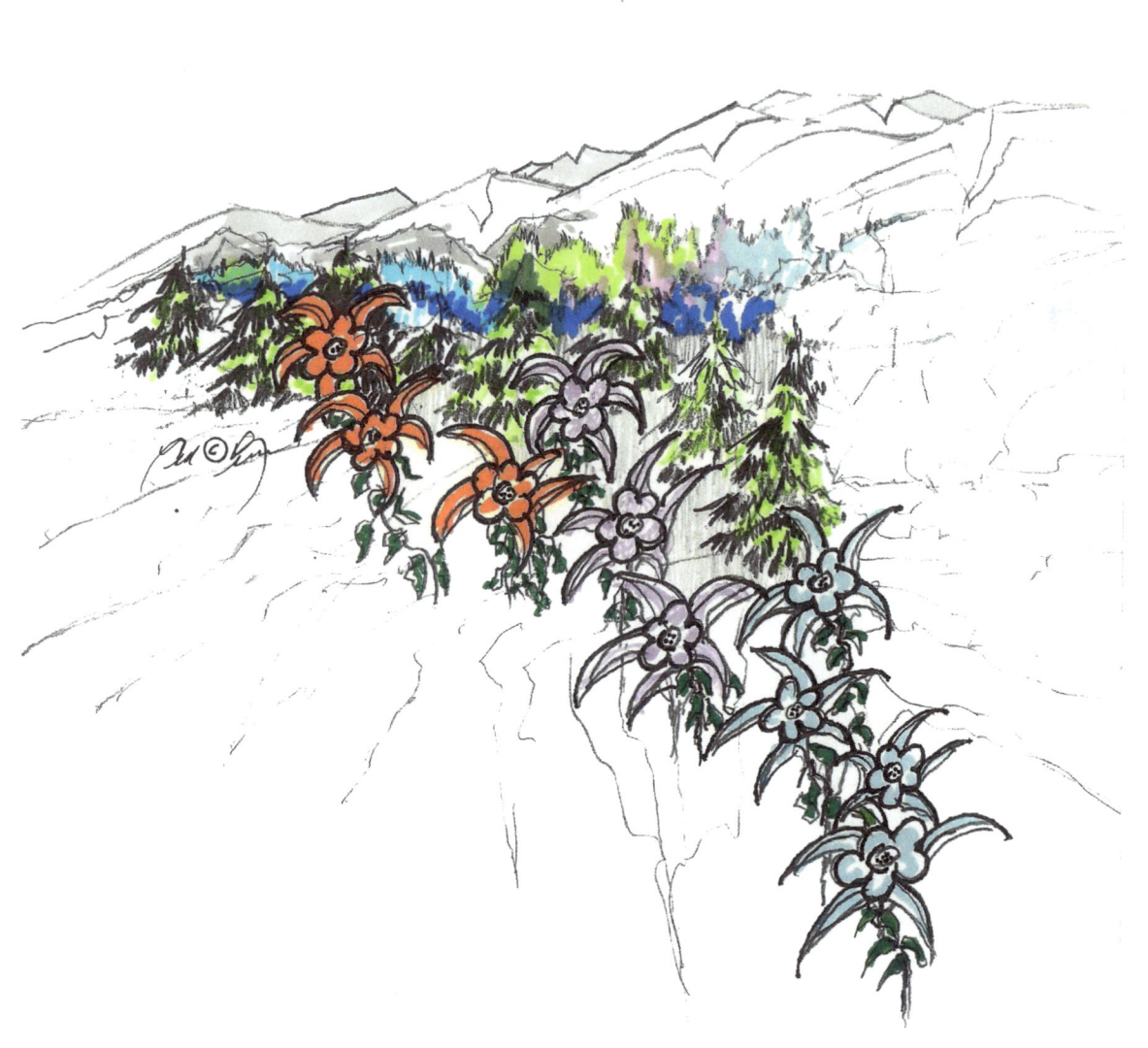

Kisses sweet
In high mountain glens
You have pushed
Though early summer snow
Only the elk they would see
Unless you will
Come travel with me
Reeboks or a stout steed
Our journey must start
Abercrombie and finch
Loaded the packs
Dried food with treats
Hoping in earnest
We will not get tired
To return down the trail
I will never know why
The altitude they picked
To return year after year
Their beauty must be seen
And scent to be smelled
Fragrances of earth
Better then mirth
Bursting in blossoms
Beyond rainbow colors
In groups they flourished
We never did pick
The camera guided by me
Recorded it all
Are travel is complete
Pictures now in the stall
Bring joy for generations
My columbines and me
They went straight
To my heart
Forever they will remain
In a weary winters night
The columbines are coming
In the new year to start
But only the elk will they see
Unless you travel with me

Indian Summer

Fifth season of the year
Cuddly warm
If you have lunch at the farm
Evenings cool to cold

Dress warm
So you can seek the stars
Spread your blanket
Fly to beyond the sky
Knowing you are one

Best time in the wilderness
During the day
On my back
Lying on sweet grass

I carve the clouds
Magic beholds
The shapes that I see
Wish you were here
Lying with me

Along the mountain stream
Placid with peace
Wild flowers galore
I stare in awe

Making the water turn
With natures placed stone
Exploding with light
Bubbles ascending

In the twilight
Smells refreshing
Night to fall
I don't mind it at all

I carry the clouds
In my minds eye
Silver linings
Later to paint

Being in joy
Seasons have changed
One more chapter
For my book of life

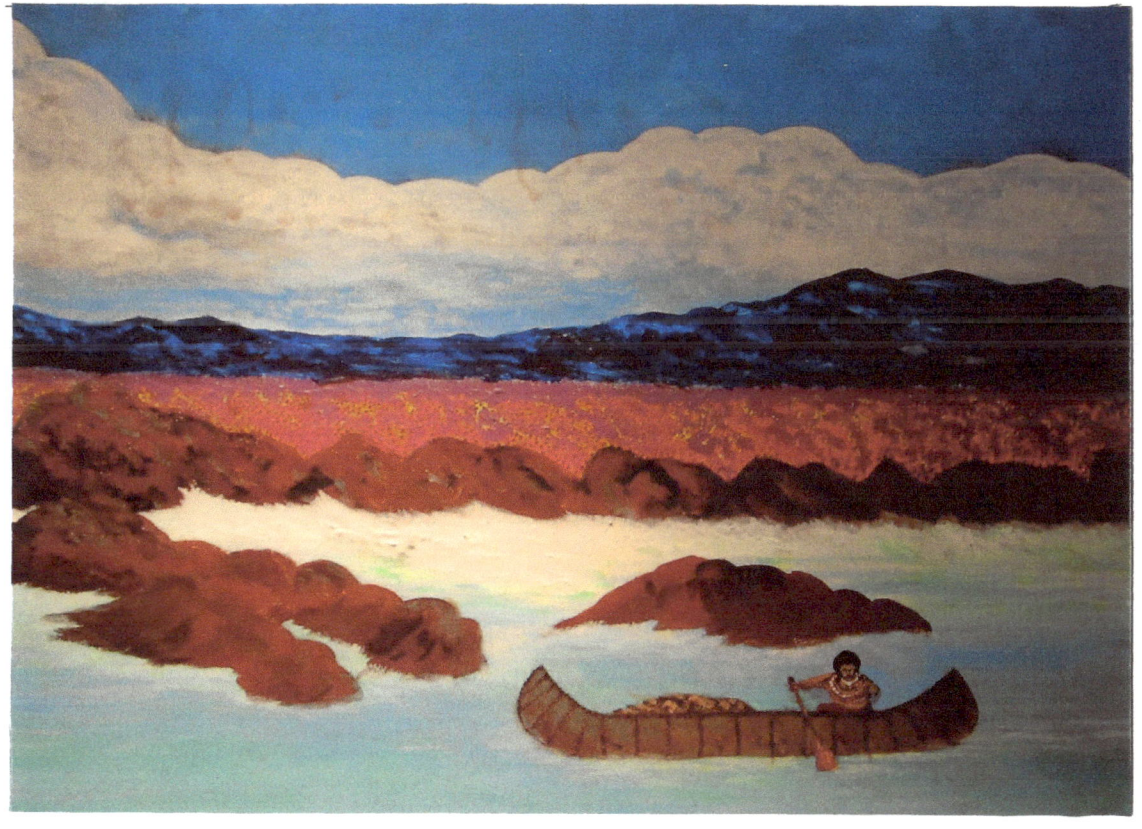

ON THE RIVER GOING HOME

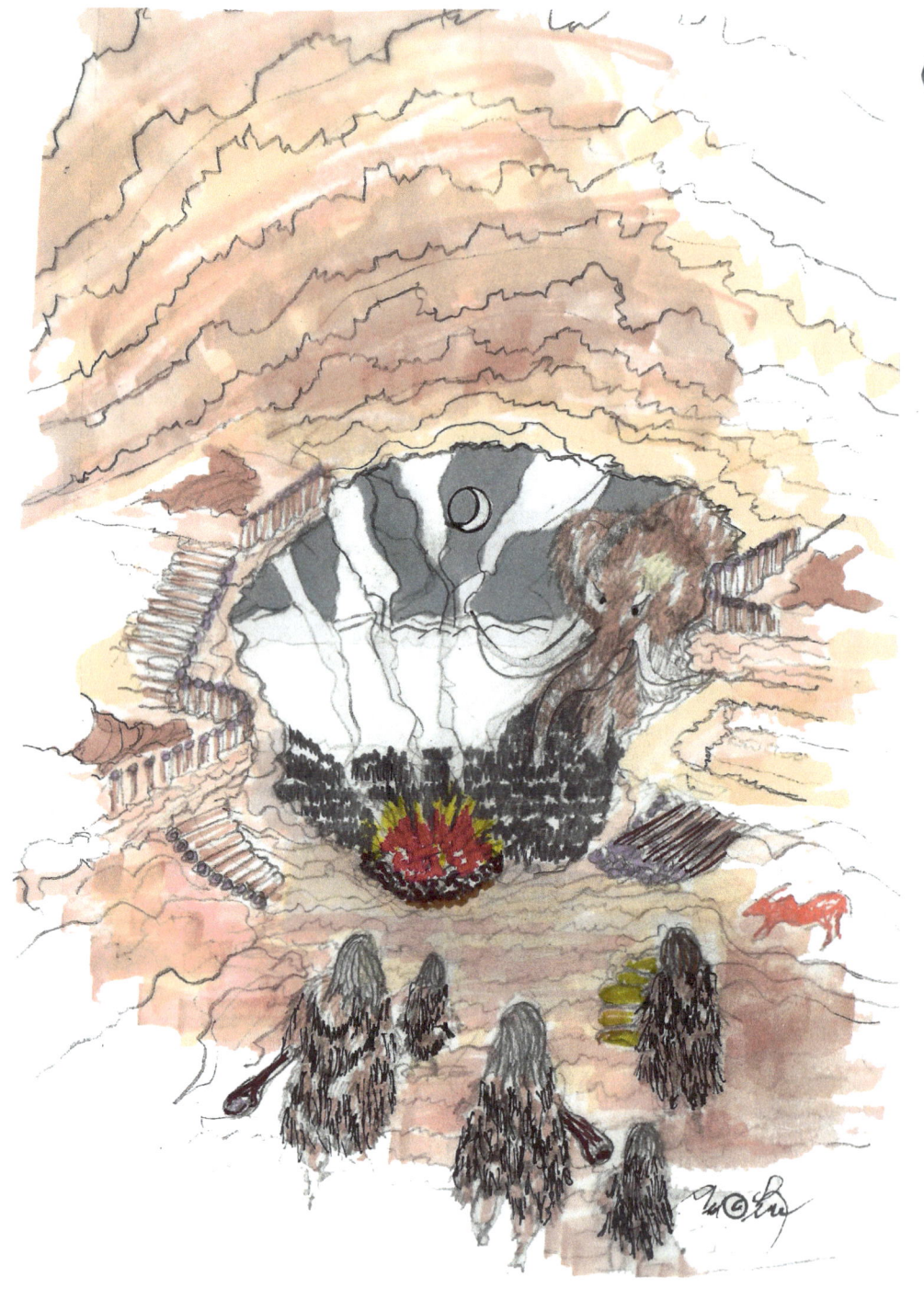

CAVEMAN/WOMAN 101

Deep in meditation
starless autumn night
A feeling entered to split my soul
I was transformed to travel
The rising sun awoke me
To a place and time millions years ago

Sitting under a huge hideous tree
A creature was looking at me
I could now see me
In the reflection of his eyes
Dressed in garb that matched the time

A fur hide covered my body
I had a full grown beard
With dirty long hair
I know now why he did flee in fright

He motioned to me with his arm
Follow me
For reasons unknown
We could and would communicate
Only in our minds telepathically

The language for him
was still many years away
Groans and grunts primeval screams
The early warning system
For those that could hear

The look in their face motions
Of arms, hands, body, legs and feet
Was the way they expressed to each other

Years back football coaches
used this technique
To tell the quarter back what to do

Name is Ugg so I renamed him Org
He lead to the entrance of his
5 room split level condo cave
Of course I knew there would be
No door or bell
Greeted by a fire hearth
With a least 15 cords
stacked fire wood
He told me he had to let
The interior decorator go

Her only contribution to him
Was to paint and draw on the walls
He introduced me as ugg ugg
As usual I renamed her Orga
He stated she was only one
of his many mates

Because so many babies die
And only a few will live
To gather food
Some to become hunters
I new then I was seeing
An extended family

How did you get the fire
Lighting had hit and burned a tree
Soon it went out
We would have to wait
Till it would strike again

With want of heat
We found a way to create it
No longer raw meat
Or cold stew in vitals long gone

To ward away the creatures
Of the night that's why
it is at the front door
How do you hunt
We sharpen stout sticks
And harden the points in the fire
Gather all hunters in the area
By shear numbers in force
We tired our game
And close in

But what of the big hairy tuskers
Only a few we will get
Sometimes many suns must pass
Before we put them away

Do you fear what I will call
Saber tooth tigers
No because we all run
in different directions

Org you are a wealth
information flows from you
I have gathered followings
Most every one in the area

To meet at special times
I created stories from
The sun, moon and stars
And all the periods of time
They would come and listen to me
Soon it required a fee
A bone, or a twig, un broken eggs
Taken from a high nest
nestled in the tree

Man"s start of religion
This thought occurred to me

Wisdom the animal creatures
Would start to search
Following the sun
To a warmer place

I new then Org and Orga
With extended family
Would follow
To give you and me life
Thru thousands of evolutions

Many of you will differ
And that's alright
Just like I went
I returned to the present day

In early dawn I did awake
Was Org and Orga just a dream
I think so

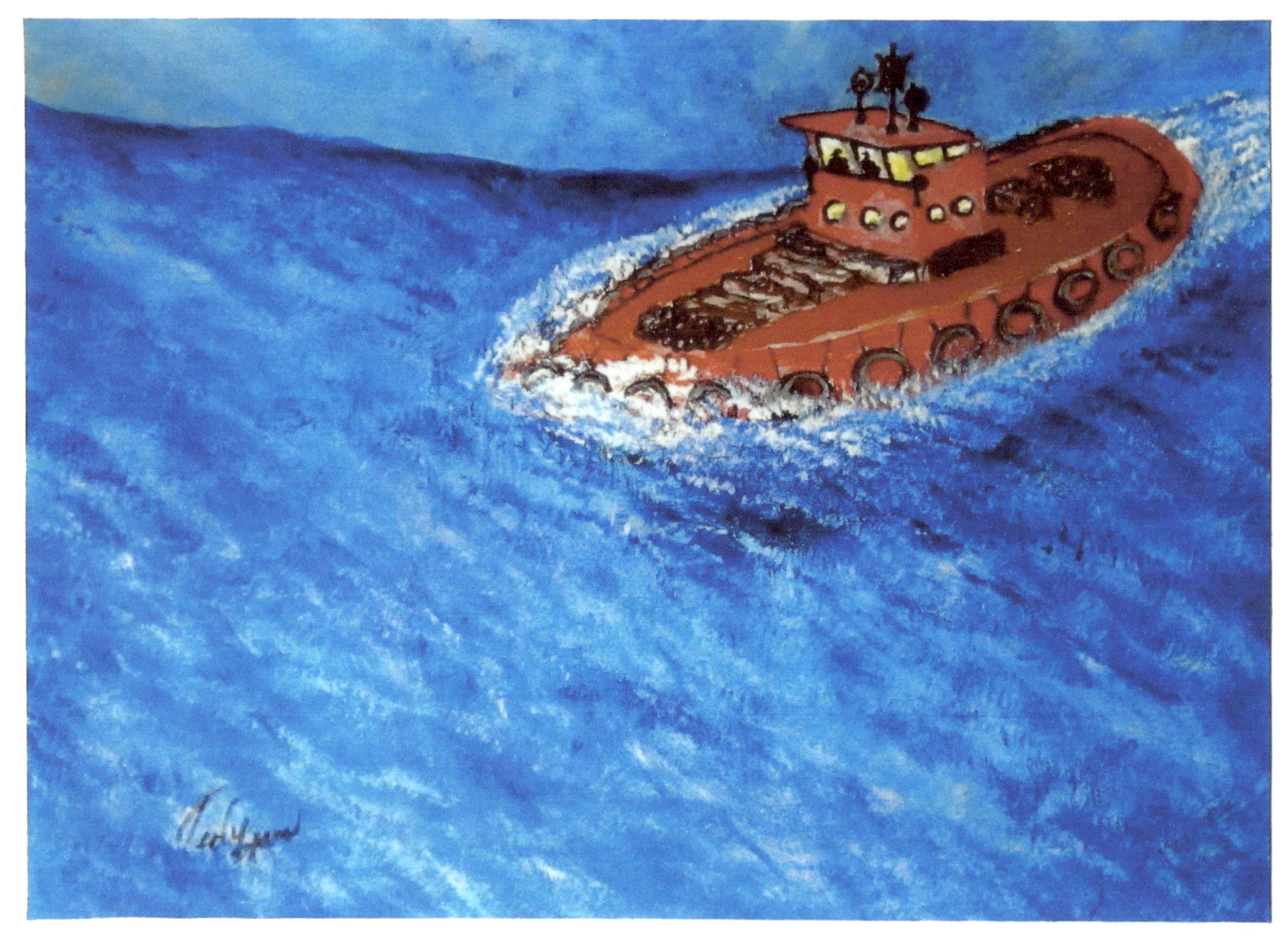

RED TUGBOAT

CAPTAIN THE SHIP IS OVER THERE

BLUE BEAR IN THE WINTER

CHAMPAGNE THE POODLE
IN HONOR OF CHAMPAGNE
THE GIRL HUSKEY SAMODE

MY LIFE BEGAN IN A WARM SPACE
CAN'T REMEMBER THE SPARK
THAT GAVE ME BEING
I DID NOT KNOW WHY IT WAS CROWDED
I DID NOT KNOW ANYTHING
ONE NIGHT MY MOTHER DROPPED
US OUT, I WOULD NEVER KNOW FATHER

FURRY BALLS ALL AROUND ME
I WAS STILL IN DARKNEST
I FOUND THE GROCERY STORE
BECAUSE MOM'S WARM MILK
WAS FLOWING
MY EYES OPENED WHEN IT WAS TIME
ONLY TO SEE MORE FURRY BALLS
GEE WIZ I HAVE PLAYMATES

THEY ALL LOOKED THE SAME AS ME
WHEN IT WAS TIME FOR THE NIPPLE RUN
IT WAS FIRST COME FIRST SERVED
MOM HAD MORE THAN ENOUGH
TO GO AROUND
OUR WONDERFUL SLEEPING BED
WAS SOFT AND IN A WELPING BOX
I WAS NOT READY TO GO EXPLORING

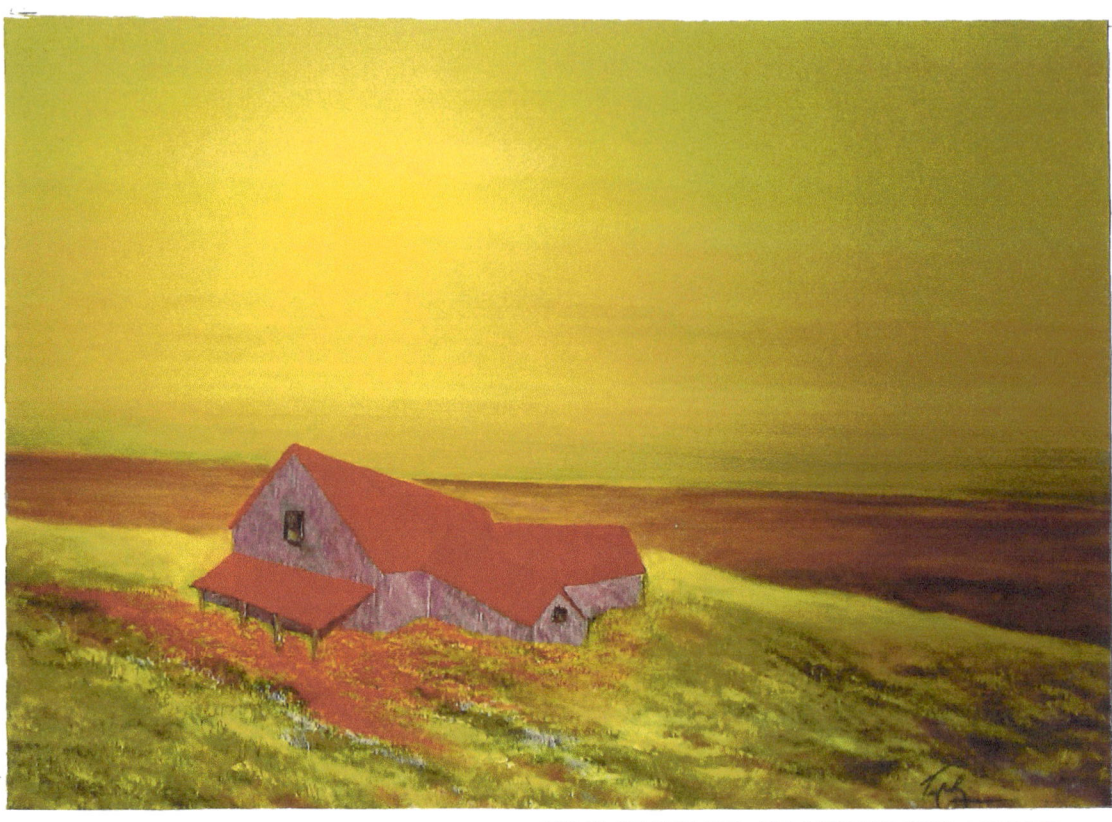

I FIRST SAW GIANTS LOOKING AT US
THEY HAD LOVE AND CARING
AND PRIDE IN THEIR EYES
AS THEY CUDDLED EACH OF US
THEY COULD TELL THE DIFFERENCE
BETWEEN BROTHERS AND SISTERS
THEY WERE STILL FURRY BALLS TO ME

AS WE DOUBLED IN SIZE
CAME THE BOWLS OF WARM MILK
WATER AND PUPPY KIBBLE TO EAT
PLAY TIME WAS FUN WE
COULD RUN ALL OVER THE PLACE
AND MAKE DEPOSITS EVERY WHERE
THE GIANTS SAID IT'S TIME TO GO

BIG HOUSE ON THE PRAIRIE
MICHAEL LANDON WAS LOOKING
FOR LITTLE HOUSE ON THE PRAIRIE

EPILOGUE
I NAMED MY NEW BLACK STANDARD
POODLE CHAMPAGNE AND HIS MATE
TIFFANY, FIRST LITTER SENT ME
TO CHINA AND JAPAN FOR 4 WEEKS.
THEY LIVED 17 HUMAN YEARS
AND ON THIS TEARFUL DAY
I ACQUIRED A WHITE STANDARD
POODLE WHICH I NAMED
TIFF TWO
THE LOVE OF MY LIFE

Pink Bows

Can make you smile
For a while
Pink Bows
On fur that flows
Pink Bows
Against shiny white
Fur
That glows
In the light
of the moon
That's gone too soon
And fades into the morning light
Too stark
The Sun
That fades the bows
Because in the light of day
Everything is too clear
Too bright
And you find yourself wishing
For Pink Bows
Glowing and illuminated
In the moonlight
Instead of
Memories ruminated
of faded
Pink Bows

Regina, Jan.29, 2013

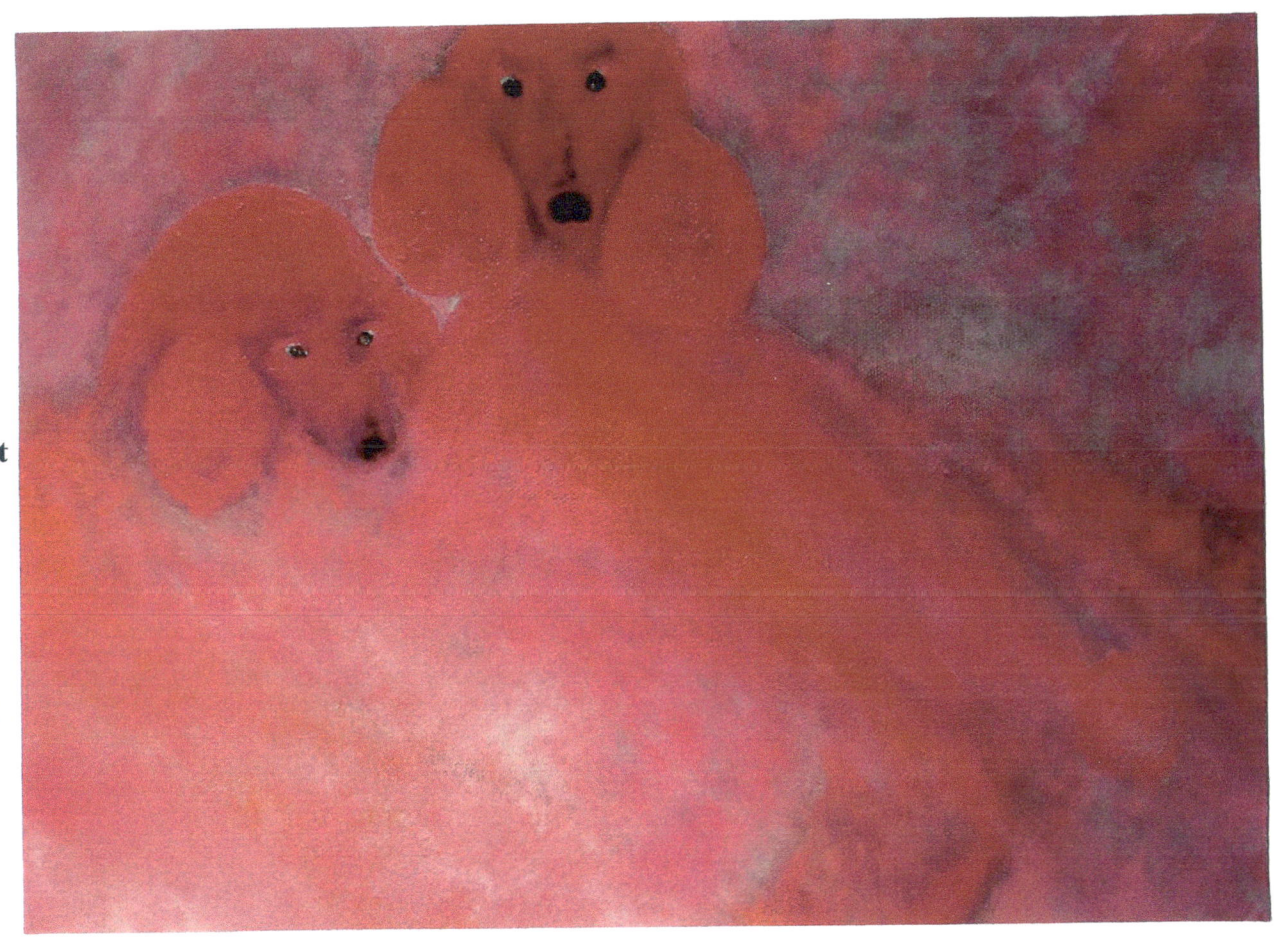

PINK POODLES
WITH PINK BOWS

CHOPPERS

They chop the air
To send them on their way
They have interesting names
Huey, Blackhawks , Jolly Green Giants
Made and flown by man
They have limitations
Not to hard to understand
Transportation is their goal
Providing access where none exists
The noise they make is horrendous
Sound proof ear muffs
To cover your ears
As usual nature wins
When it created
The HUMMINGBIRD
Multiple colored beauties
That fly the air
The maintenance required
Provided by earth
They have no need
For a manufacturing plant
Generation after generation
Bring joy to the world
Speed through the air
Puts man in despair
Zero to 100 plus or more
With a blink of an eye
Hovering still to feed and escape
Supported by tiny wings
To go up, down, sideways
And back something that
Man chopper has to rotate
180 degrees
Quite and silence
Is their mode of their flight
Nature has given us
The perfect
CHOPPER

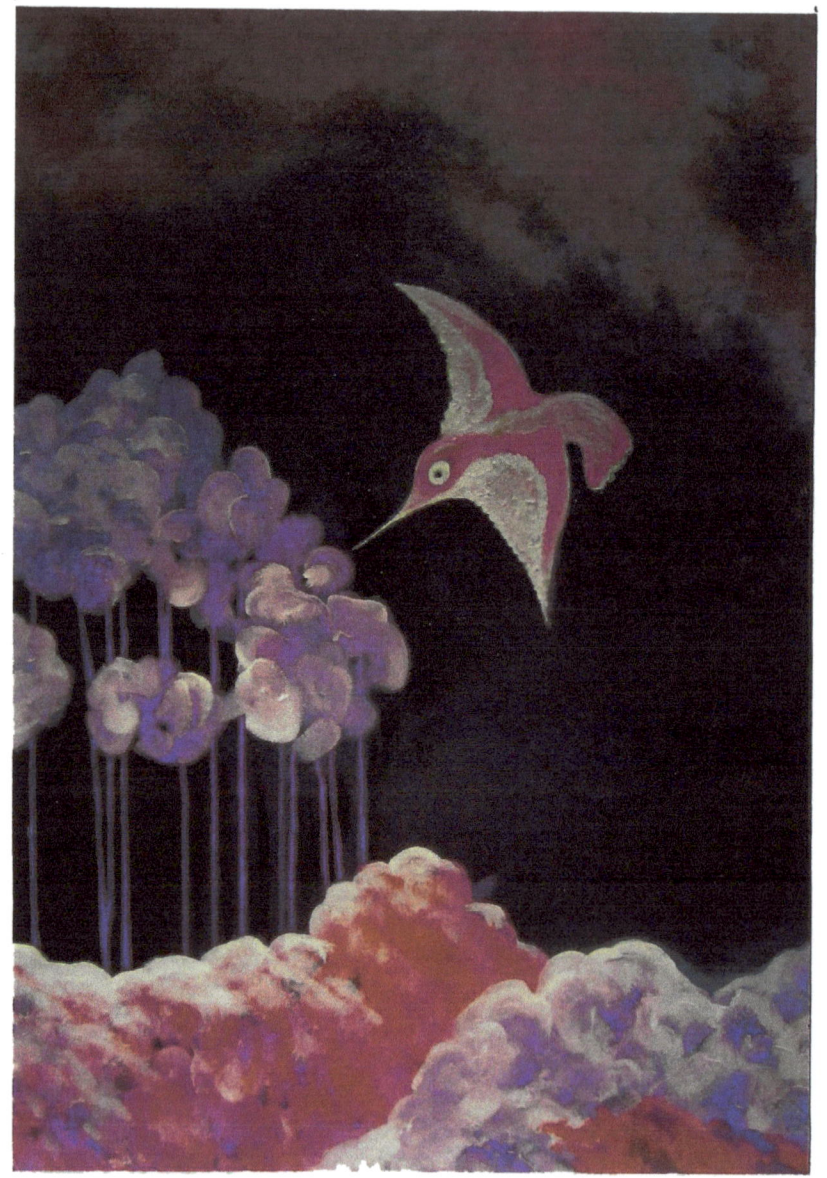

MISS IRELAND

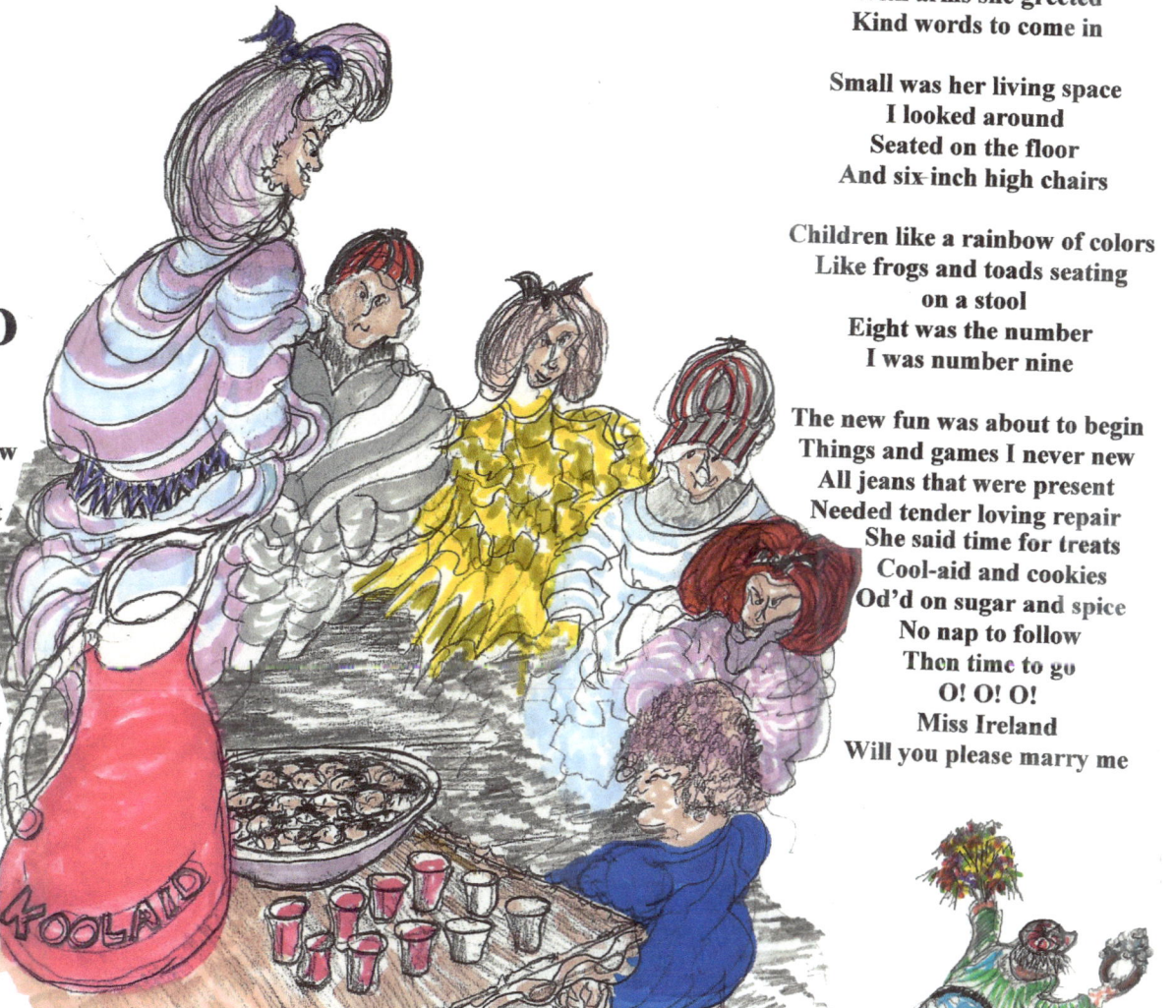

"Toto" its time to go
Where! Trudging thru a spring snow
My shoes are leather and get wet
When they dry the size they forget

Not far a matter of minutes
To kindergarten you go
Kinder-but a garden in snow?
The travel was fast

Even a new tooth could I not grow
Galisteo to booth way
The streets they were called
Up on the portal

Dad knocked at the door
Who would answer the door?
The wicketed witch to be defined
Or an angel in come to earth

When she came I almost fainted
On the portal floor
Blue eyes speckled with diamonds
Blond and silver strands
Of hair almost reaching to her thighs

A simple dress of red
Tied with a white bow
With arms she greeted
Kind words to come in

Small was her living space
I looked around
Seated on the floor
And six-inch high chairs

Children like a rainbow of colors
Like frogs and toads seating
on a stool
Eight was the number
I was number nine

The new fun was about to begin
Things and games I never new
All jeans that were present
Needed tender loving repair
She said time for treats
Cool-aid and cookies
Od'd on sugar and spice
No nap to follow
Then time to go
O! O! O!
Miss Ireland
Will you please marry me

57

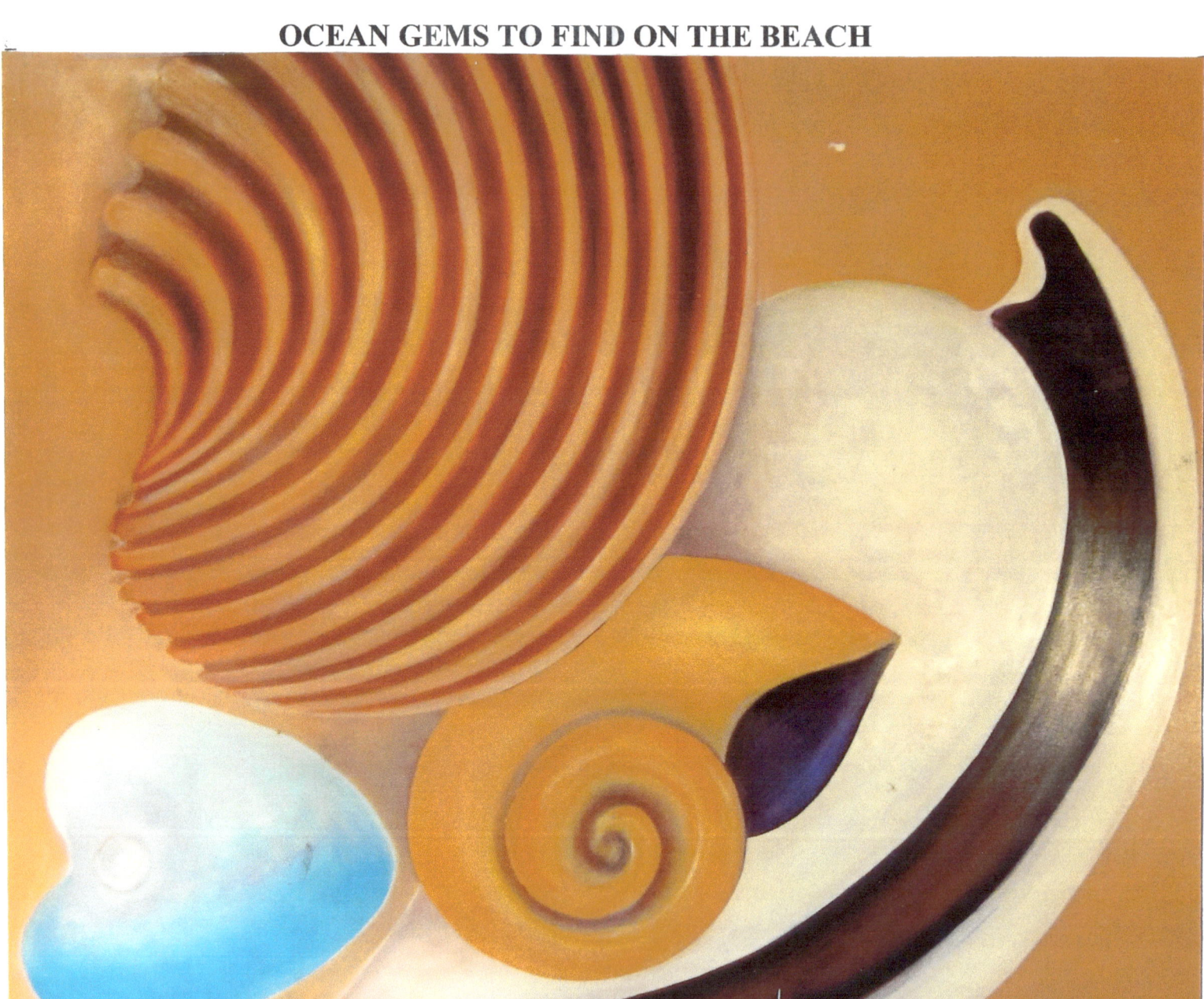

La Tuna at Leon

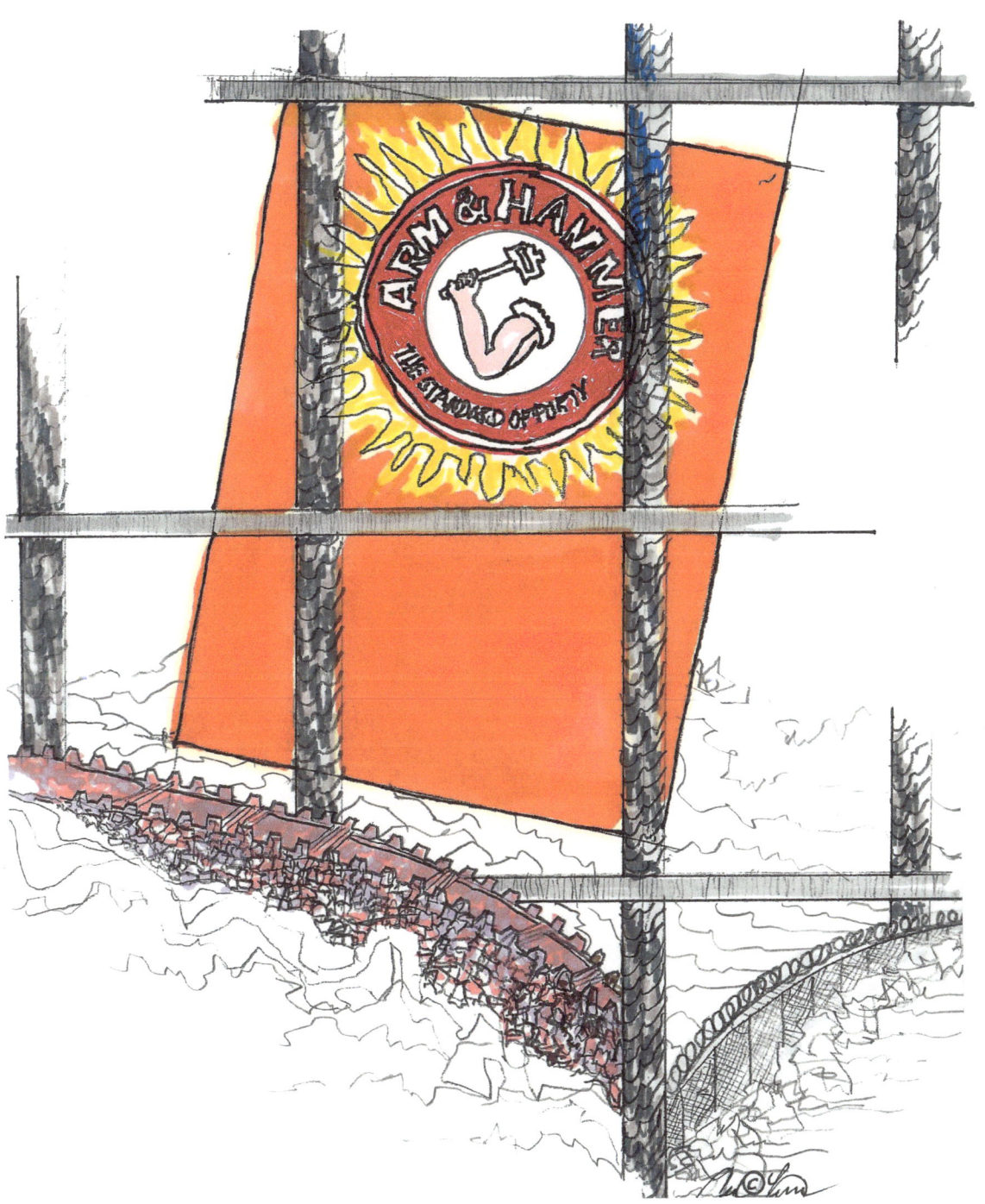

My head was in my arms
Dozing on my office desk
Cell phone rang
Vibrating soon to the office floor
Answered deep in sleep
I uttered hallo hello
Its me Bob Proctor
Our high school class
Poet laureate renown
How did you find me
The Mexicans have
Moles at Verizon
We have unlimited time
Why in all these years
Would you call me
Because of your rep
For laundering money
True in my round four legged tub
With rubber rollers and a crank
I sanitized my paper bills
Hung them on a line
in the basement to dry
Bob where are you and Edie at
A place called La Tuna at Leon
I think it is the national prison
Or national treasury
How did you get there
Tell me the story
Edie and I were on the way
To the condo we rented
In Puerto Vallarta
We choose to use back roads
Following a Mexican map
We now know never trust them

59

I almost made a full stop
At one of the Topes
When a Mexican jeep
Hiding in the trees
Jumped us and made us stop
Four Polocia dressed in black
Carrying Mexican semi automatics
They were proud I could see
The rotunned Jeffe shouted at me
We must inspecto your VW wagon
But why did you stop us
You took the topes to slow
Three went in as we stood by the side
One returned with our box of Arm and Hammer
Edie had taped the top for
Future refrigerator use in the condo
El Jeffe smiled with joy
Druggos you have
Senior Senorita your under arresto
With Mexican bailing wire
They tied right wrist to left thigh
Then left wrist to right thigh
Blew open their brown paper lunch sacks
Placed them over our heads
I could smell the chicken tacos
El Jeffe tossed the keys to the VW
To the youngest of the group
His parting words as he shouted
No No Asta la vista
We knew then the VW
And all it contained was gone forever
They set us in the back
Guard on either side
Off we went where I did not know
Off came the paper masks
The Patron greeted us
I asked where are we
Cuidad de Leon behind bars

He said he would set us free
For the amount of one million pesos
Tossed me the cell phone
One call only no abrogardos
He also informed us that
Since it was a day away from Christmas
They would be required by Mexican law
To sing Christmas carols in Mexican
On Christmas Eve
I have more than that amount
In an off shore island account
They take incoming wires
But all withdrawals must be in person
I can easily repay you and with
Expenses even a vacation
Current exchange rate
Is about $100,000 USD
Can you and will you help us
As soon as possible
Our Mexican caroling will
need a lot of work

O course I will
I would hope to have you free
Before the New Year
Please leave details to me
Adios dear friends for now

I reviewed my options in deep thought
I new that Banks have direct line to IRS
How would I explain $110,000 deposit
Never believing Banks
All my savings were in the washing machine
Under a pile of dirty socks
I would have to turn $100 bills into $1,000 bills
It would take a day to visit the local banks
I knew then I would fly to Japan or China
For an wire untraceable transaction

Some where close to the boarder
I could hide the new $1,000 bills
I had transferred the $110,000
Lined in my dirty laundry socks

I also figured it would be in a carry on
Purchased the flight ticket on the net
First stop Dallas, Direct to Norita Japan
Option to Beijing
I felt that it would be China
No self respecting Banker in Japan
Would take the smell of dirty socks
My hotel in the sky made the trip fly
First in Beijing I picked the tallest building
A kind Chinese told me it was a bank
Up to top floor to meet the president
He introduced himself as Cha Ching
He bowed and stated
His parents named after
An old fashion cash register
I was required to call him
Rapidly three times

I explained my task with the money
He had an assistant take it out of the socks

Count the money and gave me back
The $10,000 for expenses
He offered me a cup of soup
He said he would wire to money
To a favorite bank in El Paso Texas
I marveled as he did this in my presence
He gave me a secret access number
And the amount of funds transferred
This number was only known to him and me
He then said he had a vacation coming
And would like very much to visit
The new nation of China East
O you mean the United States

He also suggested that I visit the Great Wall
And he would like to meet me at the airport
In two days for our flight to El Paso
From there we would travel to
Leon with black belt body guards
Three beautiful female administrative assistants
Ming 1, Ming 3 and Ming 4
I asked what happened to Ming 2
He said she was promoted to China East
The bank limo took me to the Great Wall
Of course the concept never worked
Just bribe the gate keepers
Our high tech great wall created
On the boarder of the US and Mexico
Will never work either
The Mexicans will just get the paper work
All people of the world want a better life

Two days later we were in El Paso
At the bank we withdrew and
Changed the deposit into Pesos
With a Mexican chauffeur
Bullet proof limo we were on our way
I soon learned that the body guards
Loved Corona
When we arrived at La Tuna
No one felt any pain
The Patron greeted us as saviors
Before we make this transaction

I have three questions to ask you
Se senior porfavored numbero ono
Is La Tuna the Federally Treasury
No Senior
Is La Tuna the Federally Prison
Se Senior
Did Bob and Edie sing carols
On Christmas Eve
Se Senior
Here are your million pesos
Please get Bob and Edie
The Patron recognized the Body guards
And immediately did what I requested

Arms and cheers all around
We all bound leaps to the limo
The Cha Ching
Ming 1 and Ming 3
Now reside in China East
Ming 4 went back to
China West

THIS FITS WITH THE PREVIOUS STOREY

**CONTRACTORS CODE
NEW 2010 CONCEPTS FOR ANT**

If project has no 500% profit
Forget it
Insure you can violate all codes
And get away with it
Use lowest subs from Mexico
All labor from Wal-Mart
Refuse all liq. Damages
Buy a new pick-up
Put the title in Mexican girl friends name
If you have one
If not please contact me
Insure that all change orders
Have a 200% markup
Smile at all inspections
Call the Architect as the Suit
Insure weather is a problem
Check forecasts Dailey
Change weather as required
Submit pay request daily
Payment to off-shore account
Collect full contract amount
Before you leave
If you follow this code
Have condo available
In Porta Somewhere in Mexico
Before you leave
Give the social security number
To IRS
Of your x- wife

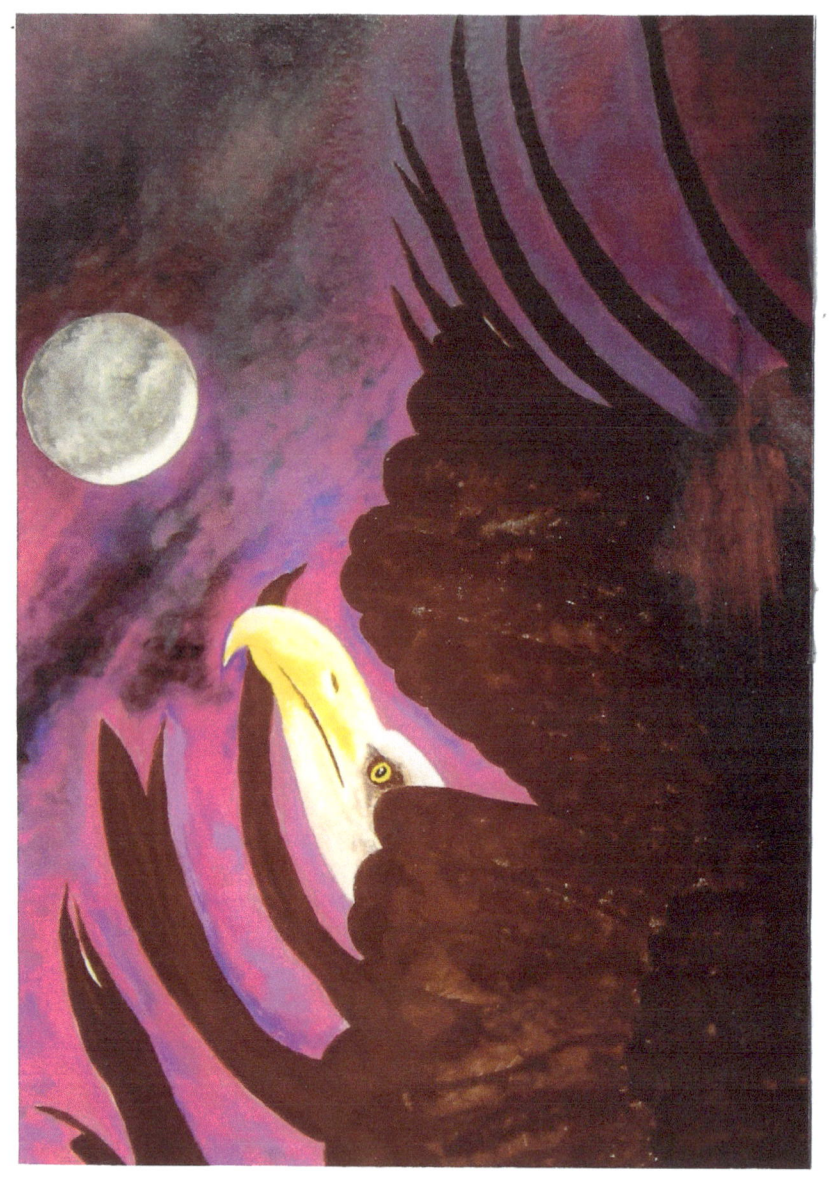

FLIGHT TO THE MOON

YOUNG WALLY
NAME SAKE WALMART
I CALL THEM
WALLYMART

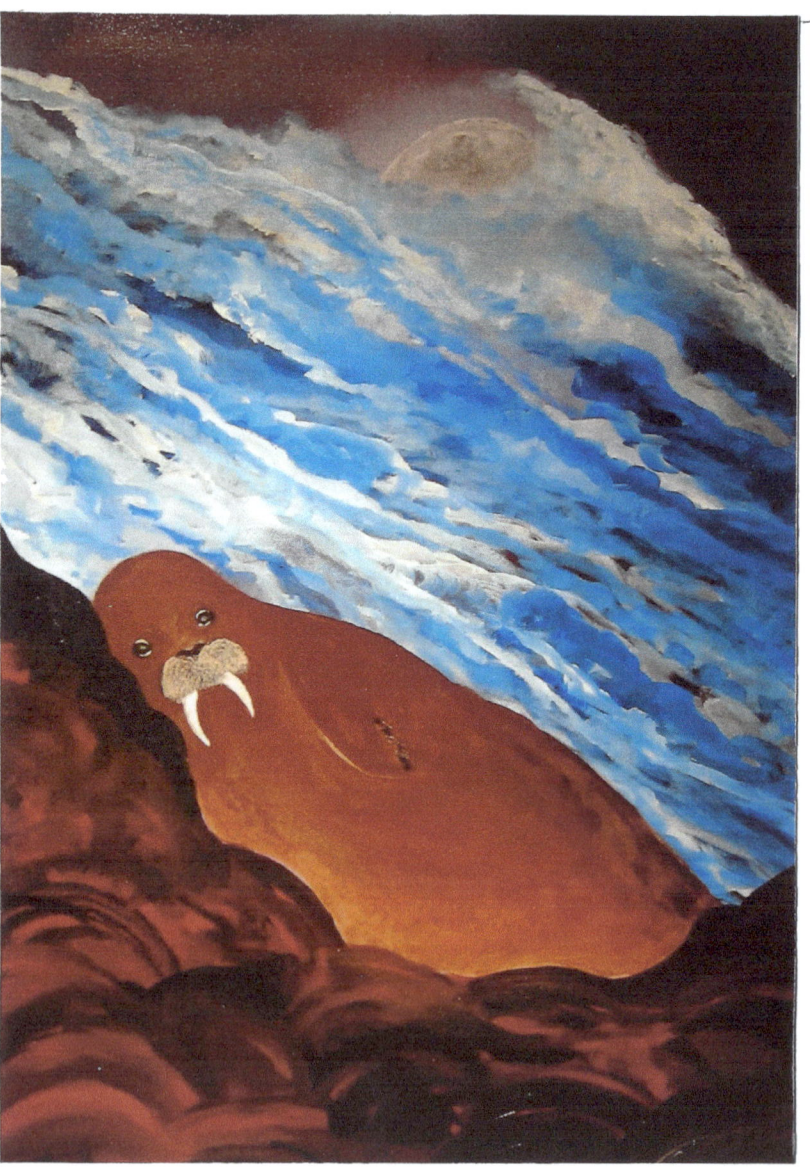

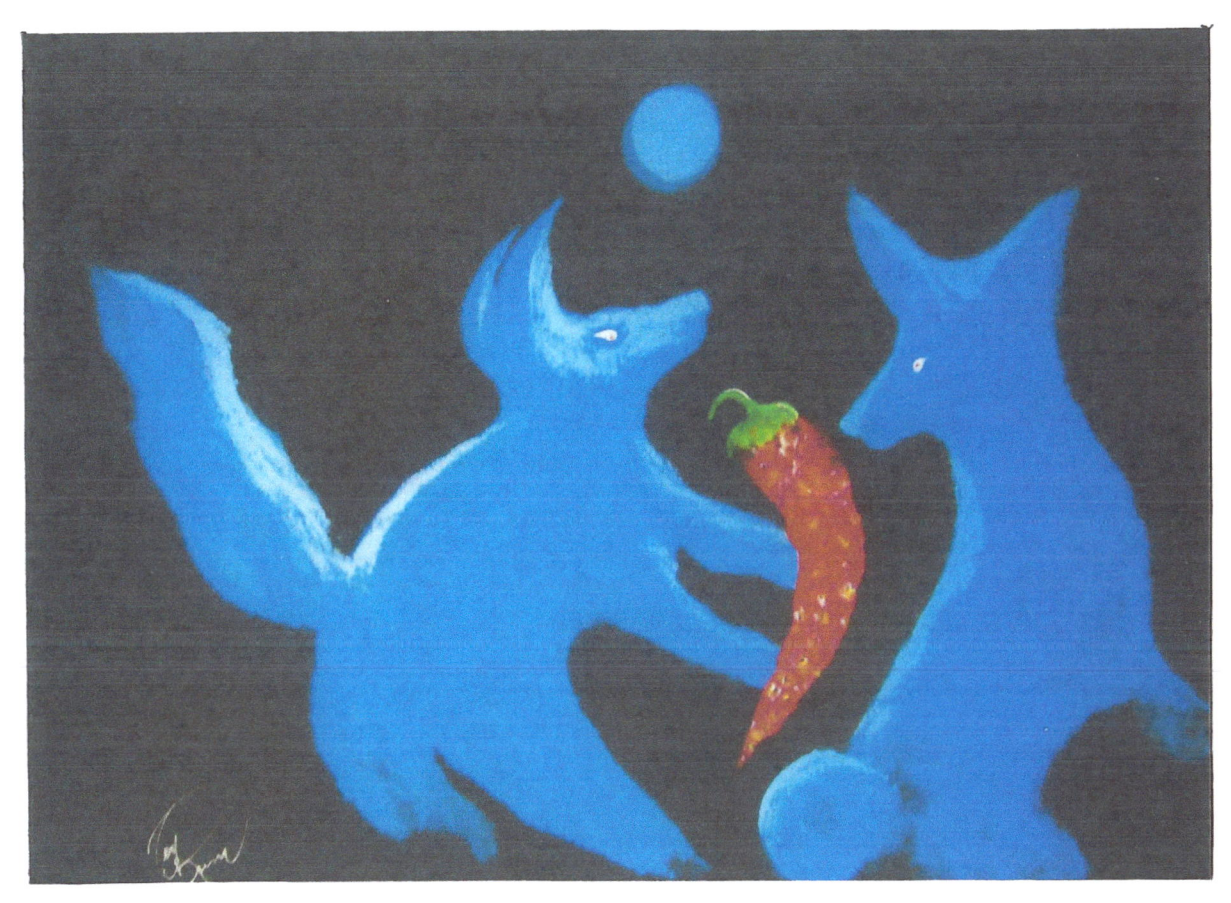

CAYOTE LOVE
NEW MEXICO STYLE

ON TOP OF OLE SMOKEY

Second verse :"all covered with snow"
Third verse: "I lost my true love for courting to slow"
If you Could check with all the lovely ladies
In my life they would assure you
I never had this issue

I love this old western song
no more verses to follow
My story I will share with you
hoping to surprise

Fern and I just finished our new home
Number one La Tierra was our postal address
On 14 acres north west of Santa fe
Complete with low tech solar water panels

The architectural students aia at UNM
Gave us an highest honor residential award

Stephanie and Kim
My daughters then requested
Dad lets get some horses for us to ride

So I fenced 4 acres built a small saddling corral
A hyperbolic roof shelter for the hay
Added a tack room it was soon to leak
We covered the saddles with visqueen

the purchase of a horse trailer was next
Bought our first timothy hay and oats
For $2.00 a bale delivered and stacked
My friends tell me it is now eight

We then begin the search
for horses to ride and love
Of course the want ads a place to start
Northern New Mexico horsemen
Will never give you details or tales
Of the horses they have for sale

So north of Espanola we did go
This quest was in the hands
of the universe
Milling in a herd they cut out
A gelded sorrel colored horse
The vaquero stated
It's a quarter horse
So the price in my mind was $.25

Second thought what happened
To the other $.75
Is he only good for a quarter of the race

With a flash of white on his nose
Of course they told us
This is the horse for you
He has been broken and trained

I wrote a hot check
would cover it later
We loaded the gelding in the trailer
All present asked what to call him
"Smokey" we all agreed that was his name

It soon became apparent he needed company
Here we go again to find another
This time we went to lower Auga Fria

A black and white with silver touches
An appaloosa gelding was our choice
Then it came again what to call him

My daughters simply stated
A magic dragon "Puff" will be his name
Three hands smaller then Smokey
Character and grace he could run

Faster than a 10 knot gale in any race
In the surrounding arroyos
Riding on sand on smokes back
Like setting on a rocking chair
So smooth the ride

Puff always won the race in the finish
He would look back and give
A horses smile
I were invited to a cattle round-up
On the Bob and Sanzanies Weil adjacent ranch
Just Smokey and me
What a boring event it turned out to be

Just turn the lead cow
To the direction you need to go
The others would follow
Herd animals after all
All of it all the ride was fun

Then the Pecos wilderness
Backcombed to me
With Walters help
A horseman and friend

We devised all of the things
Needed for a weeks ride
Smokey and puff had to carry it all

Fern on Puff and Smokey with me
My recommendation to you ride a horse
In the wilderness
You will not spoke any game
For the forms as you ride
Will melt into one

Providing you are down wind
Champagne our husky samode
On the trail would glide and dance
Thru the windfall logs

Till she spotted a deer
High tailed she would run
To hide safe and wait
Under Smokeys belly
We would then resume
our ride up the trail

A year or two later
a four day trip we did plan
For Pat wood and Foster Hyatt
Architects and friends

We would start at trail head
The Penasco entrance
ride the bald Truches peaks
I put Foster on puff and we
Rented a trail horse for Pat
Foster in full face beard
Pepper and white and wild long hair
In the riding garb he looked

Like the proverbial mountain man
We cleared north peak Truches
And on the flat trail

We encounter a small group
of backpacked hikers
Of early and late teens

The picture we presented
Straight out of the old west
Eyes wide open your could see the white
Mouths dropped with awe in their stare

I greeted them and told them this story
We are here in our monthly quest
To take from his cabin the
Mountain man
To town for his bath and delice
Foster in his mind never uttered a word
He played his role well
These kids I am sure be lived what I said

Down the trail clear of the kids
We all laughed until it hurt
To the head waters of the Pecos
Only two feet wide filled with trout
Flipping a fly you would have to hide

We choose to camp for one night
At Catherine Lake
Pat accidentally dropped
His new pentex camera
In the lake
I know its still there
Foster's brilliant watercolors
To this day adorn my walls

Smokey would take me deer hunting
I secretly hoped a deer I would never see
On north slope deadfalls
Deep in the forest
I would ease the reins

Giving him his head
He picked the trail for me

Memories and stories
So many I could pen
I must focus
bringing this to an end

I stumbled on a new love
I knew then all things must go
After a decade and four
Kim going to college
In old Durango

Found a large ranch
I new that Smokey and Puff
For the rest of their years
This is the place they must go
I could not just sell them
So I gave them away

Number one was soon sold
After Fern went away
The title company called me
We have a check for you today
On my way I would pick it up
Stated the amount $14.97 cents
This was all I had
To start my new life

Winter Nights

Cold blacker than black
It looks at me, stars hiding
Some where maybe they glow
Yet I know they are still there

My eye appears never blinking
Window for our life
Given to us
Ending our strife

A beautiful thought to convey
A wonderful life
Our universe is you
And me

Heavens shining
With light winters delight
The window of love
Within our sight

Magic is there must enjoy
Deep in thought
Living as we do
Relying on peace

Wonderment of places
Never have been to
Yet the need to go
To see new sites

Deep in revere
My down comforter wrapped
This was all caused by
Cold Winter Nights

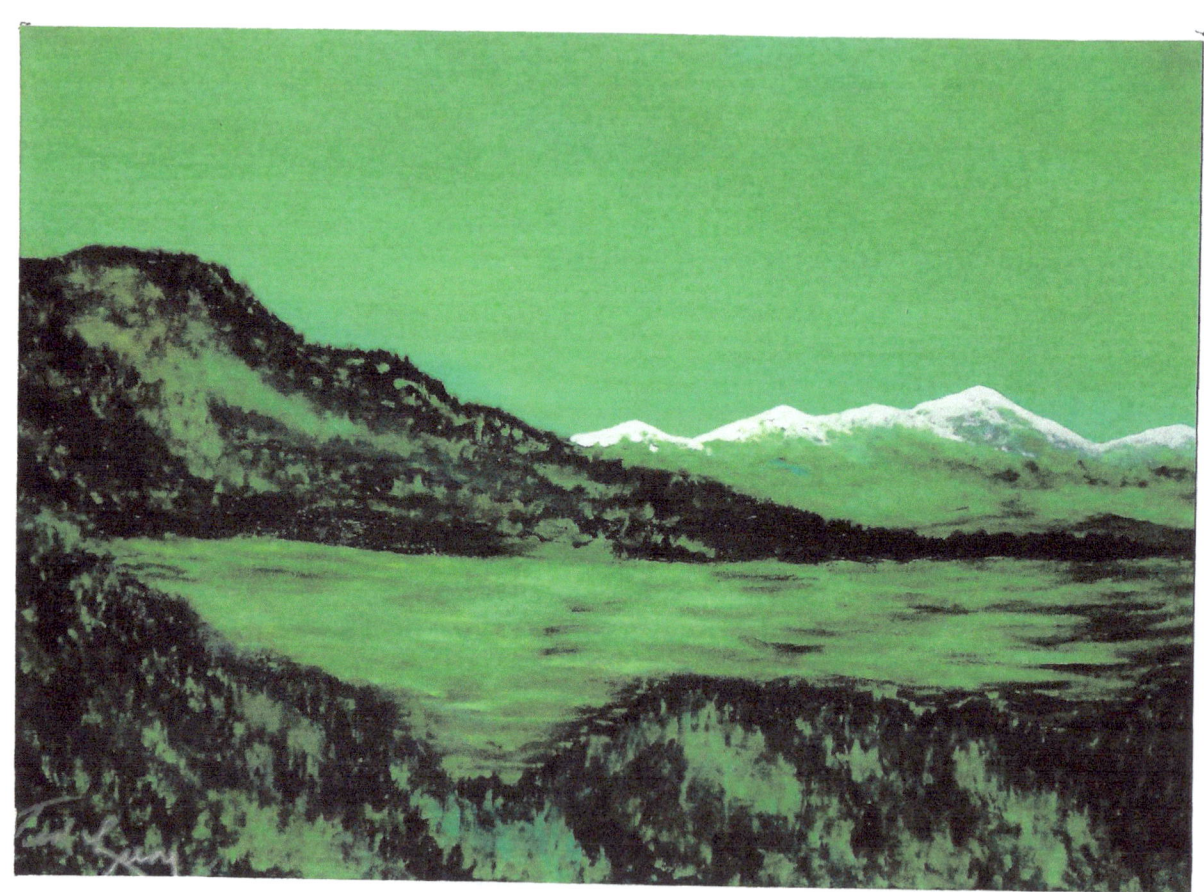

GREEN VALLEY
O HOW GREEN WAS MY VALLEY LONG AGO

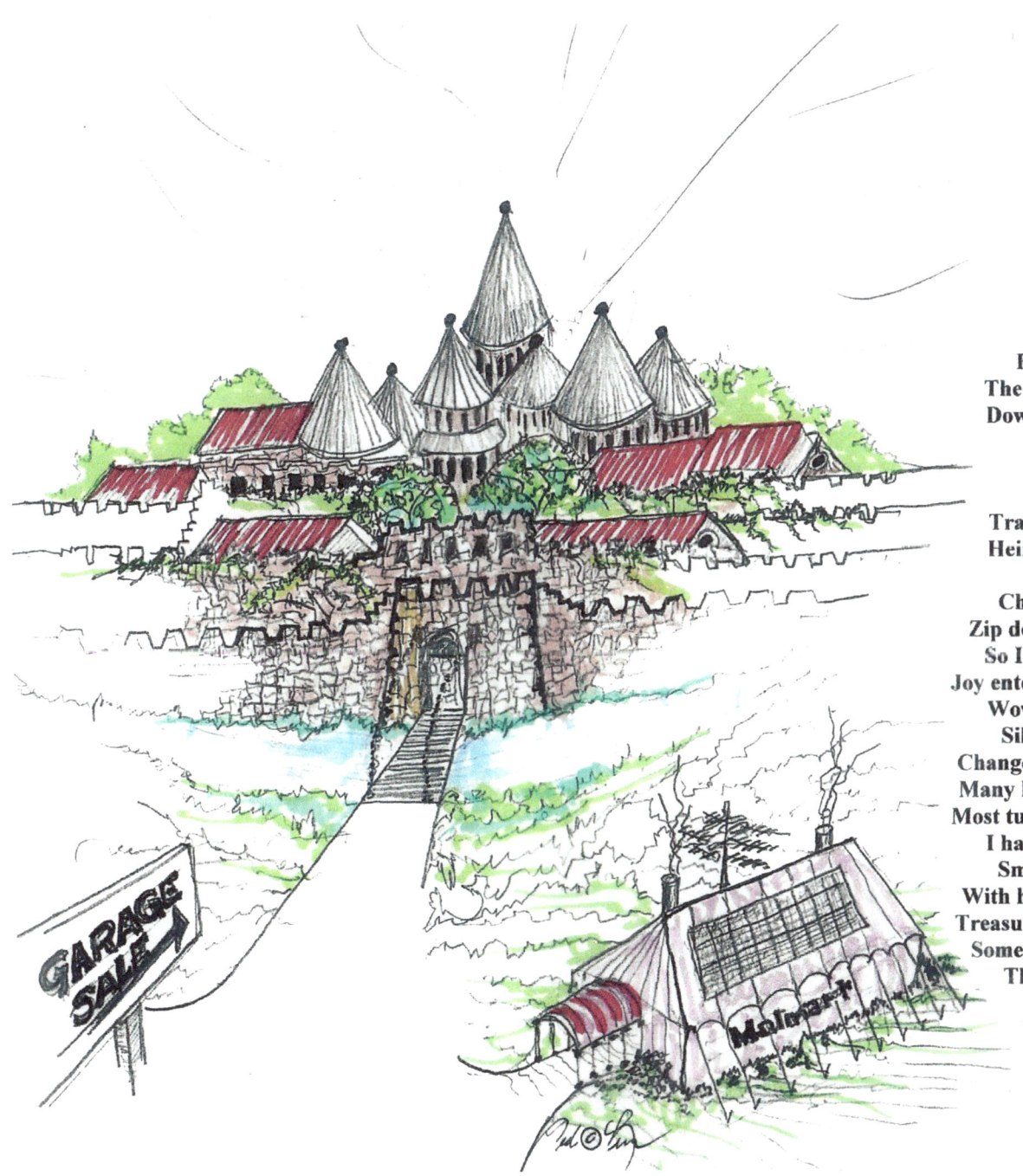

GO

Let things go
Puddles are formed
From a late spring snow
The hot sun will make them go
Down sizing buzz words today
But in what way
Homes so large
Roller skates required
Traveling from space to space
Heirlooms galore what to save
What should I let go
Choices are in the inter soul
Zip deposits at sales by the garage
So I started giving things away
Joy entered like an arrow to the heart
Wow what a good way to start
Silent message I did receive
Changed my life when I let things go
Many have been the apple of my eye
Most turned to cider I didn't even cry
I had to let them and things go
Small spaces are comforting
With heirlooms I could not through
Treasures through life, memories too
Something's you should not let go
The choice is forever yours
Welcome to freedom
When you let things go

WISDOM

Behold wisdom spoke
Time to drop the yoke
To cast you straight to prison
Or refresh your brow
With early morning dew
It will tell you
Where to find the other shoe
Tails of woe they bring you
Set their hearts a glow
It will melt like frozen snow
It may remain I hope you know
Age will grant you
A late realize of toil
The house you built
And reside within
Windows to the world
Doors to open paths
Where are you my lass
Gone with the breeze
A gentle northern wind
But there come in droves
Humanity in plight
Some with joy
Others with delight
Fear not you troubled ones
Wisdom lights the way

Theodoro Carlton Luna
Oct. 23, 2012

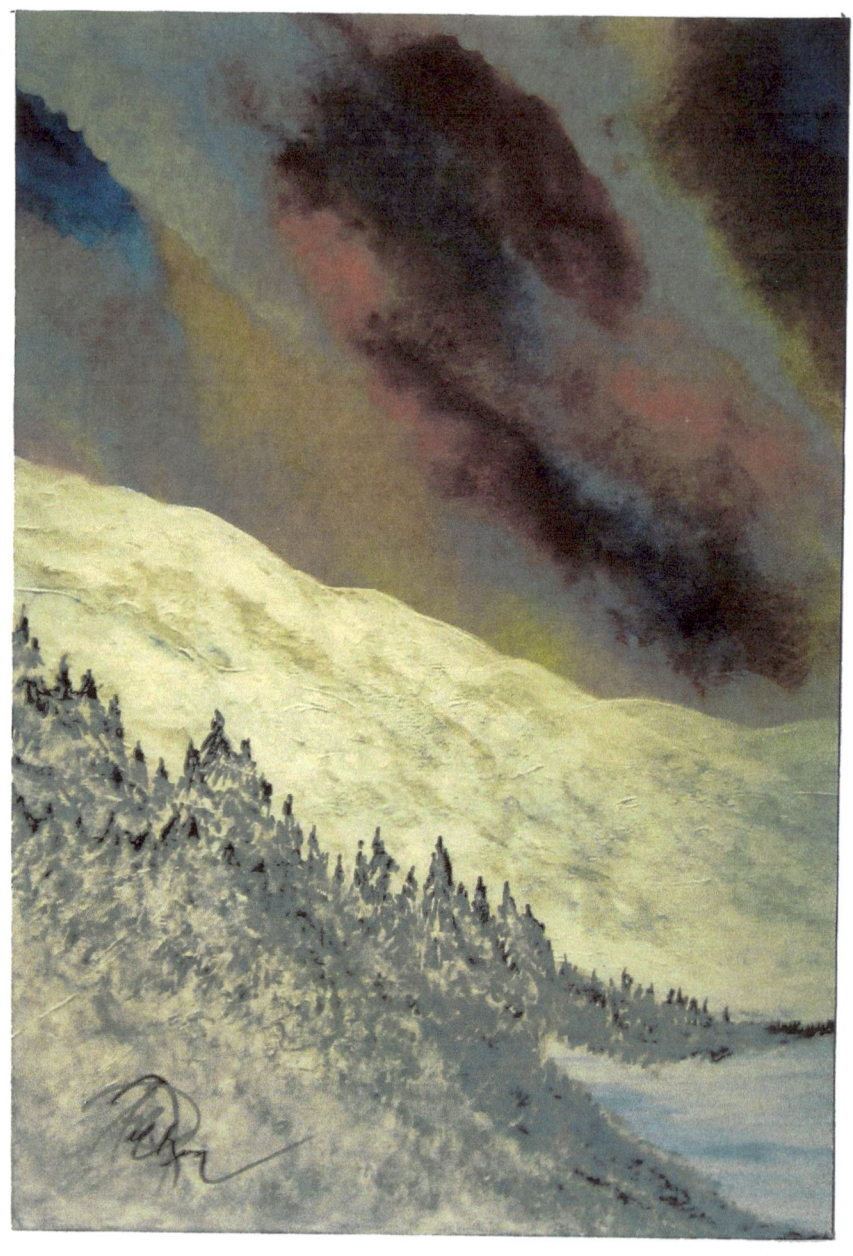

AURORA BOREALIS CONFUSED
SOME WHERE NORTH OF ALASKA

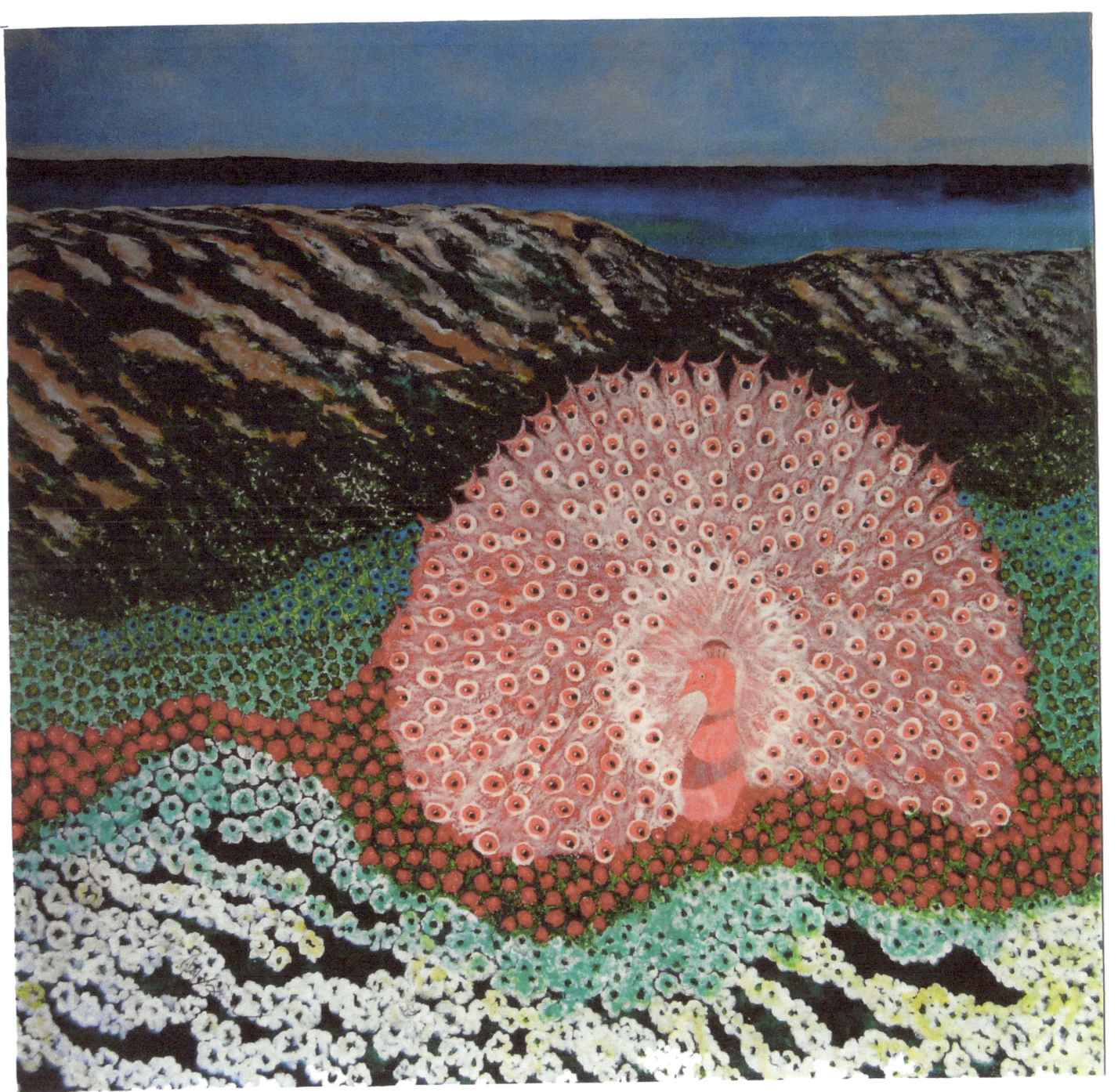

" PEACOCK "
BY THE SEA
7' X 7'
49 SQUARE
FEET
LARGEST
PAINTING
I HVE EVER
DONE

Cheeco "malo" Chacon

El Cuento Parte uno
Padre ayuda por favode
Padre nuestro no esta aqui
Desaparecido de la casa
Madre no mas con seis hijos
Enseneme para cantar
Tocar una quitarra
Los cartes hombres jugar
Padre por favode
Cheeco venis manana
De un dia paro otro
Taben el ingles de la norte
Como segunda lenyue
BuenoCheeco mi hijo

Tale two
The poor parish catholic priest
Through the years taught
Cheeco very well
To sing sweet and mellow
Or robust and loud
Strumming the guitar
A mariachi he could be
Most of all how to play
The games of cards
Poker could send you to hell
His second American
Language was well in place
The priest was raised
In Americas far East
Learned and many the
Ways of the world
Before being ordained
By the catholic church

Tale three
Cheeco grew to early manhood
The wanton wayward wind beckoning him
Go north and seek a fortune
He knew the he must say
Good bye to the northern Mexican
Hamlet dry desert blue sky
So in a flash stuffed a flower sack
Of his meager belongings
Slung it over his shoulder
Bid his Mexican family adieu
Know full well he would never return
Up through ole El Paso he would go
Never having to wade the Rio Grand
The way North was a wagon trail
Called El Camino Real
After a long days trek
He came upon a mud and straw
Big spreading ranch house
He entered through the front door
It was not locked, no one around
Of course the owners were
Rich and far away
He found more then he needed
Fine leather boots and soft socks
A Sunday's best suite complete
With white shirt and tie
A big felt hat with pure silver band
He cut off his long black hair
Next shaved the beard
He left a mustache
Curled the ends
Donned all of the new found
Items of ware
Looked at the looking glass
Could not believe his brown eyes

He took his sandals, white cotton pants
Pancho and crumpled his sombro
So it fit through the hole
In the out-house out back
Page by page from the
Sears and Roebuck catalog
He covered it well not leaving a track
He knew he must run fast
In the small corral behind the house
The horses we grazing within an open gate
He tried to catch one, but they ran to fast
Out the open gate fast as the wind
Under the shed laughing at the meelee
Munching on grass was one JackAss
Cheeco found a bridal no saddle would fit
Up on his bare back
Trying to ride as fast as he could
To the far North

Tale four
North on ole Camino Real
Within a few miles of Ole Santa Fe
The Jack stumbled and fell
Tossing Cheeco down a rocky gulch
Upward he climbed to find the
Jack dead
He new that the Coyotes would
Feast for weeks
So in stolen boots he trudged
To Ole Santa Fe
His first night he slept in the dust
Soon he found a saloon
From hardened gamblers
He learned his new trade

A wise old white headed man
Bent his ear
If fortune you seek
Take the company train
To a company town
Called Madrid
A scant 27 miles
East and to the South
Of Ole Santa Fe

Tale five

The company just wanted Black Gold
The company town was really
Tent city
It was often said only 30 square miles
Contains the Black Gold
They named the diggings well
Lucas and White Ash
Cooks mines and last
But not least Peacock
The minors numbered many
Often to hard to count
With widow makers pick
And spade they dug the
Inter laced tunnels
Shoring the ceilings with wood
Beams hung with canary's in cages
To warn of the gas if they died
And run like hell to the out side
The Indians mined meager turquoise
Till the Spanish came and stole
Everything in they way
For they were after silver and gold
They found little and went on their way
They however coined the name
Madrid for their homeland far away
For it was a noble city in Spain
The minors came from strong stock

To bend their backs and minds
Digging and loading the small
Steel and wood back wheeled carts
Stacked high with black gold
Its not known who pulled them on the
Small rail track, I would suspect
The human back
Often the minors numbers would fall
Tunnel cave ins buried alive
No one to hear the screams
Some times the Black Gold's dust
Had entered the lungs
Days were numbered then
They had not discovered a cure
Cheeco learned all this fast
With resolve and conviction
He would get his Black Gold
Not in the mines but at the table
To practice his new gamblers trade

Tale six

The only place he reckoned
Was the Mineshaft Tavern
It was really more an Old West Saloon
If an Englishman new they called it
A Tavern he would roll over dead
They place that had watered whiskey
Little did the minors know
They would split a full bottle and make two
Also serving a no class beer chilled by the earth
Cheeco had established himself
His favorite one leg round table
Set in the corner with him
Facing the patrons of the saloon
His fame soon spread often with dire dread
He did not care he was mining the Black Gold
The players mostly minors would come

Then they would go when their funds were low
Some said "he can read the back of the cards"
Of course he could he mark them well
Only he could deceiver the code
They way of the marking is still unknown today
When the last lantern went out no one about
Under the oak pine bar longest in the west
One a shelf above the floor
The sealed cards rested in decks
Like roman soldiers on the no where march
He developed a way to mark all the cards
And not a seal did he break
And so it seamed when a new deck was wanted
He would smile a inter smile no one could see
And of course his Black Gold grew
Easier then the mines drinking watered whiskey
All through the night

Tale seven

Of course the bar room ladies
Were there every night often a pretty sight
There was one a lady named "Belle"
Fiery red hair so brilliant and bright
Large green eyes when she gave you a stare
Buxom and desirable with a wonderful smile
Dressed in a short dress of red
Long silk knitted in black stockings and
Gold colored low heeled slippers
She plied her trade
If a minor would pay her toll
Off to the back room they would go
For a quick minors release
She could manage a dozen or so a night
She stashed her toll in the pillow
That rested her head
The minors soon changed her name
Now they would call her
'JEZEBELLE'

Cheeco soon paid her toll
At first liked each other then came love
Often they would sing together
As he strummed an old guitar
This was the minors delight
Bought them both drinks
Of course watered whisky
They both new they would

Continue to work their trades
It was the gathering of Black Gold
And the riches it would bring
Jezebelle soon started stuffing
Her second pillow tell it was full
Before dawn on a summers morn
She went away how and where
No one would ever know
The only thing missing
Was two stuffed pillows

Tale eight
I think its final
Cheeco pined and moaned
For he would never forget her
Jezebelle his first and only love
Gladly returned to the table
On a clear full moon night
A handsome young stranger
Came from the North
Big and strong with
Blond long hair eyes of blue
Colored as by the sky
Strapped on his right hip
A big 44 holstered tied
With rawhide string to his thigh
His purse was small he
Knew to make it grow
He would to play
The game of chance

He sequestered a seat at
Cheeco's table
Minor after minor dropped out
Till only him and Cheeco remained
The blue eyed stranger last coin set
In the middle of the round table
Surrounded on a high pile of Black Gold
He had discovered Cheeco's poker winning trick
The anger devil within burst
He stood and set his 44 free
One bullet through Cheeco's left eye
Before he fell from the chair to the floor
The blue eyed stranger was out the front bar room door
Up on his saddled steed galloping
As fast as he could for
The devil's posse would soon be chasing him

The news spread fast
A mounted posse started to form
They took a vote
For they all new he had done
The Company Town a service
They also new that the
Blue eyed strangers would
Soon meet his maker
By a crusty old out-law
With a faster draw
The bar men stuffed Cheeco
In a big coal canvas bag
Tied the end with one knot
And tossed him head first
Into the broken deep earth
One kindly old bar man
Said with such grace
Lets give him an epitaph
I'll get an old board
Paint and brush
And so it was
here is what they wrote

Here lies
Cheeco "malo" Chacon
Struck dead by
A blue stranger
One bullet through his
Left eye
God give his cheating
Heart, mind,spirit and soul
No rest or peace
Let him wonder in the
Black gold tunnels
For eternity

Jezebelle's in spirit still lives today
On main street
Serving ice cream and treats
In her soda fountain store

I KNOW THIS TALE IS TRUE
FOR THE BAR STOOL
AT THE TAVERN
TOLD ME SO
AND SO WILL YOU

Theodoro Corona Luna
1888 ???
Copyrighted 2012

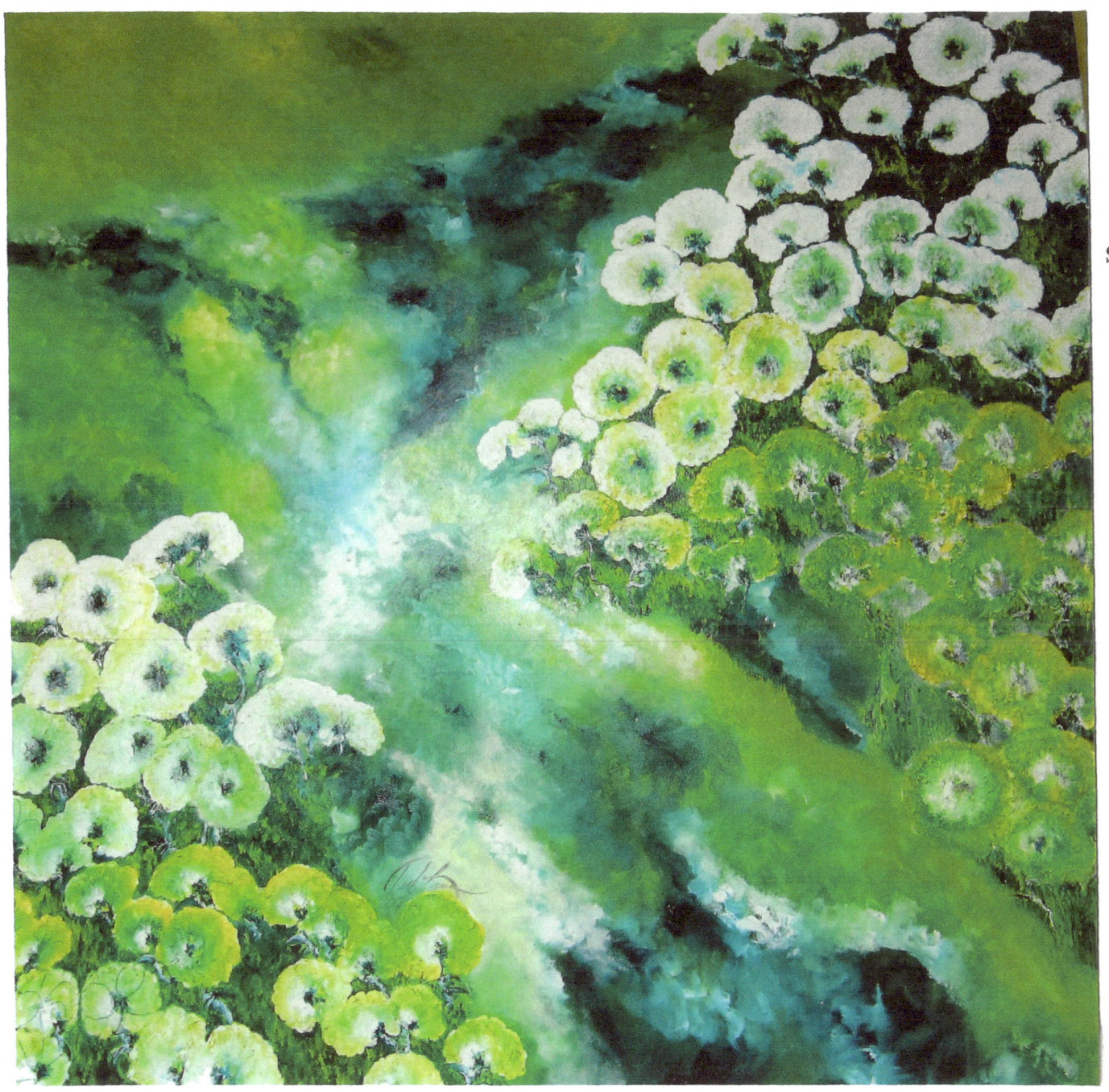

WILD DAISYS

A PICNIC IN THE MEADOW
KFC CHICKEN
CHAMPAGNE IN GLASSES
SPREAD ON WOOL BLANKET
MY NEW LOVE
WITH EYES OF BLUE
BLOND ROLLING HAIR
SHOES STILL WET
FROM CROSSING
THE STREAM
SHE IS EVERY MANS
DREAM
NO ONE IN SIGHT
A JOY AND DELIGHT
THE BOTTLE WAS EMPTY
I AM GLAD I HAD TWO
LATE SUMMER
AFTERNOON
NOT A CARE
IN THE WORLD
LOVE BLOOMS THE
BEST IN A SEA
OF WILD DAISYS
PLEASE GO
JUST NORTH OF SANTA FE
ON THE WAY TO
THE SKI BASIN
THIS STOREY IS TRUE
IF YOU DON'T BELIEVE ME
I'LL GIVE YOU
MY WET SHOES

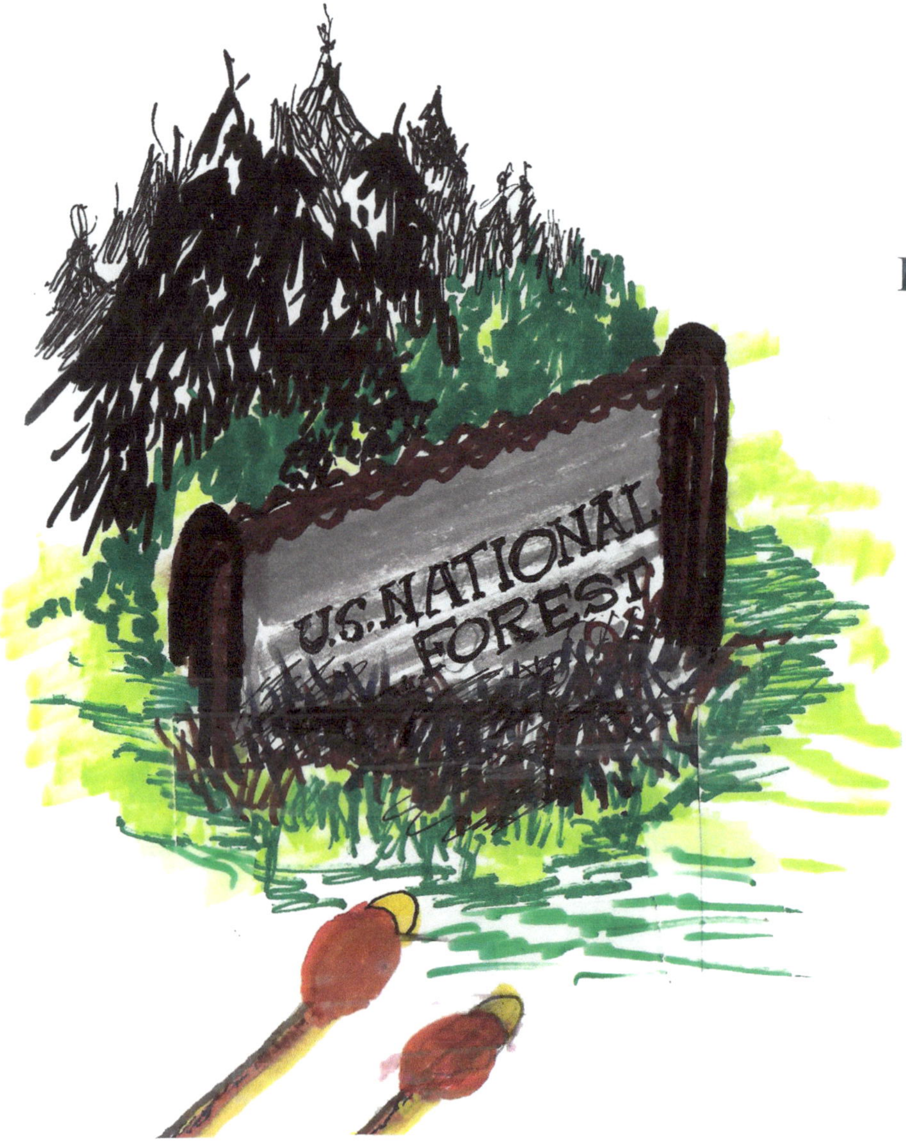

ALIANZA
REIES LOPEZ TIJERINA
RAID
RIO ARRIBA COUNTY COURTHOUSE
NORTHERN
NEW MEXICO
JUNE 5, 1967

A FACTUAL HISTORICAL TRUE STOREY
LARGE AREAS OF NORTHERN NEW MEXICO
WERE THE ILLEGAL SPOILS OF COLONIAL INVASION
AIDED BY OFFICIALS ROBBING SCORES OF LAND GRANT
COMMUNITIES OF THEIR LAND
ENTER TIJERINA FOLK HERO
THE ALIANZA ACTIVIST

AFTER THE RAID A SUBSEQUENT MANHUNT
WAS THE LARGEST IN NEW MEXICO
TIJERINA ABDUCTED TWO MEN
TIJERANA AND FOLLOWERS WERE LATER ARRESTED
THEY MADE BAIL WHEN A COURT DATE WAS SET.

I WAS SITTING IN MY CANVAS DIRECTORS CHAIR
CONTEMPLATING THE BLOSSOMS ON MY APPLE TREE
ON A VERY EARLY MORNING WHEN THE PHONE RANG
GOOD MORNING TED LUNA ARCHITECT I ANSWERED
MR. LUNA THIS IS ALFONSO SANCHEZ
DISTRICT ATTORNEY OF RIO ARRIBA COUNTY
HE SAID I WOULD LIKE TO MEET WITH YOU
I NEED YOUR HELP ON A VERY SPECIAL PROJECT

HERE IS WHAT REIES
AND HIS FOLLOWERS
DID TO START IT ALL

74

WE MET AND HE INFORMED ME OF THE UP COMING TRIAL
OF REIES LOPEZ TIJERINA
HE COMMISIONED ME TO BUILD A MODEL OF
THE RIO ARRIBA COUNTY COURT TO BE USED AT THE TRIAL
WE SIGNED A SIMPLE CONTRACT

BACK IN SANTA FE I CALLED MY FRIEND AND PHOTOGRAPHER
BOB NUGENT, WE DEVELOPED A WAY TO TAKE PHOTOS
OF BUILDING ELEVATIONS AND PUT THEM TO SCALE
ON BACK TO THE COURTHOUSE
WHILE BOB DID THE PHOTO WORK
I TRIED TO FIND PLANS ON THE BUILDING
THEY DID NOT EXIST, SO I HAD TO
DO ASBUILT DRAWINGS OF EACH FLOOR
WITH MEASUREMENTS FOR EXACT DEMENSIONS
OF EACH SPACE AND NAME THEM

IN MY OFFICE I HAD ONE WINDOW THAT FACED THE SIDEWALK
OUT FRONT WHICH AT THAT TIME WAS 232 HILLSIDE IN SANTA FE
AS I WAS WORKING ON THE MODEL
A FACE APPEARED AT THE WINDOW
IT WAS REIES LOPEZ TIJERINA
HE NEVER SMILED JUST WALKED AWAY

THE MODEL THANKS TO BOB WAS VERY
EASY TO BUILD, JUST GLUING THE PHOTOS TO
MAT BOARD, AND EACH FLOOR HAD TO
MAKE THE ROOF REMOVABLE TO SHOW THE INTERIOR
I DELIVERED THE MODEL TO ALFONSO
HE WAS VERY PLEASE AND GAVE ME A CHECK
HE TOLD ME WHEN THE TRIAL DATE WAS
AND WANTED ME TO BE THE EXPERT WITNESS

THE TRIAL WAS SET THE JURY SELECTED AND SEATED
AFTER OPENING REMARKS WERE FINISHED
ALFONSO CALLED ME TO THE STAND
ALONG WITH THE MODEL
HE WENT THRU A SMALL RESUME OF
MY PROFESSIONAL LIFE AND ASKED
THE AUTHENTICATION OF THE MODEL
HE SHOWED THE JUDGE AND JURY
IT WAS ENTERED INTO EVIDENCE
AS EXHIBIT ONE

CROSS EXAMINATION THE TIJARINA'S ATTORNEY
GENERALLY QUESTIONED ME AND HE
ENDED BY ASKING ME THE COLOR OF THE COURT HOUSE
I SIMPLEY SAID PINK, NO FURTHER QUESTIONS

THIS WAS MY FIRST APPEARANCE AS AN EXPERT WITNESS
LITTLE DID I KNOW THERE WOULD BE MANY MORE
TIJERINA WAS SENTENCE TO FEDERAL PRISON
HIS CAUSE WAS JUST HE JUST DID IT THE WRONG WAY

TED C. LUNA
ARCHITECT-PLANNER

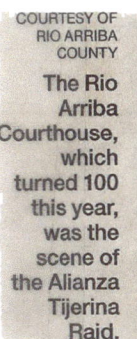
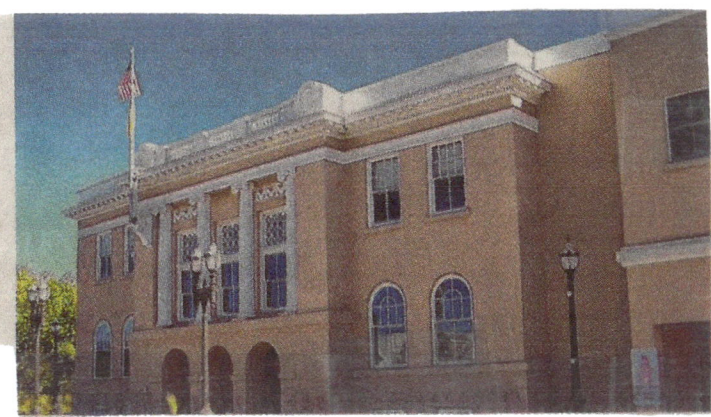

COURTEZ OF RIO ARRIBA COUNTY

The Rio Arriba Courthouse, which turned 100 this year, was the scene of the Alianza Tijerina Raid.

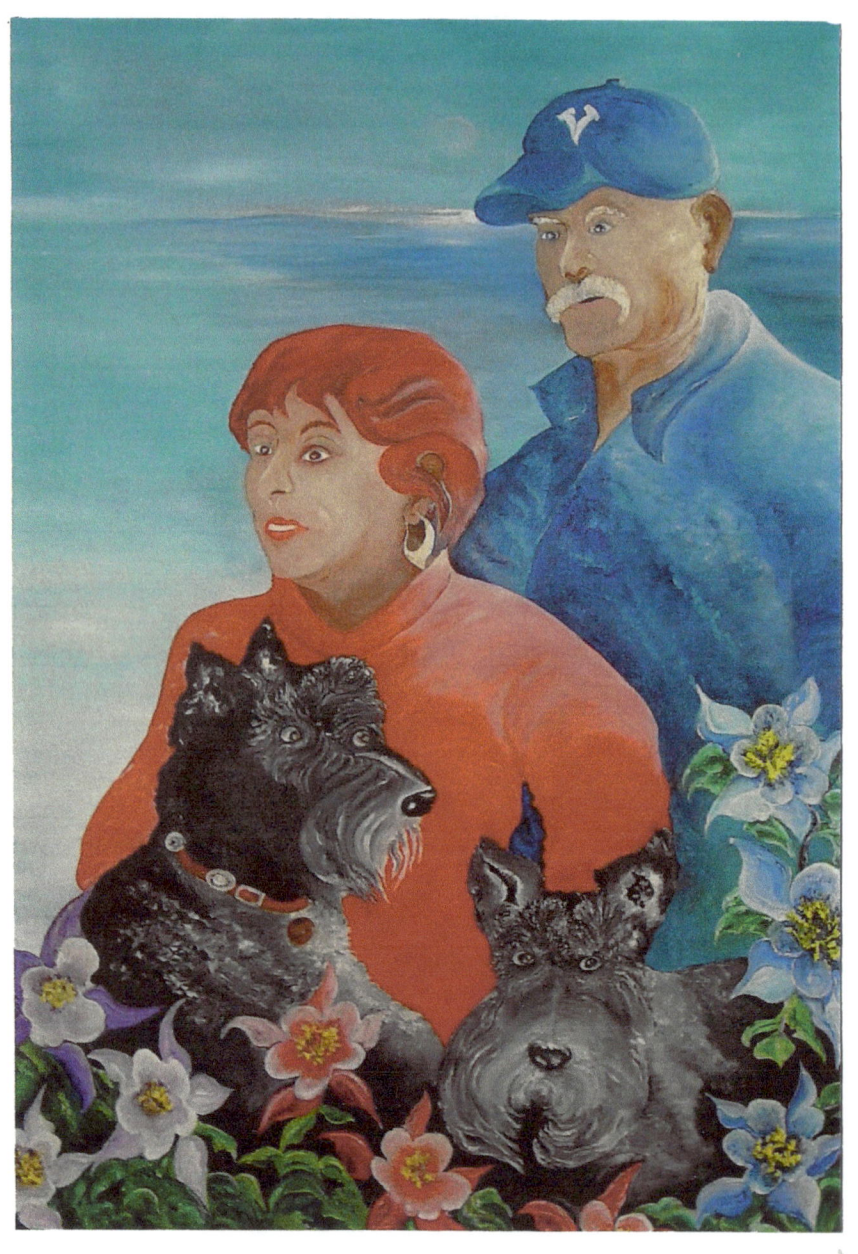

MY VERY SAD STOREY

GINGER A CONCERT VIOLINIST
LARRY A GLOBLE FREIGHT PILOT
LIVING SOUTH EAST OF SANTA FE
HIGH UP IN BEAUTIFUL MOUNTAIN HOME
NEEDED A MASTER BEDROOM
I DESIGNED AND THEY BUILT IT
WE WERE FRIENDS FOR A YEAR
GINGER ASK ME TO PAINT
THEIR TWO FEMALE SCOTTISH DOGS
WHEN RACHAEL AND I DELIVERED
THE PAINTING GINGER WAS VERY PLEASED
IN CELEBRATION WE WENT TO THE
SANTA FE COUNTRY CLUB FOR LUNCH
DURING LUNCH I ASKED FOR
A REASONABLE FEE FOR THE PAINTING
GINGER BLEW UP AND CALLED ME
NAMES I HAVE NEVER HEARD OF
SHE IMMEDIATLEY DEPARTED
RACHEAL AND I LOOKED AT EACH OTHER
WE JUST COULD NOT BELIEVE HER ACTIONS
IN HER MIND SHE WANTED IT FOR FREE
I CALLED HER MANY TIMES
AND OFFERED IT FOR FREE
SHE FOR WHATEVER REASON NEVER
WOULD TALK TO ME, THEY NEVER WANTED
TO SEE ME AGAIN
I PAINTED THEM OUT OF THE PAINTING
DONATED IT FOR GALA SILENT AUCTION
TO WATER MELON MTN. RANCH
A WONDERFUL RESCUE ANIMAL
NO KILL FACILITY HERE IN
ALBUQUERQUE
IT SOLD

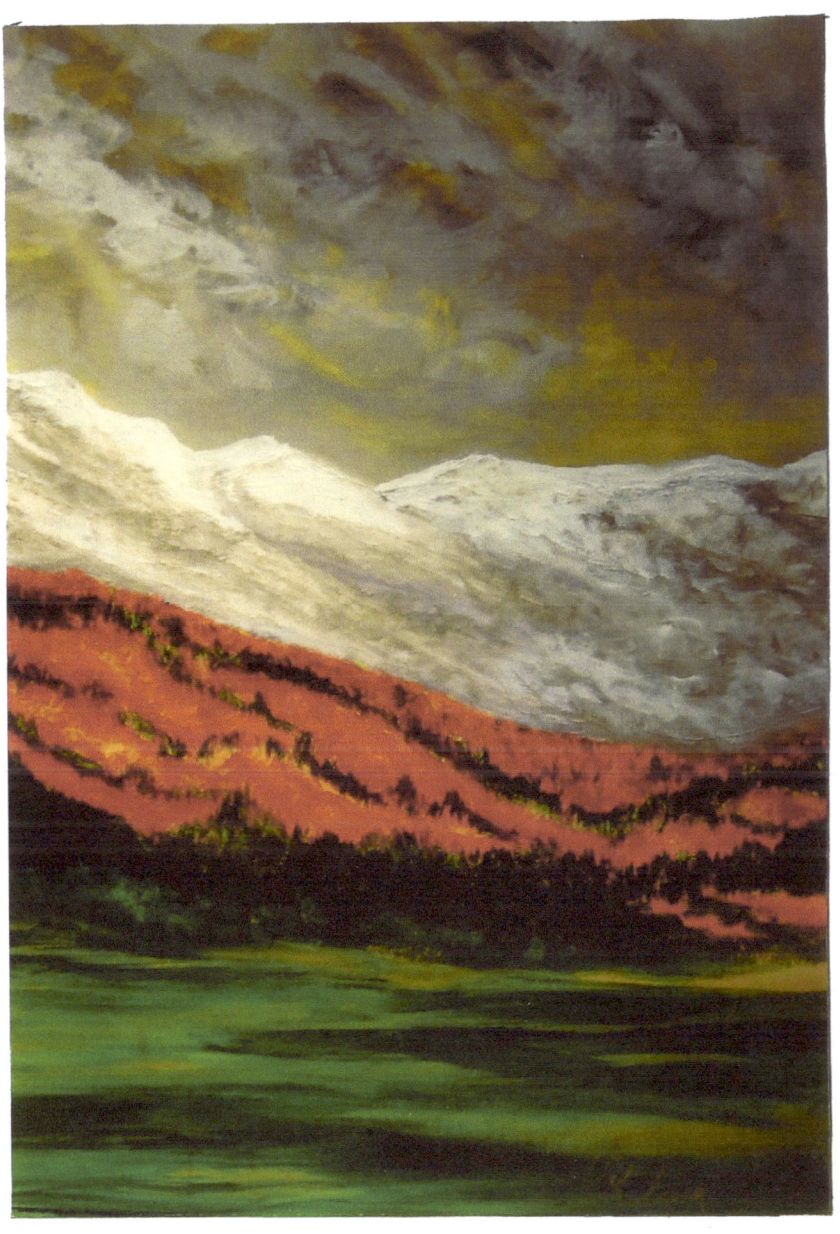

FIRST SNOW

Clear crystals
Turning white
In first morning light
Gently to the earth
Floating through crisp air
Laden gray skies
Sun well hidden
The cleansing of spirit
Transformation
Beauty for all to see
A master paint brush
Some times by the sea

White jewels
Spaced in between
Gathering new blankets
Warm as could be
Colors changing
Becoming one
Welcome First Snow
You mean so much
To me

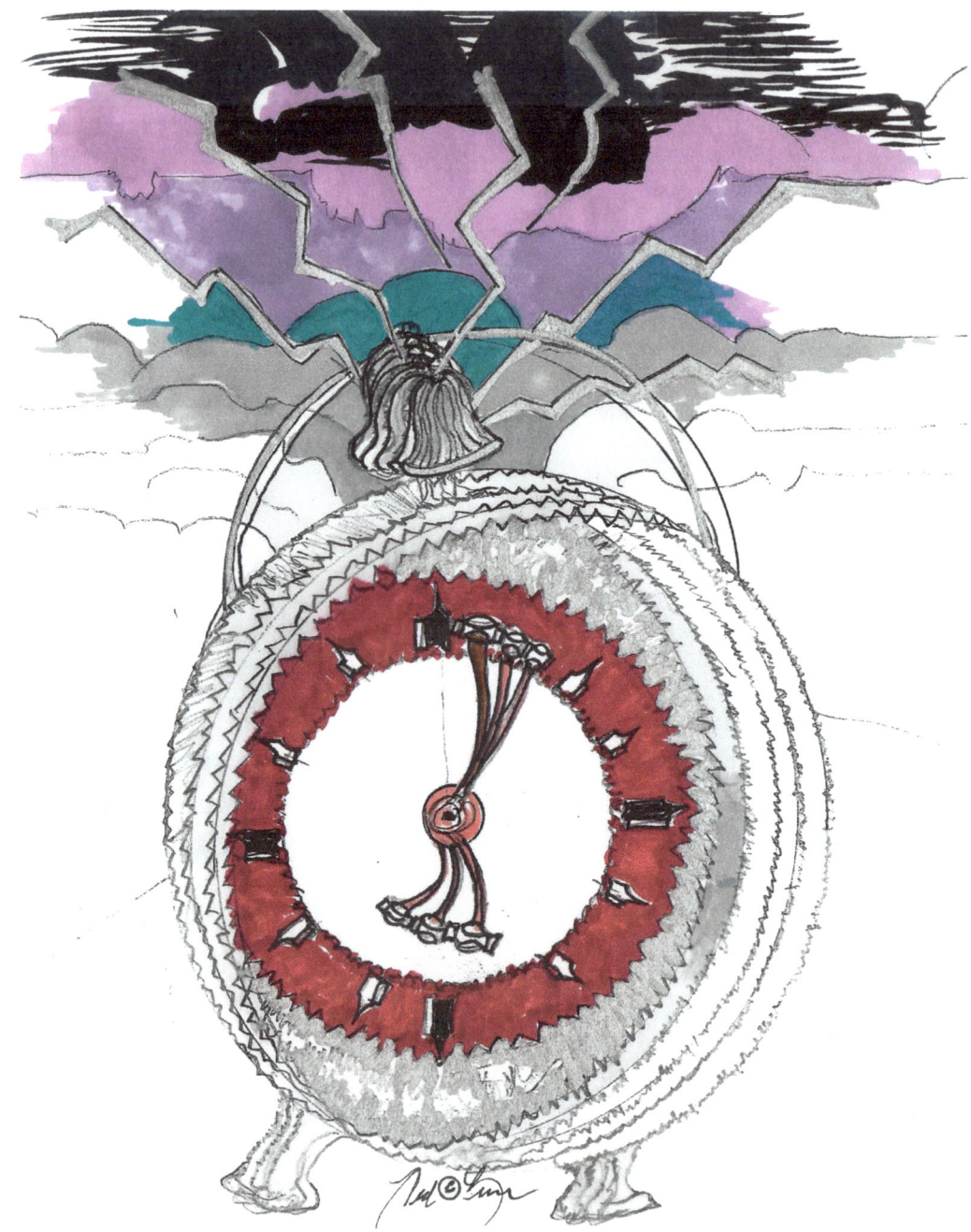

THE CLOCK

The stroke
Thunder at early dawn
The curtain fell
On the theatre of my mind
The lighting struck
As I reached for the clock
Salience finally
My present to begin
The day is mine
A gift to be sure
No more will I endure
For I will live for today
Beauty to create
With only love
Depends on what I ate
Schedule asunder
Priority's bold
Visions to see
I am happy
I'm not a tree
Weather so fine
And I am not blind
Universal joy
Is what the day
Brings to me

SALMON

In the head waters
The river unknown
12 to 24 inches deep
Mother spawned her eggs
Father to complete

The cycle is done
Remorse not present
Their life went away
A cycle to repeat

Fryes you soon become
Your journey to the sea
Because you are small
And travel so fast

Few adventures will you see
Brothers and sisters
In a covey you go
How did you know
The river leads to the sea

You will spend years
Growing big and strong
You will shun the nets
That some time
Brings you to me

Hidden yearnings soon to arise
How do find the river
That lead me to the sea
Nature in its wisdom
Found it for me

The journey is full of perils
Bears manmade falls
I marvel at your being
As you swim and climb
Struggling up stream
You find your way back
To the brook
That adorned you
With life

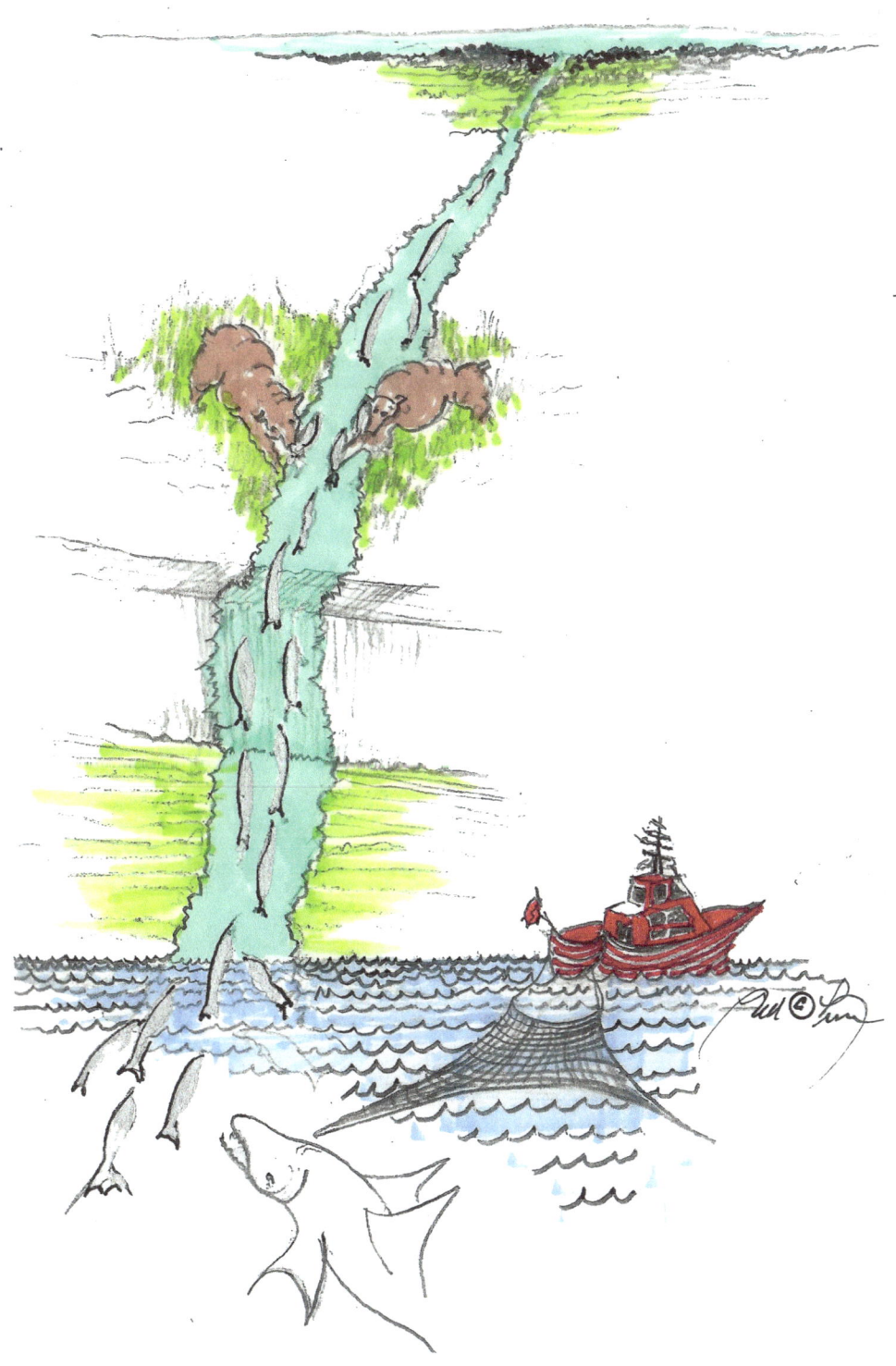

9

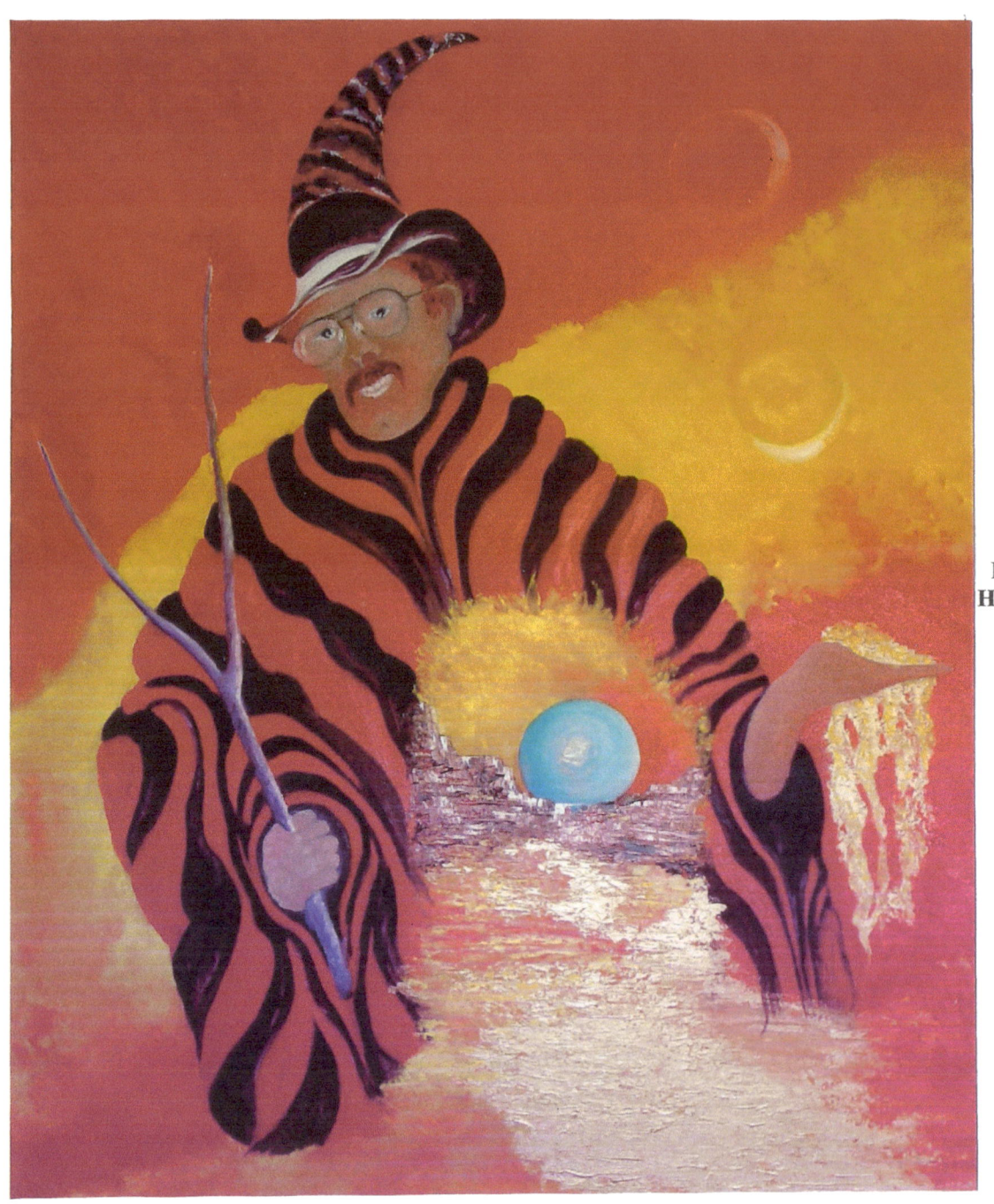

WIZARD OF THE NORTH
CHARLES (CHUCK) BRYANT
A LIFE LONG FRIEND
MARRIED TO JOANNA
FIRST SAW HER IN DIAPERS
PLAYING THE YARD
ACROSS THE STREET
WHAT A BEAUTIFUL LADY
CHUCK WITH HIS DEVING STICK
COULD FIND WATER WHERE
NONE EXISTED THUS HIS NICK NAME
HE COULD PEER IN HIS CRISTALS BALL
AND MAKE GOOD THINGS HAPPEN
HE IS AN ICON MASTER BUILDER
OF VERY HIGH LEVEL HOMES
THROGH THE YEARS WE HAVE
WORKED TOGETHER
HE IS ALL SO THE BEST
MASTER DEVELOPERS
SANGRE DECRISTO ESTATES
TESQUE HILLS IN TESUQUE
WE HAVE SO MANY MUTUAL
TALES I COULD TELL
HE CALLS ME THE
WIZARD OF THE SOUTH

FRIENDS

Walking through life
Some things require
Holding thoughts shared
Always to hear

The way life lives
Your hand in mine
I feel your presence
Yesteryears long gone

Because of you
Loved ones come
And yet some go
Days come then they go

New or old some things remain
Heartfelt sharing
Always when I think of you
You make me dance

In the annals of my being
Bringing me joy
As I share my seeing
My horizons expand

With you in my thoughts
Changing nothing
And yet everything
For you are my
Friend

HARLEY AND ME

Mechnical creatures
Spice of life
Taking you where your feet
Will never go
A bike they are called
For wheels are only two
They added an engine
To make the ride swift

In years to come they added gears
Your freedom of flight
On dirt and gravel trails and roads
An eternity later
With asphalt they would be sealed
This memory i will keep
To share with you

Stories of harley and mc
Jack johnson kept his shop
Lived in a triailer a 50 foot hop away
From his dealership
Lower auga fria street
In dear old santa fe

He sequested me one day
And this is what he had to say
Ted its time to ride my way
Starting with taking in trade my
Brit twin cylinder 500 bsa

My first tour on a paved highway
Off i went from santa fe
Lawton oklahoma to spend time
With sister peggy and max

My last ride of pleasure on the bsa

Father conned the bank
With his word clinch the deal
After school i did pump gas
At his station a few blocks from home
17 cents a gallon
I new i would pump many millions

Timley payments due
For harley and me
Freshman in high school
Chuck and i were bored to death
So one day in early summer
We put each other to the test

He rode a brit thriumph
I never let him know
He was a better rider than me
He said once around the federal oval
That bordered high school
Traffic no where to be seen

After lunch for all to see
No one was really interested
This race would be mine
We defined the starting line
Reviving the engines
A leap of faith i did not know
Lived in me

It was a blurer so fast it went
Across the finish he looked
Back and smiled at me
My macho said to me
Lets do it again
Repeat of the first lap
The finish the same

HARLEY CHUCK AND ME
SANTA FE HIGH SCHOOL DAYS

Ha ta hey Ted what are you doing
Chopping my store bought Harley
I bought the biggest knobby tires
Both front and back
Next went the fenders
I left a little on the back
Windscreen to store
Went to a single seat
Painted it safety yellow
satisfying the macho in me

I could walk it on the back tire
And race down the street
We had become one
My true love girl friend
In time would become my first wife
She burned her ankle
On the hot exhaust pipe
scars to remain to this day

We have five riders
Including you and me
To the Borrego trail
We must conquer
Tesuque is the trail head
Up to Hyde park

Late blooming spring
Easy riding this was a lark
Till elevation we gained
North side slopes
Still covered with snow
Deeper then the ocean

Peppered with new fallen trees
We lifted each bike
Pushed them through the snow
Twilight soon came
Followed by the dark

We gathered wood for a fire
To last through the night
Blazing and warm
Knapping only to turn over
Front warm back cold
Later I would learn
To build two fires
And lie in-between
I vowed then once and for all
On the road safe and sound

Raising my fist
middle finger extended
Forever goodbye to the
Devil that lives in
Borrego trail

Chuck lets ride an enduro
Are you sure that's her name
Endurance you bum
Man and machine for 100 miles
Palo duro canyon

West Texas was the scene
We spent our life savings
registering for the race
Gold trophies would crown
The first five
That proved they
Could finish the race

We would ride single file
Chuck leading sometimes me
Thru desert sand so fine
Rocks and hills up and down
Sweating buckets as we went

On a tough hill
Chuck dropped his steed
Sand filled the air cleaner
Power no more but it still ran
He said to me finish the race
A mile back I saw a road

I had half the course
To travel alone
I did finish came in last
So this was
our west Texas blast
Some memories do last

When they say
Its time for a new reality
I joined naval air
Reasons are clear
Good food clean sheets
foxholes never to dig
My new world
About to unfold
I traded
My beloved yellow Harley
for a green 49 ford
Many years later
Harley would find
And inter my life again
But when and why
Time or place
I simply did not know

HARLEY DAVA AND ME

Suzanne and I as we dined
Angel fire country club
A lady came to greet us
With sweetness and bold
I was told you are
The architect that created
The Vietnam Veterans National Memorial

You could not know how you changed my life
Dava Shumsky Ansell is my name
A few years pasted Suzanne
Sending her to go our separate ways
No lady in my life I felt single again

In my Santa fe office
My secretary told me
This is a call you must receive
Hi this is Dava
Do you remember me we met a few years ago
Victor and I have just been given a huey
Please come up and tell us what to do
She was working at the chapel

I would be up in a day or two
It would only take two days to fall in love
She was a lady from the east
Been riding Harleys for 10 years or so
She called her black beauty Harley" baby"

Chuck bought a rice burner
And lent it to me
To ride and chase Dava around
For new world would unfolded in me
She had planned for her 2 week vacation
To tour northwestern states
To Canada and end with the rally in Sturgis

The rice burner we knew had to go
In the journal an add caught me eye
An 1997 Electra glide Harley
Loaded beyond the gilds
Except for a windscreen wiper
Left to right to clear the shield

H/d in wisdom of their years
Decided that speed would do the deed
In rain or snow
Most riders know if you must go
You always ride slow

He and his wife had planned
A ride the weekend the chapel to see
We will meet you in the parking lot
Hopefully for your new red Harley to be
I have known love at first fright

Red Harley entered my heart like a spear
Spirit and soul followed immediately
Time as always soon came
Our odyssey tour to unfold

Bedrolls anchored and tools might we need
Clear riding on a glorious day
Till we hit Colorado
Then turned to rain all of the way

Next morning to aspen we rode
Through elevation 12,000 that
Defined independence pass
I put on john Denver
Now I really knew why he named it
Rocky mountain high

Her years of experience in touring
She gave me this gift
Prepared touring on a Harley
What a wonderful way to be and see
It had become my reality

Only back roads would we travel
Up through west Yellowstone
Old faithful on time we spent not a dime

Soon we were in Montana
20 miles out of butte
Smoke from the forest fires
Dark bellowing black and gray
We could breath or the road to see

Turned back to Bozeman
For lunch and maybe call it a day
Attacking each other at lunch
She yelled you must go and I will too
To finish the tour in our separate ways

In the parking lot we did embrace
Her and I new the anger was over
It had nothing to do with her or me
Frustrated because our tour

Was cut short

On through billings turning south
To south Dakota rapid city
Deadwood spearfish and Sturgis
To ride in the biggest
Motorcycle rally in the world

Following morning we would ride
Up to Sundance then on to devils tower
We new a race track had a rally
Four or five miles west of Sundance
We search for the driveway

Then went in front of a large motor home
We made it travel so slow
Dava spotted it to the left
I gave her the 5 second lead
As a good rider will allow
Then she turned I almost slowed to a stop
What happened next I will never forget

The sound of terror
Rubber trying to brake
He t-boned her Harley at 55 mph
In to the saddle bag inches from her leg
She flew like a rocket straight up in the air

Baby went tumbling
In side circles to the bar ditch to rest
The rider in the bike that hit her
Vaulted over the handle bars
No one wore a helmet it
Was strapped to the rack

Doing summersaults his wife still on bike
As an eagle I flew to Dava side
I saw her landing hip first then her head
Pray to the lord she's not dead
Out like a the turn of a switch

I talked to her she could not hear
Placing my leather chaps under her head
I talked and I talked her connection to life
Couple in the motor home called 911

Emt just four miles away
Came so fast and called officers
State troopers they new what to do
I counted 11 when the all showed up
Emt and I brought dava around

Shock was her relief she seemed not in pain

They treated the other couple
They took all three sirens screaming
To a small hospital in Sundance
Second treatment was there
Dava awake her pain did arrive

A kind sargent called a tow truck
He and I would help load
What was left of the bikes
The driver suggested to me
He would take them to the h/d
Dealership 85 miles away in rapid city

We all cleared the road
Thanked the couple in their motor home
To Sundance I rode Dava to see
I was happy to see her alert
The doctor told me
He was sending all three
For care and pain management
To rapid city regional hospital

I then had a lonely 85 mile ride
I met Dava in the emergency room
We waited two hours for a doctor
When did come his orders were clear
Up to the 5th floor your admitted now
Evaluation and killers of pain
They gave her something I did not know

Turned out first 5 days
Of little food mostly sleep
I set in the chair the first day or two
By her clean white bed
It then became clear to me
She never knew I was there

For days I would see riders wife's and friends
Motorcycle accidents hurt in the big area
This was not a pleasant experience for me

Holiday express for 9 days was my home
We had come so far
For sights to enjoy and see
To Sturgis I would ride
Alone Harley and me
6 blocks from the main street
I parked Harley on a residential grass
Five dollars a day

I was sure it would be only one
Riders in shades of black
Scantly glad females
Motorcycles represented
From every nation in the world

I had one draft beer
No more would I drink
When you love your Harley and your life
That's always been my limit
I would start my own private tour

When you ride in a group
All you will ever see is the bike
Fore and aft or to your side
Concerned with safety
You cannot enjoy the countryside

Presidential immortality carved in stone
Only in an earthquake would
Make them close their eyes
A short 8 miles away
I greeted Oglada Lakota
Chief crazy horse mounted on his steed
I cannot find the words
To express my feeling
So I empty my pocket and took a stone

In my south Dakota travels the days melted
I rode through the grassed plains
Where dances with the wolfs became alive
Thanks Kevin your story is still great
Buffalo free to roam and mate

In badlands national park
I slowed to let the herd cross
When a huge bull spotted red Harley
Instincts warned me his was ready to mate
I twisted the go handle raced away
Two curves later the wild donkeys came
They offered no mating call that I could discern
I was save and sound headed back to holiday

Many more travels would Harley and me take

I spent more time with Dava
She finally could talk
Aided by a walker walk
They were ready to dismissed her
With a ton of pain killers to take as needed

I had called my partner and friend
Luckily Dava's expedition with trailer in tow
He would come and we loaded the Harleys

Back to angel fire we go
Baby she deemed only one place to restore
Chic's dealership in Albuquerque
Her final bill in excess of 12k
Brought baby's new being

Her spirit restored
She had to hire a Wyoming attorney
To plead her case
In Cheyenne she found him
His first words to her
The rider in fault had Dairyland Insurance
Milk cows had formed the company
The settlement came after two years

The lawyer stated because of state laws
It would be small any other state
It would have been twenty times bigger

Living in angle fire
We would take twilight rides
Around enchanted circle
We would stop and play pool
Mostly she seemed gifted
With cue in her hand

Drinking only one prescribed beer
Bull o' the woods saloon
In red river still exists
If you will go say hi for us to all
For they never would know
Red Harley Dava and me
For reasons that were many
She needed to sell baby
So I created an ad in the daily newspaper
It did its work for the first couple arrived
Fell in love and wanted baby
By the stoke of my words
It yielded dava a few thousand more

Jeans and things was the name of her store
Her 12 years of wishing
Her dream finally came true
This was something she always knew

As my life goes through passages
After 8 years or less
I had moved back to Santa fe

Dava to remain in angle fire
I new then I would return
Just to Harley and me

This is the longest story
That I have ever written
I will bring it I promise
To closure and hope
We are still friends
So hang in
The end is in sight

I know now I should have given
A loving name to red Harley
"Red Bird"
He had given me 48,000 miles
Of safe flight
The time soon came to part
Chuck my life long best friend
He had always loved Red Bird
So he bought it from me

Red bird sits in nobility
Waxed and shined
In sangre de cristo estates
Chuck in his wisdom
Granted me life time
Riding rights
So ends my tale
Just Red Bird not me
Maybe

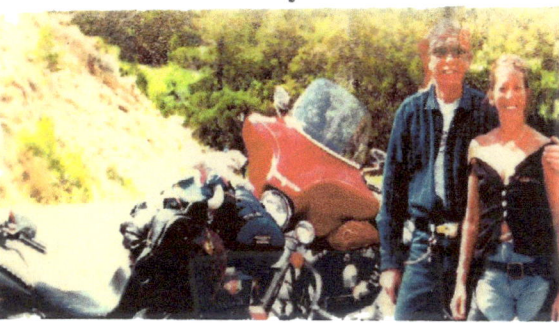

LAKODA FUNNERAL

A GATHERING OF ALL THE ANIMALS AND
HUMAN SPIRITS AND TRIBE
WORDS ARE SPOKEN
WITH SPECIAL CEREMONIES
TO ACKNOWLEDGE THE PASSAGE
UP ON POLES LADEN
WITH DRYED WOOD KINDELING
THE REMAINS REST
TORCHES WILL START THE FIRE
FLAMES OF ALL COLORS
CONSUME EVERYTHING
AND TURNS TO ASHES
THE PEOPLE KNOW
THE WINDS WILL SPREAD THEM
THROUGH OUT THEIR NATION

IN OUR CURRENT WORLD
MANY PEOPLE CHOOSE TO BE
CERMATED
SOME WANT THE ASHES
TO BE BLOWEN WITH THE WIND
IN PLACES OF THEIR CHOOSING

THE NATIVE AMERICANS
HAVE ADOPTED
WHITE MANS WAYS

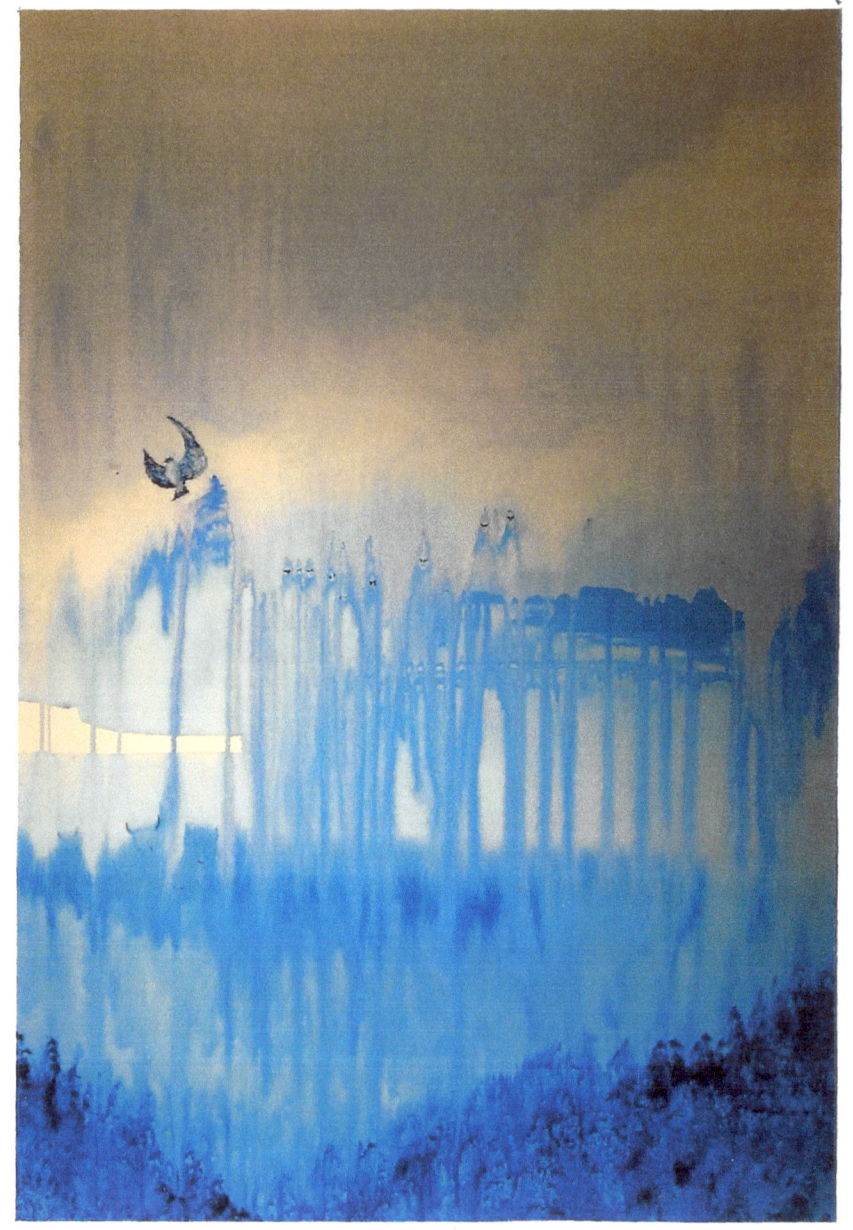

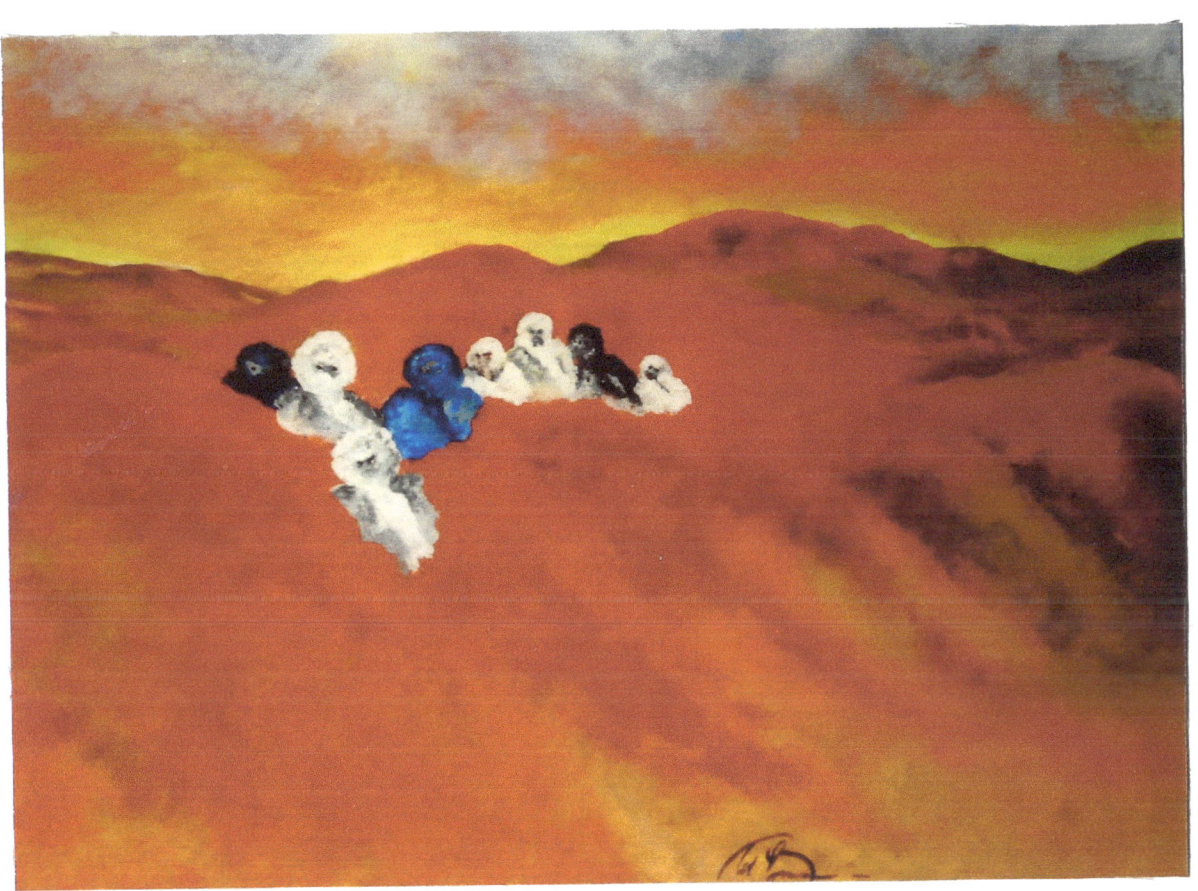

SUNRISE DESERT SEARCH
ABDUAL WHERE DID THE CAMELS GO
FOLLOW THE TRACKS YOU FOOL
THE WIND LAST NIGHT ERASED THEM

NUMBERS

The ancient CPA was bored
I will develop a system
To put numbers to time
He spun his abacus
Well into the night
When he was done
He would take it
To the mighty one
In hope of improving
His plight
Proud of his achievement
And on bended knee
He presented his system
I have numbers
a time for seconds
Minutes are next
Hours will follow
And then the day
After the weeks will enter
And then the months
And finally the years
The are numbers attached
So a measure can be made
The mighty one grinned
You fool life has no measure
Many are young at the start
This will stay until
They come to see me
Many are old at the start
When they enter my world
Time has no numbers that count
You just lost a rung
On the corporate ladder
GET OUT

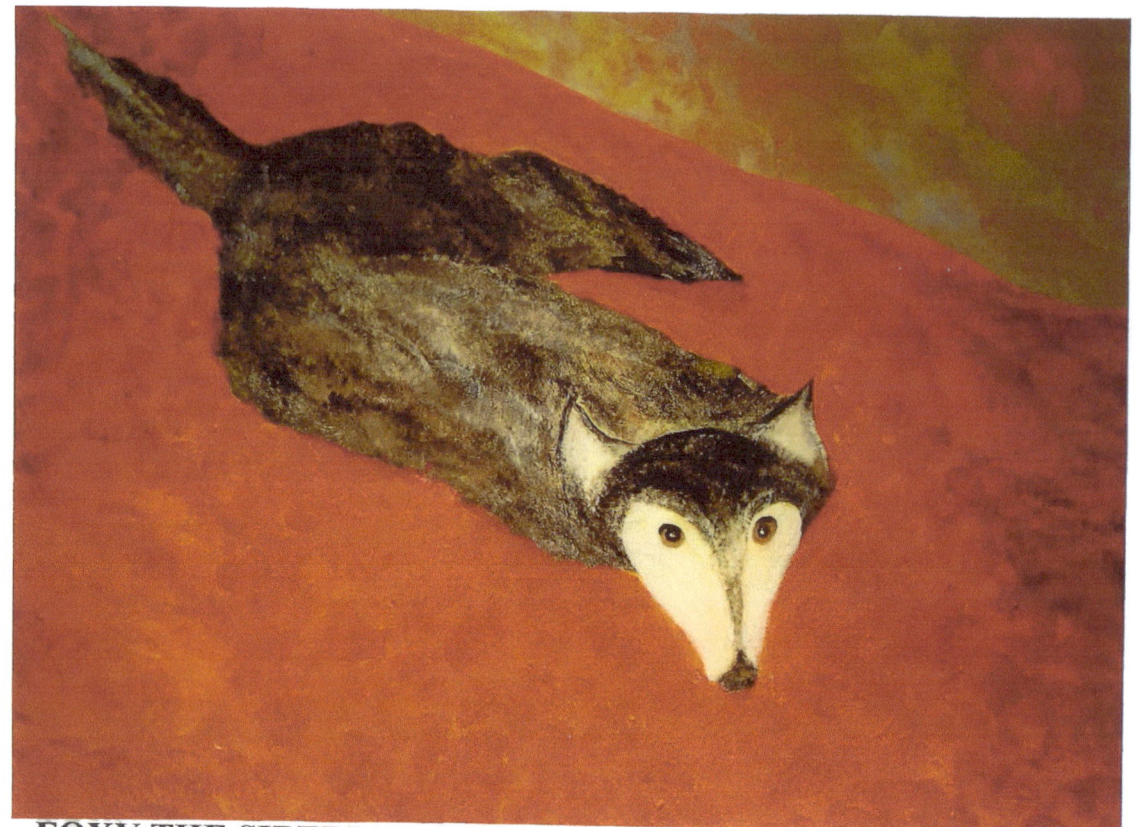

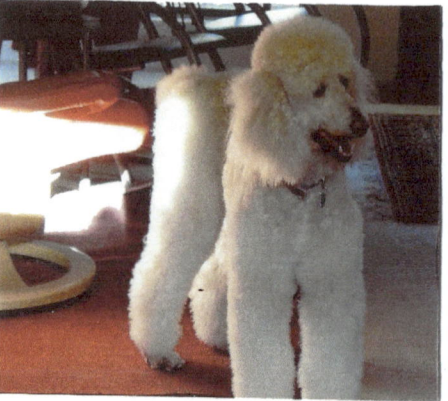

MOTHERS DAY

Mommy!

You make my day
When you dance through the door
I know treats are on the way
This is your day once a year
It does not seem fair
Can't we clear the calendar year
We love and play
Lots of petting too
Coddles with words of joy
Soon I seek my favorite toy
Thanking you always
For your my doctor
Keeping me healthy
My heart grows fonder
24/7
In the ground or pot
Plant my gift to you
With love water and
Miraclegrow
Say a prayer that
It won't snow
I love you for your being
My mommy to me

FOXY THE SIBERIAN HUSKEY
REGINA AND I HAVE MUTUAL CUSTODY
FOXY TAUGHT TIFF 2 TO SWIM
AT ELEPHANT BUTTE LAKE

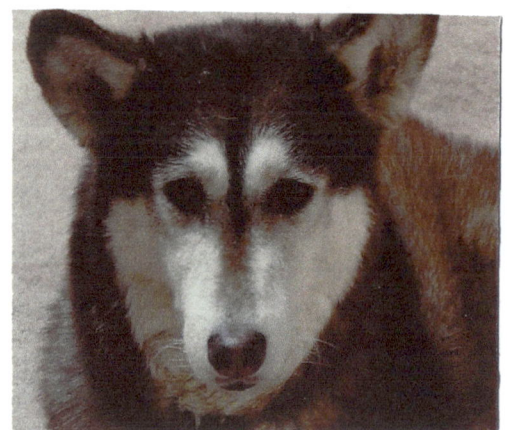

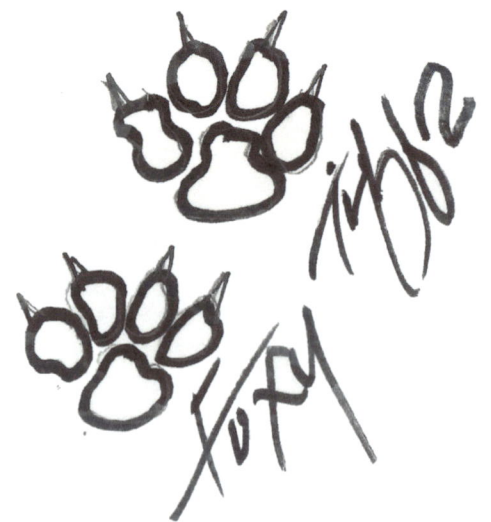

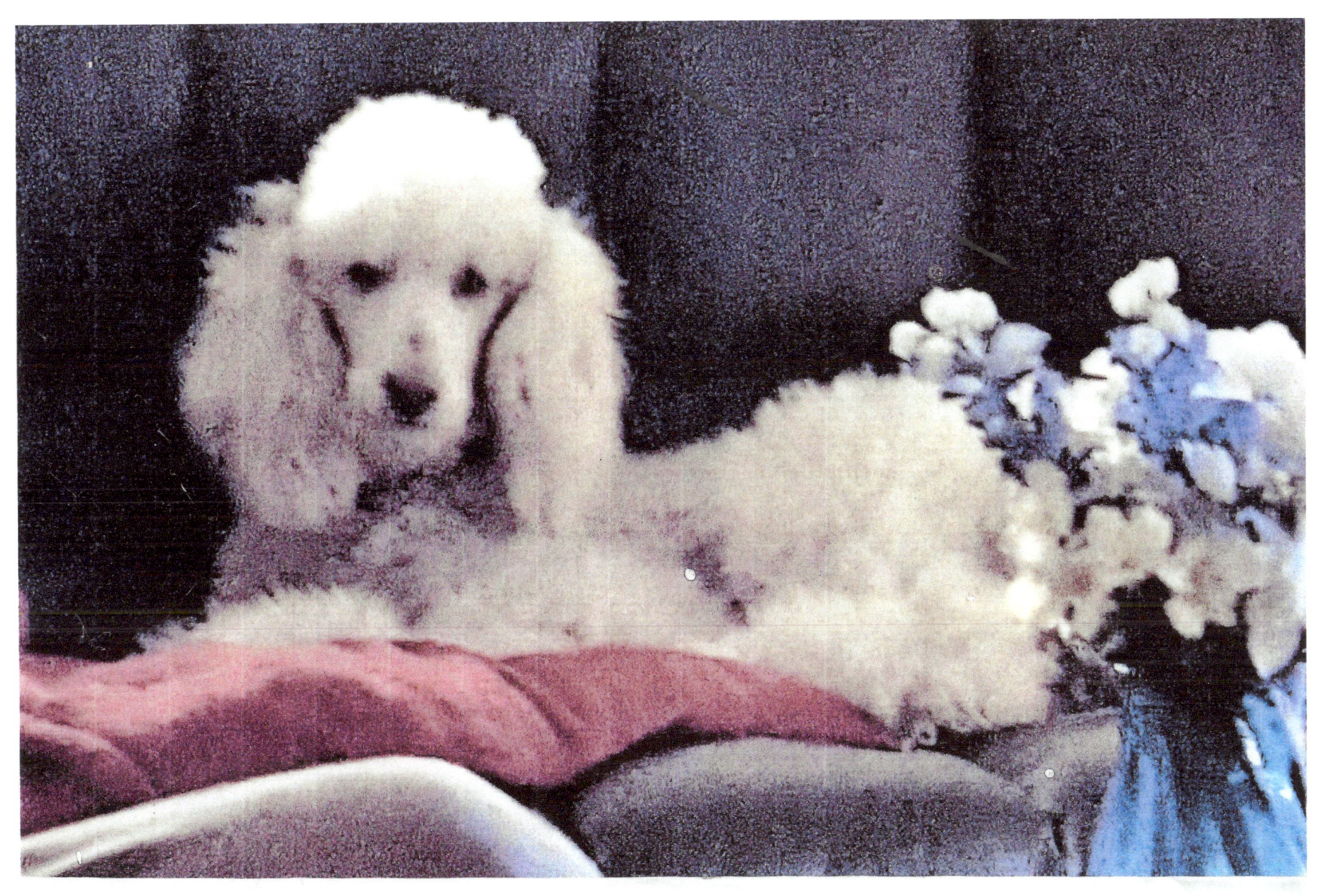

TIFFANY 2, TIF 2

Souls all glad
Like gladiators of old
High-tech shielding
Helmets must cost gold
Coaches to inspire
Organizations so bold
Ladders to climb
For the sake of each soul

Injuries occur
As in life by accident
Difference is
The doctor comes to you

A team it is called
No reference to horses
It started before puberty
Studying the law

When the law is broken
Instant judgment is given
Officials of the court
Proclaim the fine

A red flag gets thrown
To the supreme court for ruling
Two verdicts only
Stands or overturned

The fine may stand
Or overturned
Justice is swift
No time in jail

Life starts anew
With the snap from the center
Just as it should be
For you and me

60 minutes or more
Possibilities unlimited
Movements called plays
Just as in life
The theatre of the field
Awaits the new production
Just as our passages
From chapter to chapter

Its wonderful to know
That 60 minutes
Can change to 240 minutes
Adding time to our
love of life

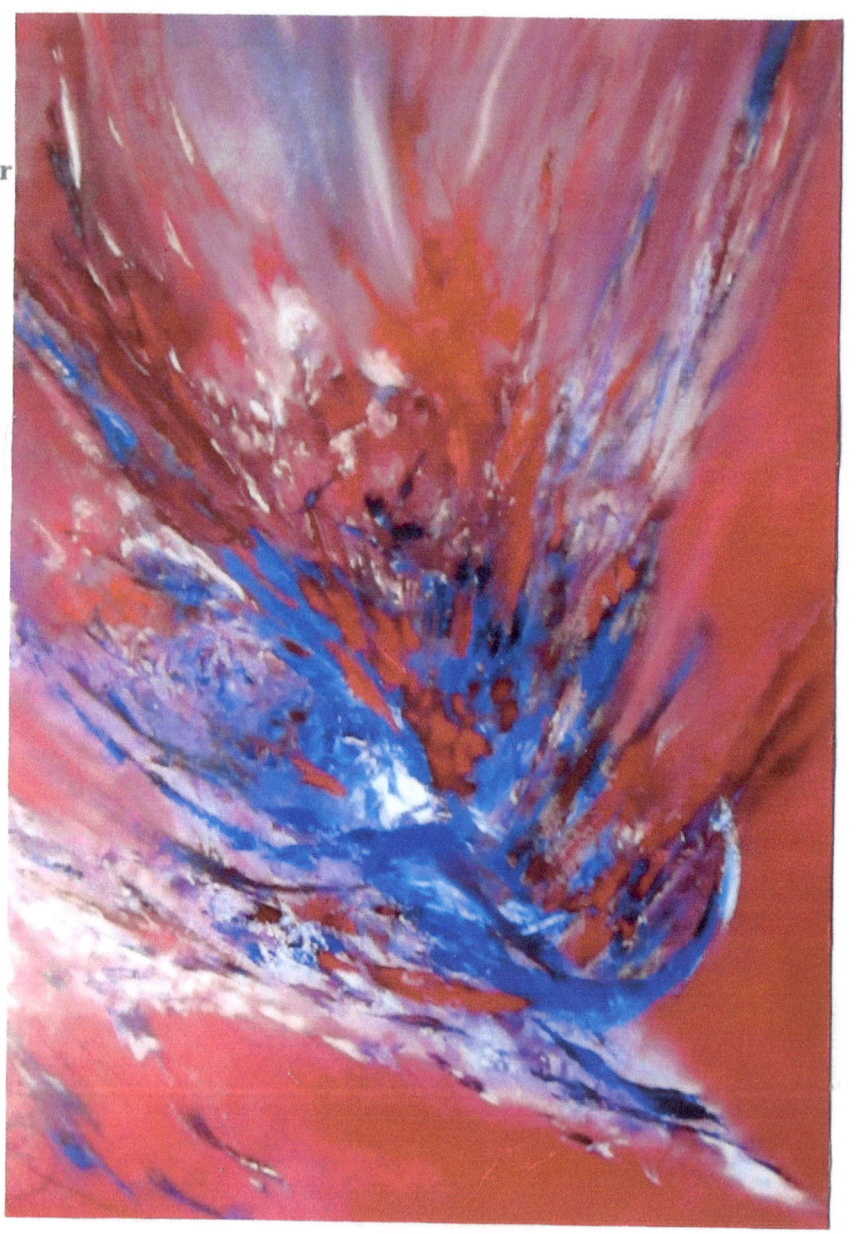

ENERGY
FOR OUR LOVE OF LIFE
THE UNIVERSAL GIFT

Football

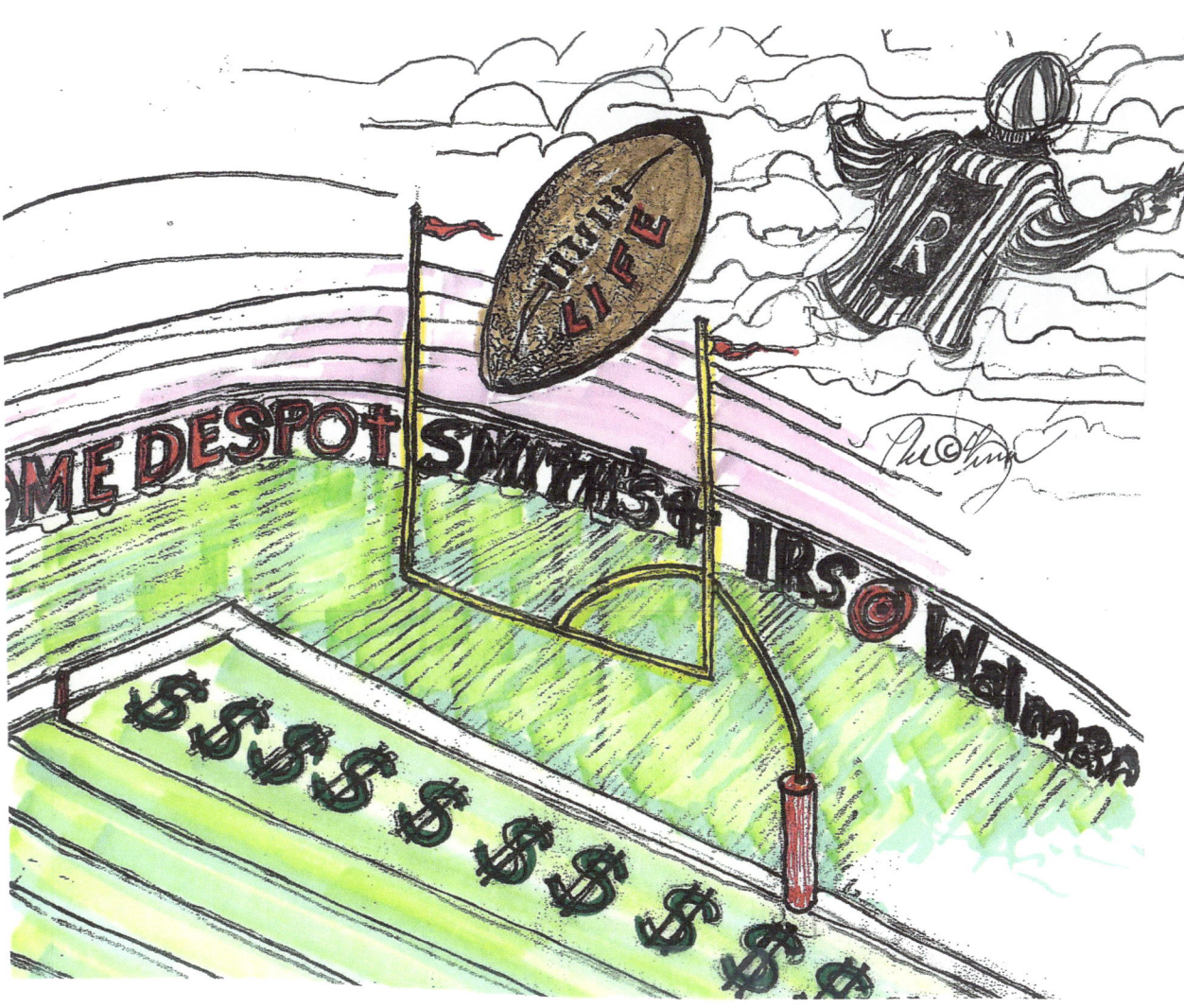

Only a game?
Now a multi-billion elusion
However I wish
Life could be like football

Kick-off born again
60 minute life span
Sudden death
To be born again

The rules become law
Jury and judges in place
To see who breaks the law
Attorney's only in the bleachers

Time outs are allowed
We call them vacations
4 quarters just like the seasons
Each with the change of direction

The number is twelve
Started 2009 years ago
Had to double the number
Called offense and defense

We all play
At one time or another
Each side of the line
Winning or losing

losing is winning
winning is losing
At times there is a tie
Over time can redeem

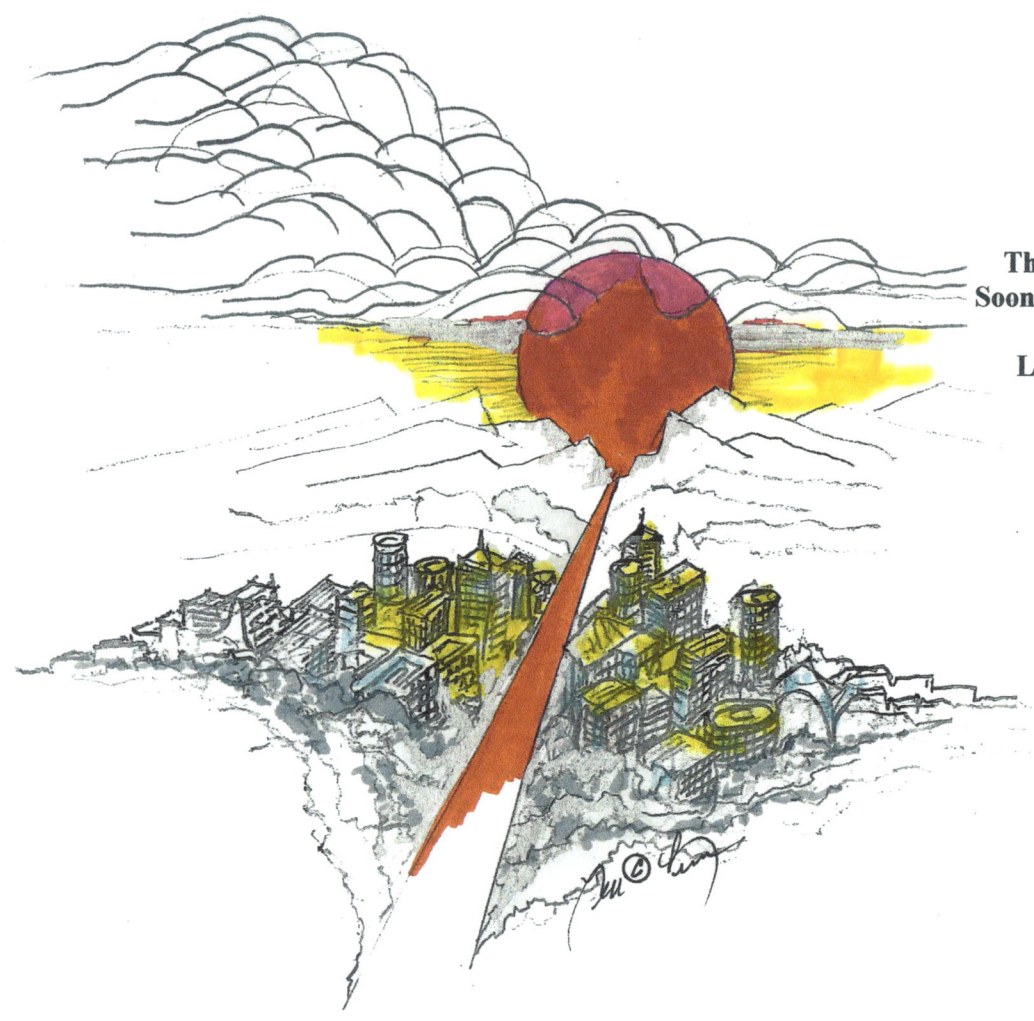

TODAY

The grapes cling to the vine
Soon to be made into sweet wine
I don't want to recall
Life nailed me to the wall

Things of the past
Never to last
Yielded unfit
Seas of sailing
Finding no port

Sky's unchanging
Clouds to wonder
Were shall I be
When can I be

Stars disappear
Morning bright
Sun is stunning
Much to my delight

Adding to life
Story's to create
Feelings to feel
No internal strife

Forgetting and resolve
Is finding freedom
Peace and tranquility
Just to enjoy being

Drifting thought life
Gone is the darkness
A binding hold
Soaring to heights

Like an eagle in flight
Wind gliding through feathers
Life is only
today

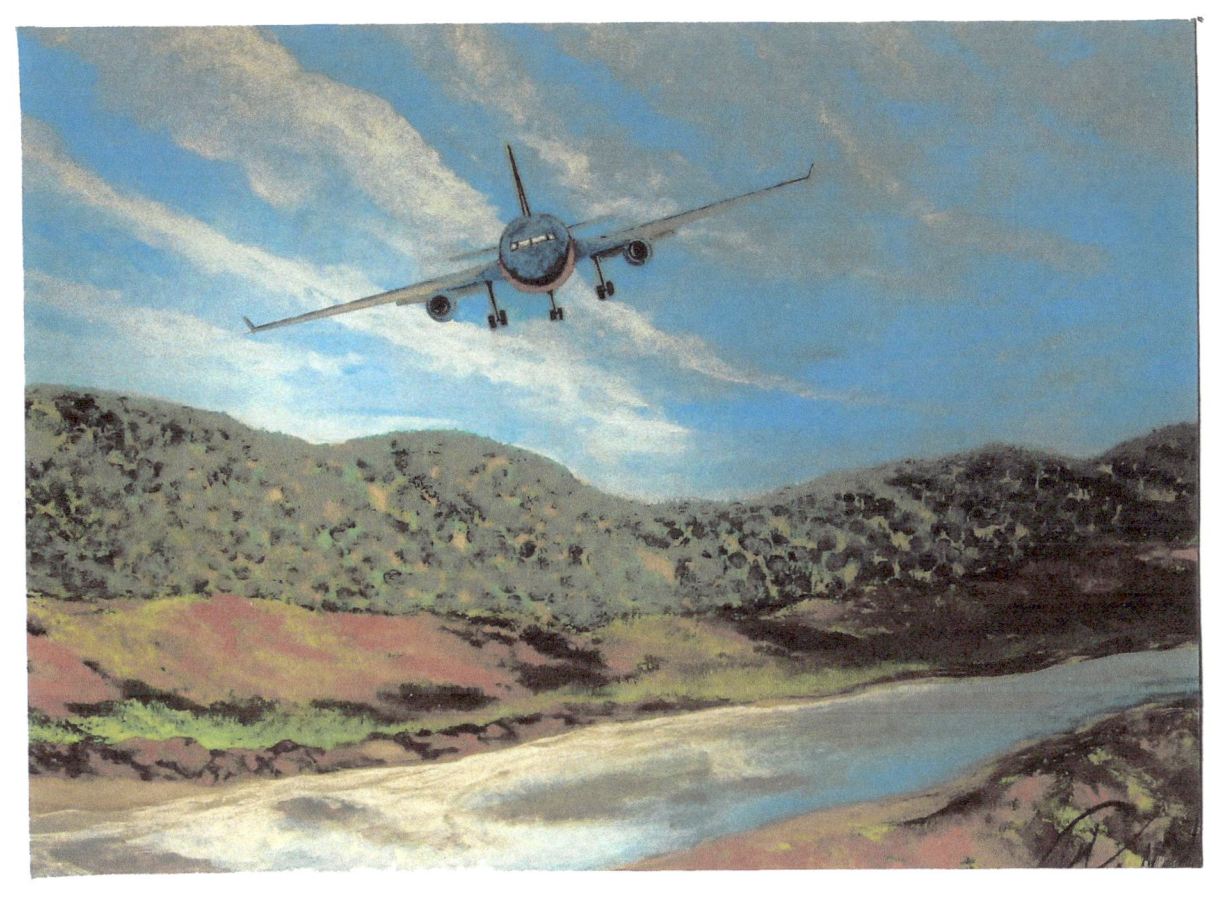

SOUTHBEST LANDING PATTERN OVER THE RIO GRANDE
I HAVE ALWAYS LOVED PLANES
IN THE YEARS I SPENT IN US NAVEL AVIATION
MY PLANE HAD PROPELLERS

KRISTIN WADE VON BEHNES, RN
GRAND DAUGHTER

WHERE DID YOU TRAIN
I DON'T REMEMBER
O! YES ITS SOMETHING LIKE UNM
WE SPENT THE FIRST WEEK
IN A FROG POND LEARNING
HOW TO READ
DOCTORS HANDWRITTING
WHAT QUALITIES WERE REQUIRED
A LOVE OF HUMANITY,
UNDERSTANDING, COMPANSION,
EMPATHY, GRACE
AND A FEW OTHERS LIKE TOUCH
MOST OF ALL BEING COME IN
CRISIS OR CHAOS
YOU COULD NOT FAKE IT
SOUNDS LIKE THE REQURMENTS
FOR AN ANGEL,
I'V BEEN CALLED THAT
ACADEMICALLY YOU MANY LAURALS
I TOOK A PATH BEYOND THE BOX
GETTING ALL OF THE CREDENTIALS
UNM DID NOT WANT ME TO GO
I AM NOW AT UNM HOSPTIAL
THE BEST IN THE STATE
THANKS KRIS
YOU HAVE DEFINED
THE NOBLE PROFESSION

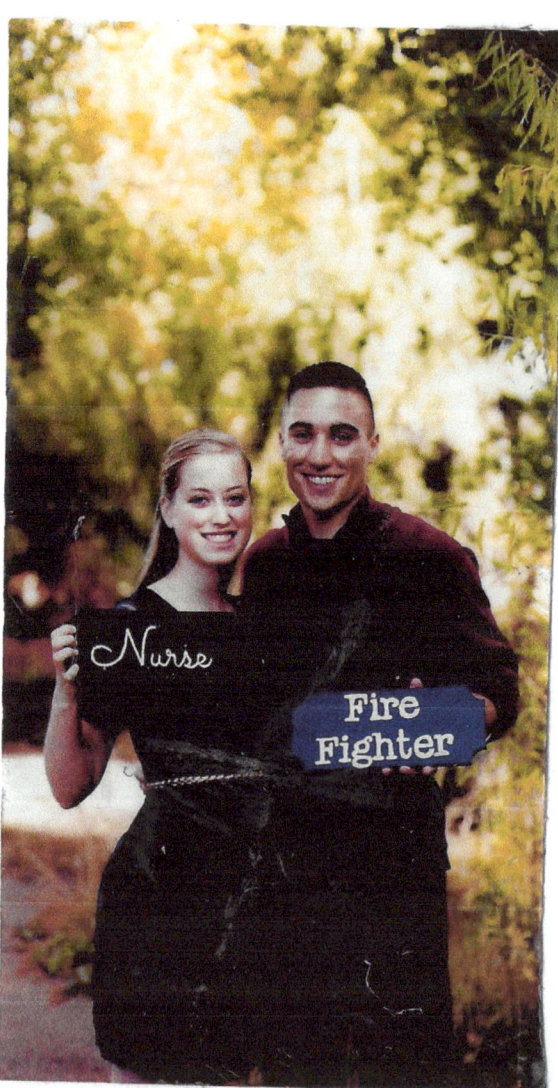

KENTON VON BEHNES
ADOPTED SON

WHERE THERES SMOKE
SORRY SIR WE PUT THE FIRE OUT
WHAT DOES EMT MEAN
HOPE YOU WILL NEVER FIND OUT
YOU GUYS SAVE LIVES
WE TRY AND DO THE PROPERTY TOO
HOW DO GUYS TRAIN
FAST FORWARD ON THE INTERNET
HOW MANY YEARS ON THE INTERNET
SORRY SIR IS A STATIONS SECRET
HOW ARE YOUR LEADERS SELECTED
POLITICS AND RANK AND FILE
BUT THEY ARE ALL TOP LEADERS
IN TIME TO COME
I WILL BE ONE OF THEM
WHAT ARE YOUR DUTIES
AT THE STATION
WE ARE CALLED MR CLEAN
AND CHEFS EXTRAONDAIR
HOW DO YOU KEEP YOUR
TRUCK AND EQUIPMENT SO CLEAN
NOT TOO MANY CALLS
THANK YOU KENNY
I NOW KNOW ITS CALLED
A NOBLE PROFESSION

NOBLE PROFESSIONS

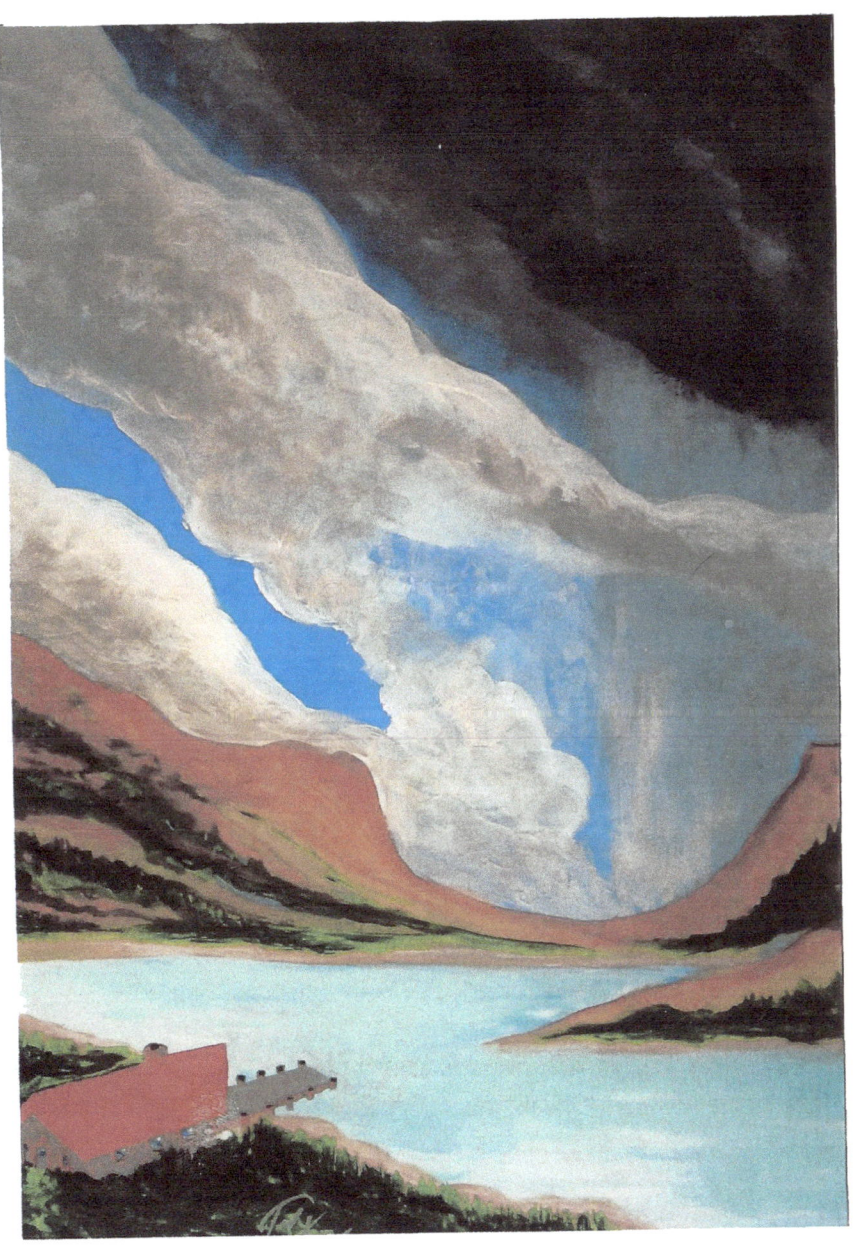

New Mexico Rains

The flat lands
To the mountains
Vision ever clear
Yet distance has meaning
For nature to began
I call them gatherings
Water laden to feed
A parched land
The horizon is defined
As in a evening dream
Ready for awaking
When the curtain goes up
Music is in my heart
For this great start
Towers of showers
Plummet the earth
Boiling with mists
Like halos of royalty
Sparks of energy
Fill the horizon
It transfers to my being
Smelling pungent
It's not the air
But deeper than that
I am in tune
With the universe

SUZANNE
WITH CHAMPAGNE AND TIFFANY
EV ESPANOLA VALLEY
"SO"FOR 8 YEARS

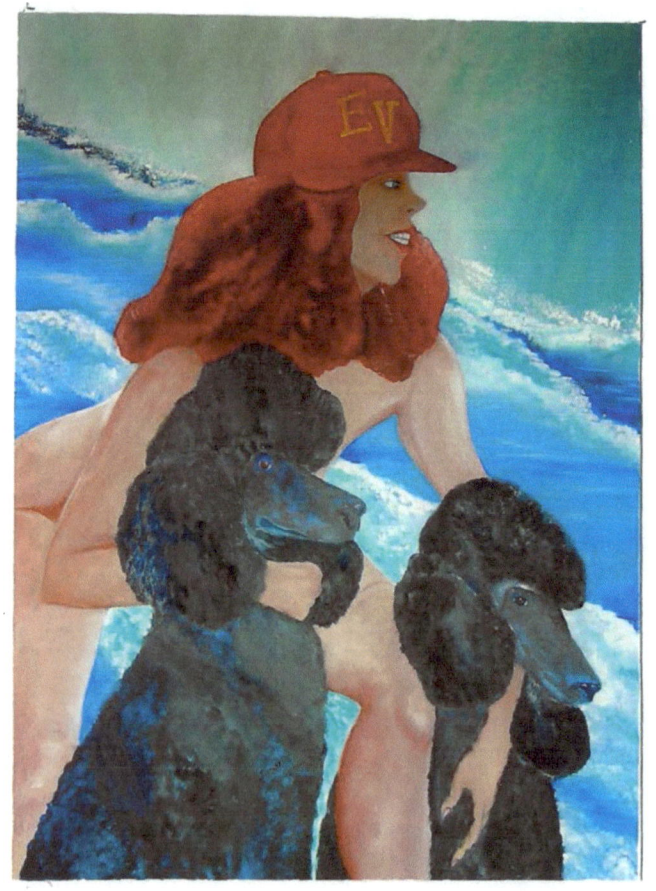

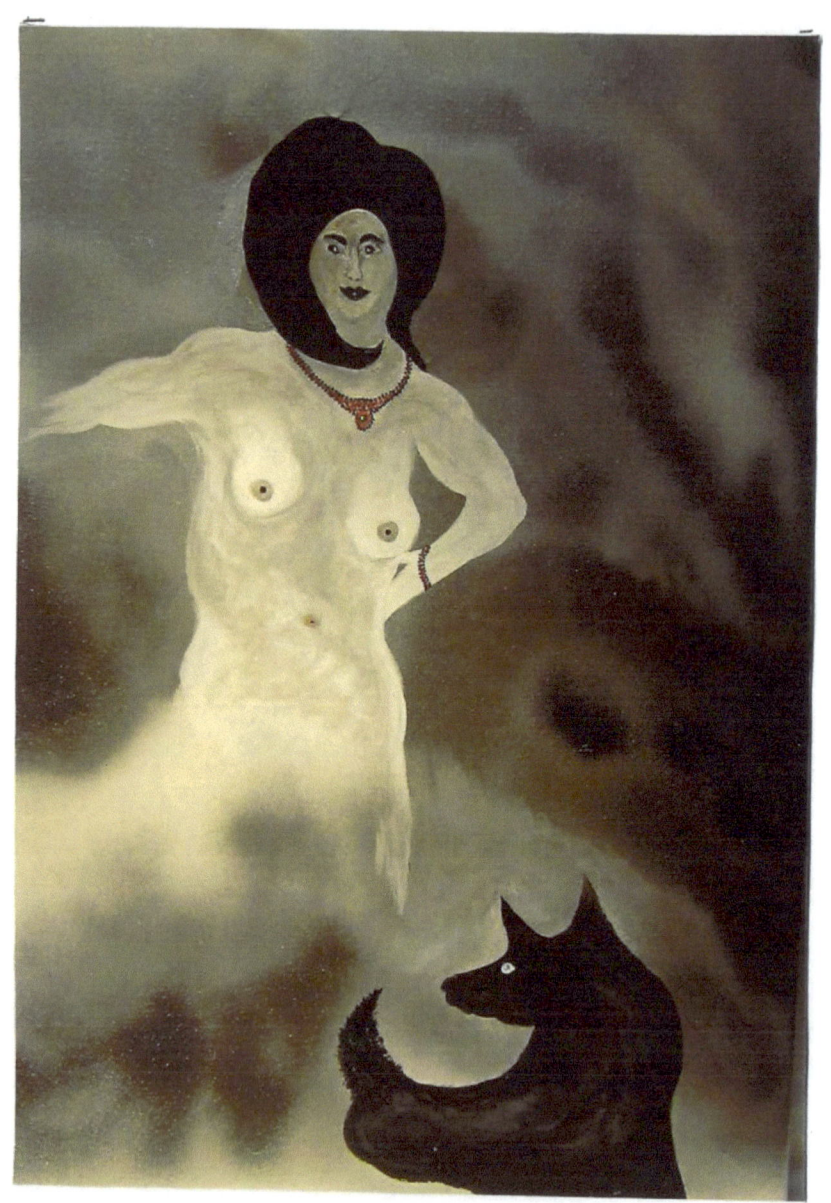

LADY FROM IRELAND
A DREAM WISH

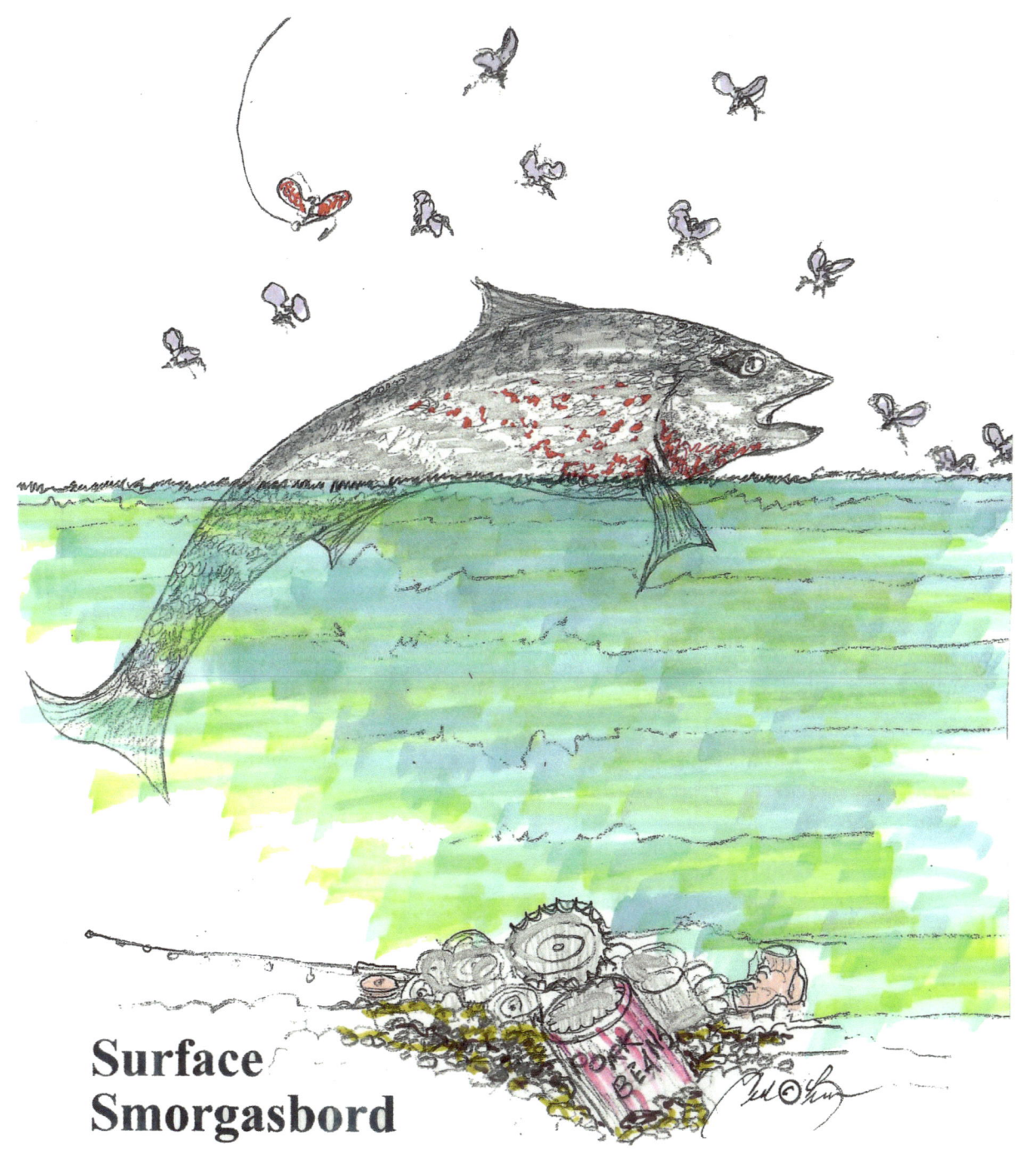

Surface Smorgasbord

Noon day heat
Lurking in deep water
Power naps
They sleep

Streams rivers and lakes
Waking for pre dawn
Or early twilight
Exercise of feeding

Young and old
They love the hatching
Of flying insects
Meals supreme

Jumping in water
Circular pools leaving
Up thought the air
With no thought of breathing

Feeding as no tomorrow
What joy they know
Catching a morsel
Back down to enjoy

Finned creatures
With scale skin
Swifter then lighting
Eyes that can see

Both you and me
Intelligence ratio
Hard to define
Seems they forget

When caught on the line
When you realize
Back to the water
They don't remember

97

The jumping fight
Why the meal was dry
The barb less hook
Released from their lip

Once again at home
Soon to strike again
Depending on the fly
That catches they fancy
Think like a trout
The pros teach
After they have sold you
Rod real and waders

Cast the line
Make the fly fly through the air
Dance it on the surface
Or soon in the trees
No fish there

In the mountain stream high
Focusing for the hunt
You become one
Listening to the water
Looking for pools
Below the rapids

Where to go
Up stream or down
Hiding before you cast
Doesn't matter

The need for lunch
Soon gives you a break
With an empty creel
Except for a bottle of wine

Polarized sun glasses
Now sit on the grass
Sun shinning down
Spaces in between

On your back
Pine needles you repose
You are soon asleep
Your thoughts are not deep

Dreams never come
Sun burned you might get
Power nap is over
Up on your feet

From your vest
Considering the fly card
You have given most a bath
But what will it take
Still can't think like a trout
My brain is to big
On the way home
I shop at Albertson's
A north Atlantic salmon
Is dinner tonight

CHAMPAGNE
With Regina

It filled our flutes
Sitting in a dirt and rock garden
With high tech candlelight
Listing to classical music
In chilled Indian summer night
To contemplate the day
The present beauty
In all its glory
No one can ever take away
An early fine dinner
At the HOLLOW
The ghost town of Madrid
Reborn in majestic magic
Don't go away

A dot on no map
Convoyed with galleries
Lead to a search for
Eldorado's lost treasure
She found her golden dream
By shear chance
The fox on canvas lived
Speckled with snow
The price to bid and buy
Light as a feather
Necked to the eye
True love hit and held
Fair beautiful lass
Bought it anyway

Bathed in serenity
As contemplating things unknown
Where did the coal miners go
Warmth filled the clear air
To gaze to the universe
With earthly thoughts unanswered
But we tried anyway
Gliding clouds danced
Very thin they crowed
Peeping through holes
The moon almost on its back
Moon beams waltzed
Through it all
Realizing the trees to tall
Stars pierced the dark blue sky
Useless to count
Bathing the earth
The theater was ours
The play just beginning
Actors all
The empty bottle spent
Sleep bosoms await the bed
My love there is no other way
To prepare for tomorrow
The presents of another day.

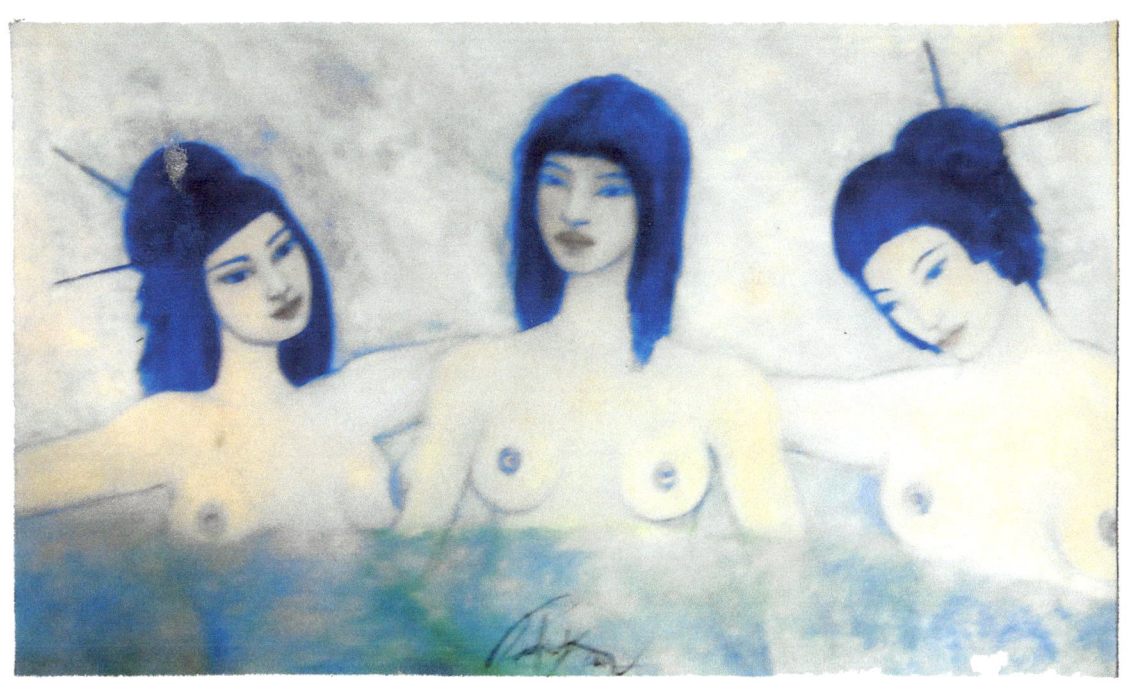

LOVELY JAPANESE LADYS

MY FLIGHT OUT OF BEIJING TO NORETA AIRPORT IN JAPAN SEEMED VERY SHORT. THE AIRPORT HAD A DIRECT CONNECTION TO THE BULLET HIGH SPEED TRAIN. I WANTED TO FORGO THE CITY OF TOKYO. LOOKING OUT THE WINDOW THE LANDSCAPE, VILLAGES WENT BY LIKE A CYBER SPACE FAST FORWARD. MY RYOKAN (BED AND BREAKFAST) RESERVATION WAS IN KYOTO. ARRIVED IN THE RAIN HUNGREY. THE HOSTESS SAID NO FOOD THIE LATE AND TOLD ME ABOUT A RESTURANT 4 BLOCKS DOWN. THEY WOULD NOT LET ME IN BECAUSE I WAS STILL IN MY WET WHITE FLIGHT SUIT. I CHECKED OUT OF THE RYOKAN THE NEXT MORNING. I HAVE CAMPED BETTER IN THE PECOS WILDERNESS. I LOVED KYOTOS TAXI SERVICE. DRIVERS IN WHITE SUITS, GLOVES. ALL THE HOTELS WERE FULL. WE WENT BACK TO THE TRAIN STATION TO A BEAUTIFUL HIGH RISE HOTEL. THEY HAD ONE ROOM LEFT ON THE 12TH FLOOR. IT WAS FOR THE HANDICAP. I LOVED IT AND USED IT AS HOME BASE FOR THE REST OF MY STAY IN JAPAN. THE MANY CITYS I VISTED WERE USERFRIEND TO GET TO FROM THERE. THE BEAUTY OF KYOTO, OSAKA AND MANY OTHER PLACES I CAN'T REMEMBER NAMES WAS OUTSTANDING. THE OLDER JAPANESE TRADITIONAL PEOPLE WERE SNOBBISH. ALL OTHERS WERE WARM AND FRIENDLY. NUDITY HAS NO STIGMA, WHAT IS VERY PRIVATE ARE EMOTIONS. HERE IN THE USA WE HAVE THIS THE OTHER WAY AROUND. SO MANY THINGS I DID, I NEVER VISTED THEIR FINE SPAS. AFTER I PAINTED THE ABOVE PAINTING I WISH I WOULD HAVE.

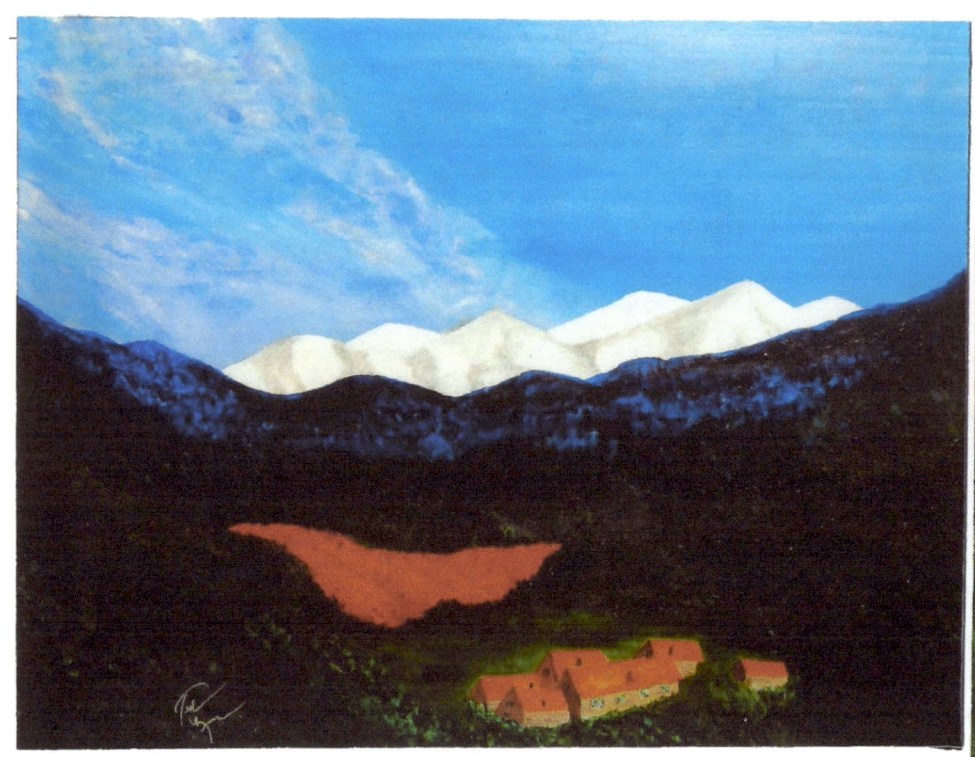

MORA NEW MEXICO
BACK SIDE OF THE PECOS
WILDERNESS MOUNTAINS

ROCK OUTCROPPINGS
ON THE MOUNTAIN MIXED WITH TREES
IN THE FOREST AT SUN RISE

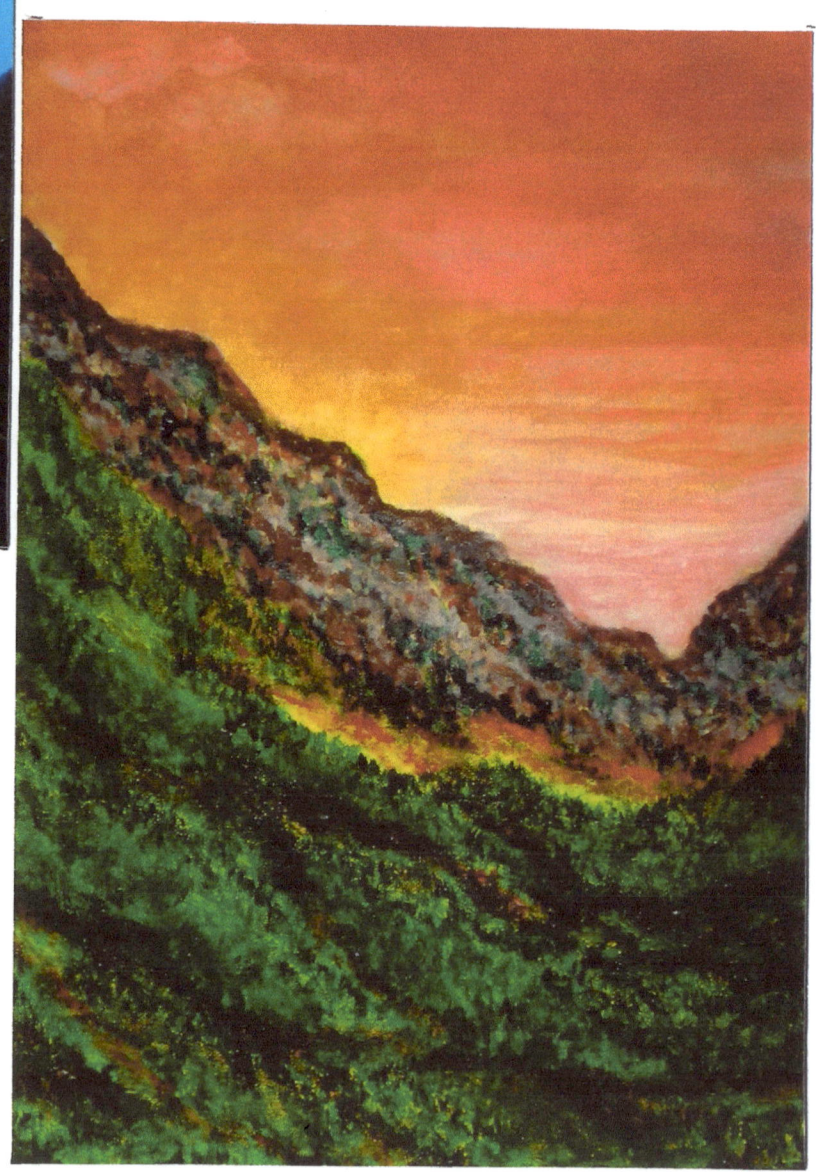

TUNNELS

SIPPING MY MORNING MAGIC LIPTON
FROM A HONEY LACED TIN CUP
MY BACK AGAINEST A MAJESTIC PINE
PREDAWN BLACK SKY
IN REVERE AND
WILDERNESS PEACE
WISHING TO RECLINE MY SELF
THE LUSH GRASS CALLING
SOON

I WOULD BE ON MY BACK ON THE GRASS
CUSHIONED BY THE MORNING DEW
IN PRESTINE MEADOW MOUNTAIN TOP
THE FOREST OF BLACK AND GREEN
ALL SALUTING THE SKY
GENTLE WINDS
ASPENS DANCING UP,DOWN, LEFT AND RIGHT
TEARS OF BEAUTY
HAPPINESS AND JOY
SOAK MY SUN BURNED FACE

MY HORSES FEEDING NEAR BY
NOT A WHINNIE OR A SIGH
TETHERED TO AVOID A LONG WALL
POKER WHISKEY LADEN NIGHT
COMPANIONS STILL SOUND ASLEEP
DAWN GREETING WITH THE SUN
GREY TURNS TO BLUE
SPICED WITH MODELED CLOUDS
MY JOURNEY SOON TO START
COME JOIN ME

IT'S NOT TOO FAR
WE WILL EXPLORE
THE TUNNELS IN THE SKY
I HAVE NO MAP
THE CHOICES ARE CLEAR
BIG, WIDE AND NARROW
NO CANARIES WILL DIE
OUR MINDS ARE THE ONLY GUIDE
ALL WILL UNFOLD

WITH A SMILE WE WERE LIFTED
FROM ALL WORLDLY TIES
ANGELS COULD NOT FLY
AS GRACEFUL AS YOU AND I
OUR ODESSEY IS STARTING
IN THE TUNNELS OF THE SKY
SILVER WHITE RAIN CLOUDS
WAITING OUR CHOOSEN TURN
A RIVER FLOWING TURNS INTO A SEA

A FOUR MASTED TALL SAILING SHIP
FULL SAILS FIRM AND STOUT
WOLLY TAMALE
ITS THE CUTTYSARK
I KNEW IT WAS IN A BOTTLE
LAST NIGHT
IT BECKON'S YOU AND ME
NO RUSTY CREW ABOARD
YOU TAKE THE HELM
I'LL TAKE THE LONG GLASS
TO SEE WHAT I CAN SEE
POINT TO THE NORTH
I SHOUTED WITH GLEE
JUMP IN THE WHALER
I'LL WORK THE OARS

ICES FLOWS A COMING
FROM THE NORTH SEA
NOW OCEAN WAVES
FRIGHTEN US
I WILL PUT TO SHORE
WHILE WE CAN STILL BE
THE HOT SAND ON THE BEACH
WITH NO LADYS IN SIGHT
NOT MUCH A SAILORS DELIGHT
THE PALMS ARE PURPLE
NO COCONUTS HANGING
WE TOOK THE WRONG TURN
IN THIS TUNNEL
LURKING AND OUT OF SIGHT
THE DRAGON SPIT WATER
INSTEAD OF FIRE
A ROYAL IT WAS
FIVE CLAWS EACH ON FIVE LEGS
ENTER MY KINGDOM
STAY FOR A VIST
WATCH ME DANCE
I'LL SEND YOU IN A TRANCE
PUFF AND IT WAS GONE
IT WAS THE MAGIC DRAGON

OUT OF THE BLUE
WE KNEW NOT WHAT TO EXPECT
FLYING IN THE CONCORD
NO ONE ABOARD
I'LL PILOT IT
YOU RIDE SHOTGUN
IN THE RIGHT SEAT
BACK ON THE WHEEL
AS FAR AS IT COULD GO

LET'S GO SEE THE UNIVERSE
I'LL GIVE YOU A SMILING STAR
AND ONE FOR ME

PLANETS ,METEORS, SUNS GOLORE
DISTANANCE STARS STILL WINKING
WHAT A GLORYIOUS SCENE TO BE
THE AVIATION FUEL WAS GONE
THE INSTRUMENT LIGHT TURNED RED
SENDING US BACK TO EARTH
O-WELL
IT WAS A WONDERFUL TRIP
PARACHUTES APPEARED
WE LAUGHTED WE DO NOT NEED
NEW TUNNELS TO SEEK
AWAY WE WENT BUT

THE BLACK STORM CLOUDS
HAVE GATHERED RAIN TO FOLLOW
FLASHES OF LIGHT HURT MY EYES
THE ROAR OF THE GODS
CLOSED THE TUNNELS IN THE SKY
SO FOR NOW WE HAVE TO SAY ALOHA
HAVE NO FEAR MY FRIEND
THE TUNNELS WILL RETURN
I WILL SEEK YOU AGAIN MY FRIEND
TO EXPLORE
THE TUNNELS IN THE SKY

THEODORO CORONA LUNA
8/29/2014

Snow Prayer

Winter snow you have not come
So it means you can't go
Your designer flakes crystal clear
Dancing in the air your not here

Snowmen women nowhere to be found
Children in tears
Where are the white blankets
That cover the earth

Please bring the winters gentle touch
We all are missing it so much
I uttered this prayer
Then falling in deep sleep

The morning was dark
I opened the blinds
And there it was
My powers had prevailed

At least 12 inches of snow
And still falling
Like snow fairy's
They would gather on the stage

Having to wait
With anticipation hurting
For the last of the crystals
To end their flight

By ways and high ways to clear
Walks on the side
Creating small mountains of snow
Ice will form tomorrow
When the sun will shine

DOGS AND CATS

Man's best friend
Has four legs
You are in his/hers tender care
The universal gift to man

We should always use the word Kazam
Instant change of reality
Magical metamorphous
The universe uses it daily

Rocky Mountain High
I tried to see fire in the sky
Had to watch the road
Harley and me

Mall Mart live Better
If I can make it through the parking lot
Lost my coupons
O-well I will be here another day

I have a Dream
Nothing to do with little Bo-Peep
In forty years
It came true

Jihad to infidels
Hope we can find some
Our way the only way
To go where?

Growing Old, we are old
What happened to the days
They went away
There is no reprieve

PACE THE
PERFECT RHYTHM

Pace in truncated rhythm
Pace in perfect rhythm
Threshold at your front door
Left and right you must go
Earth in glimmer to be hold
Pace in perfect rhythm

History speculates we walked on all four
It slowed the pace of perfect rhythm
So we stood erect
Behold the perfect rhythm

Glories places await our being
Judgmental we cannot be in places unseen
It all begins with the perfect rhythm
So to Replenish our soul we must go

Though the skies and oceans
One must glide
Once to land on the land
The perfect rhythm
Explodes in your mind

You not where to go
Books of travel did not know
One things is sure
Beings of the earth
Are all the same

Cultures and race is no disgrace
Joy of life exists in us all
Nations of war must find peace
If not joy will not exist

They must find
The perfect rhythm
This I know
Tread the perfect rhythm
Tell all you know

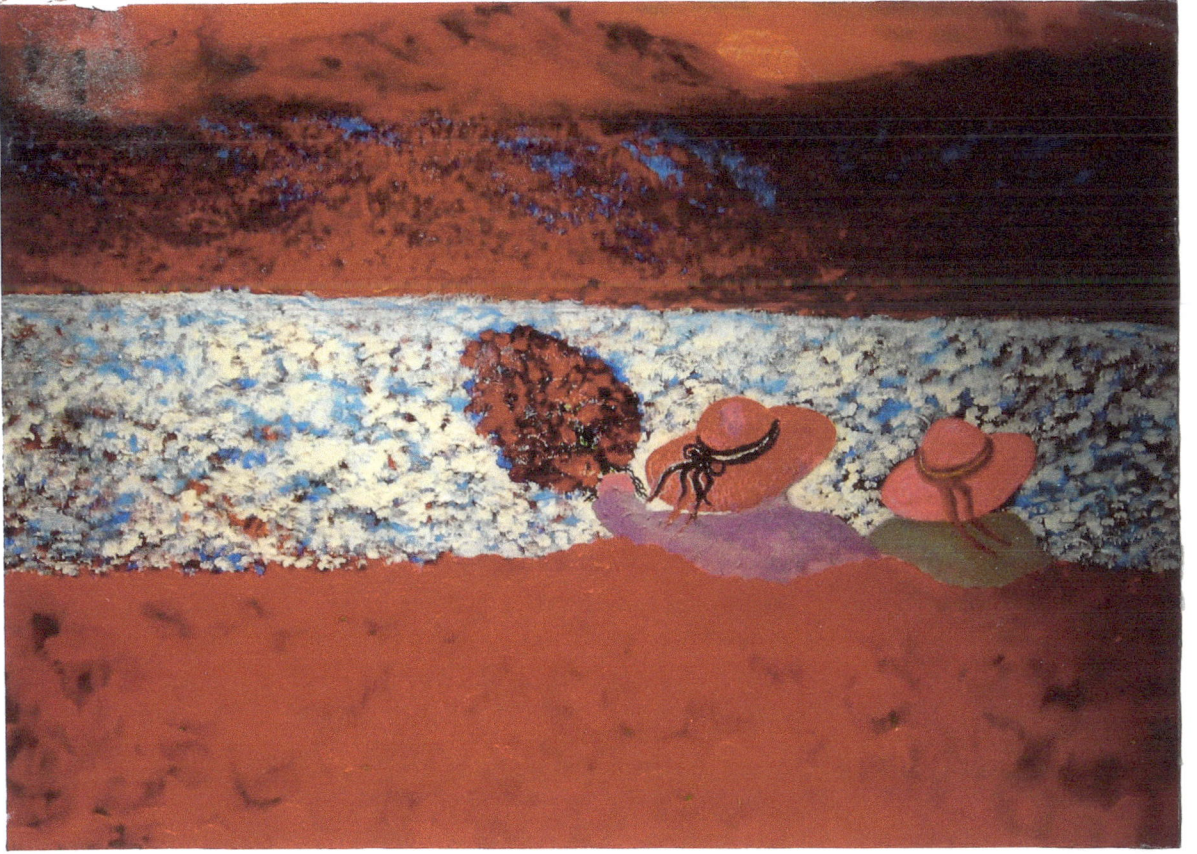

SUNRISE SISTERS
WITH BOUQUET OF ROSES
TO WELCOME THE SUN

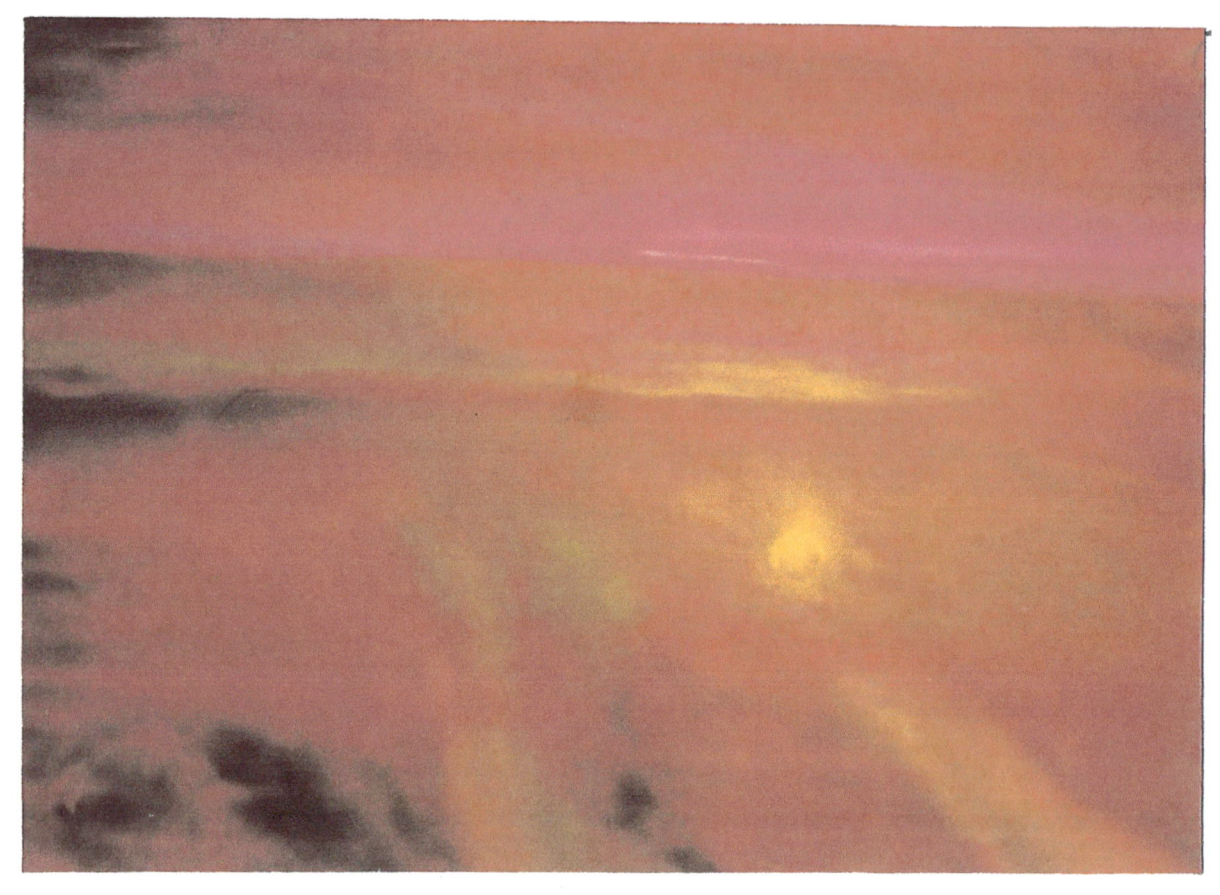

GLOBAL WARMING WARNING
UNIVERSAL NATURAL FORCES
WITH AIDE OF THE PLANETS MASS HUMANITY
WHEN ALL OF THE NATIONS OF THE WORLD
TRY TO RESOLVE THIS WARNING
THE NATURE OF THE UNIVERSE WILL ALWAYS PREVAIL
WE WILL GO THE WAY OF THE DINOSAURS
SORRY FOR THIS OMEN
HOPE NOT WHILE I'M STILL BREATHING

GOLFHEIMER'S

A few symptoms

You have had a hard week at the office
Flip open your day timer and discover its only Monday
You look at your watch, you have been in the office
10 minutes.

Your foursome has a 10:00 am tee time on Wednesday
So you take the day off, since you figure it's the weekend.
You go home and go to bed, setting the alarm clock for 10:15
It wakes you and your rush to the club.

When you get there the parking lot is empty, so you
Call your wife on the cell and she informs you that
Your at the wrong club one day early.

Next morning you set the alarm at 5:00 am
Taking a cold shower, forgetting you have hot water
The drive to the club takes 2 hours, you been going in circles
You get to the club and park in the Handicapped space
Since you have a white handkerchief hanging from the rear view mirror

Opening the trunk you see a strange bag tag
These are John's clubs, o-well I liked his better
You go to the pro-shop and get a bucket of balls
Heading to the putting green you tee up and
Start hitting your driver, the pro runs shouting
The range is over there, I wondered why the
Pins were so close together .

The rest of your group arrives and you are
On the first tee. You start introducing yourself
we have been playing together for 20 years
And you still don't know their names.
Its time to pick honors, so you reach for your
Tee's and flip them in the air, they are still in the package.

They name the game "buck skins" When did the
Club get deer, and who skins them.
Your partners hit perfect drives in the middle of the fairway

Your drive faded to the right, bounced once and landed
In the club swimming pool.

You take the cart straight down the fairway and hit the
Best ball, your partner comes over and informed you that you had
Hit his ball, I said that's all right you can hit mine.
you drive the cart straight down the fairway
Don't you remember the 90-degree rule?
I thought 90 degrees was a straight line.

Your ball lands 25 yards below the green
Your not sure what to hit, so you take a 3-wood
Grabbing the club by the head, you swing and
Your ball lands 2' from the pin.
You walk up and salute the flag and take your visor
Off and place it over your heart and start
Singing the National Anthem

Your partners cheer, and ask you to mark your ball
So you walk up and pick it up and take your red
Sharpie out and put an x on it.
It's a Texas give me, but I thought we are in New Mexico!
You have won the first "Buck skin" with a par and
You ask where is the Buck?

Having won the honors, you proudly tee up on a
Par-3, you take out your putter and announce
P stands for putter and you have 3 of them in your bag.
Your fourth putt lands on the green, you 3 putt with the
Flag still in, you are asked for your score and you
Automatically call out 3!!! I only 3 putted you state.

Next hole is a par-5 and your drive lands in the lake.
You take off all your clothes and dive in taking the
Water wedge with you you find lots of balls
Holding your breath, you thank all of your under
Water training you did in Mexico. You pick one
And scare all of the ducks swimming on the lake

Your partners are already on the green rolling
Over with laughter. One partner announces that

He is in for a Birdie and the other one says his in
For an Eagle. You look up at the sky and then
Down at the green and you can see neither

All you remember were the Ducks and why were these
They not named after the ducks?
You ask them to explain the meaning, no one can
So you offer an explanation, well when you sink
The putt you whistle like a bird or soar like an
Eagle.

You can't remember the rest of the course until
You made the turn. You ask your partners why its
Called a turn? They inform you that's where the front
Turns into the back. Your state I cannot tell the difference.

You are looking forward to playing the 19th hole.
For your share of the "Buck skins" and coning your
Partners for a press. You find the sign in the club
House that designates the 19th hole. You search for
The tee box, the bartender asks what are you looking
For and you tell him. He points in the direction of
The women's locker room stating, they keep all sorts
Of secrets in there.

Your partners tally the scores and inform you that
The true meaning of Buck skins, so you reach into
Your wallet and automatically start giving out
$10.00 bills for each skin. Of course the winner
buys the drinks. You order to shots of milk
drink up and head to the parking lot. Your clubs
are still on the cart.

Driving home you notice a red flashing light in
Your rear view mirror and wonder when they
Started putting stoplights in the rear view mirrors.
The state trooper finally pulls you and asks if you
Have been drinking, of course you say, had two
Shots of milk at the club, well he said your
Left signal is on and you have been driving
25 mph in a 75 mph interstate.

The only known cure for "Golfheimers" is
The tolerance of your partners!!!!

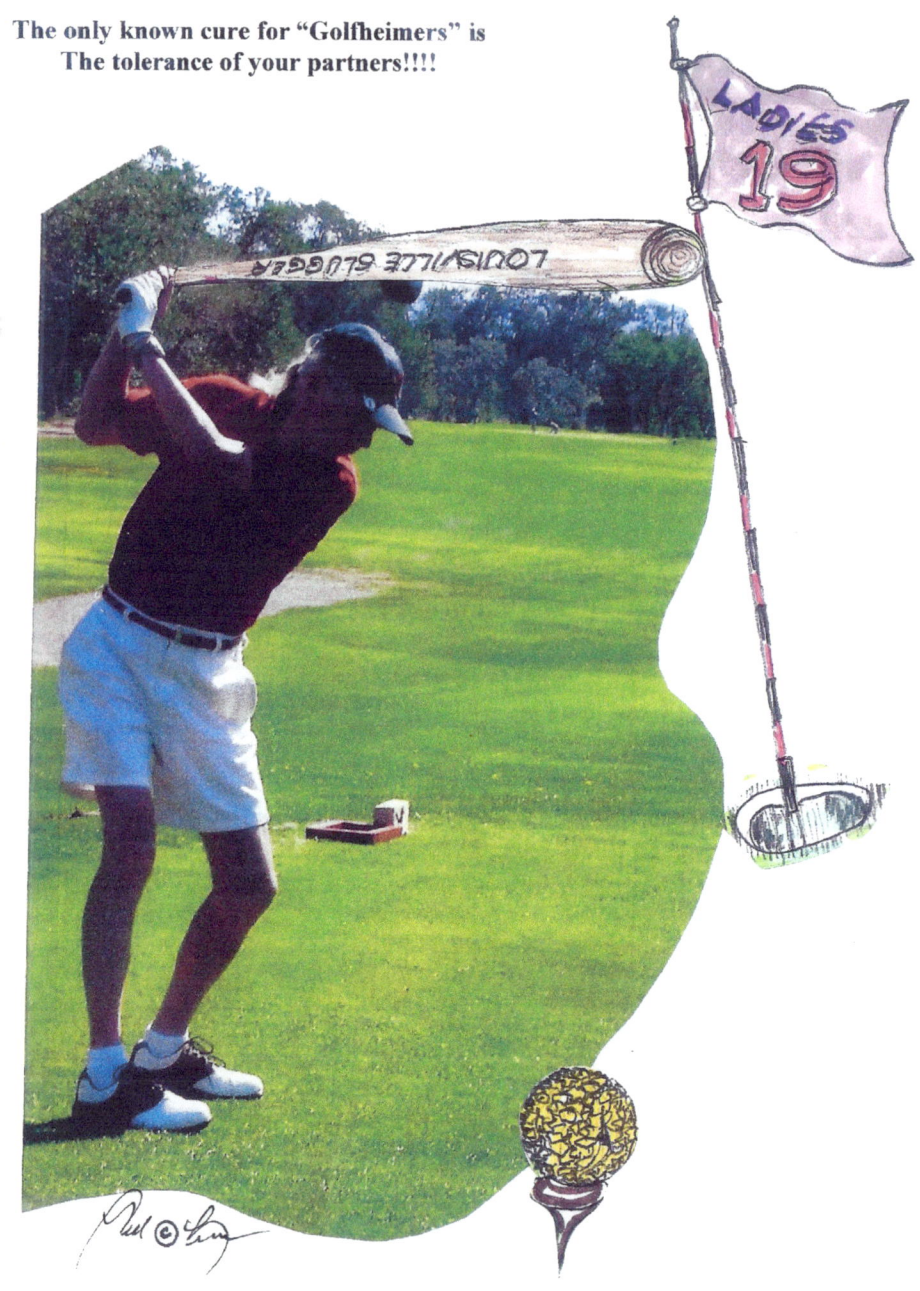

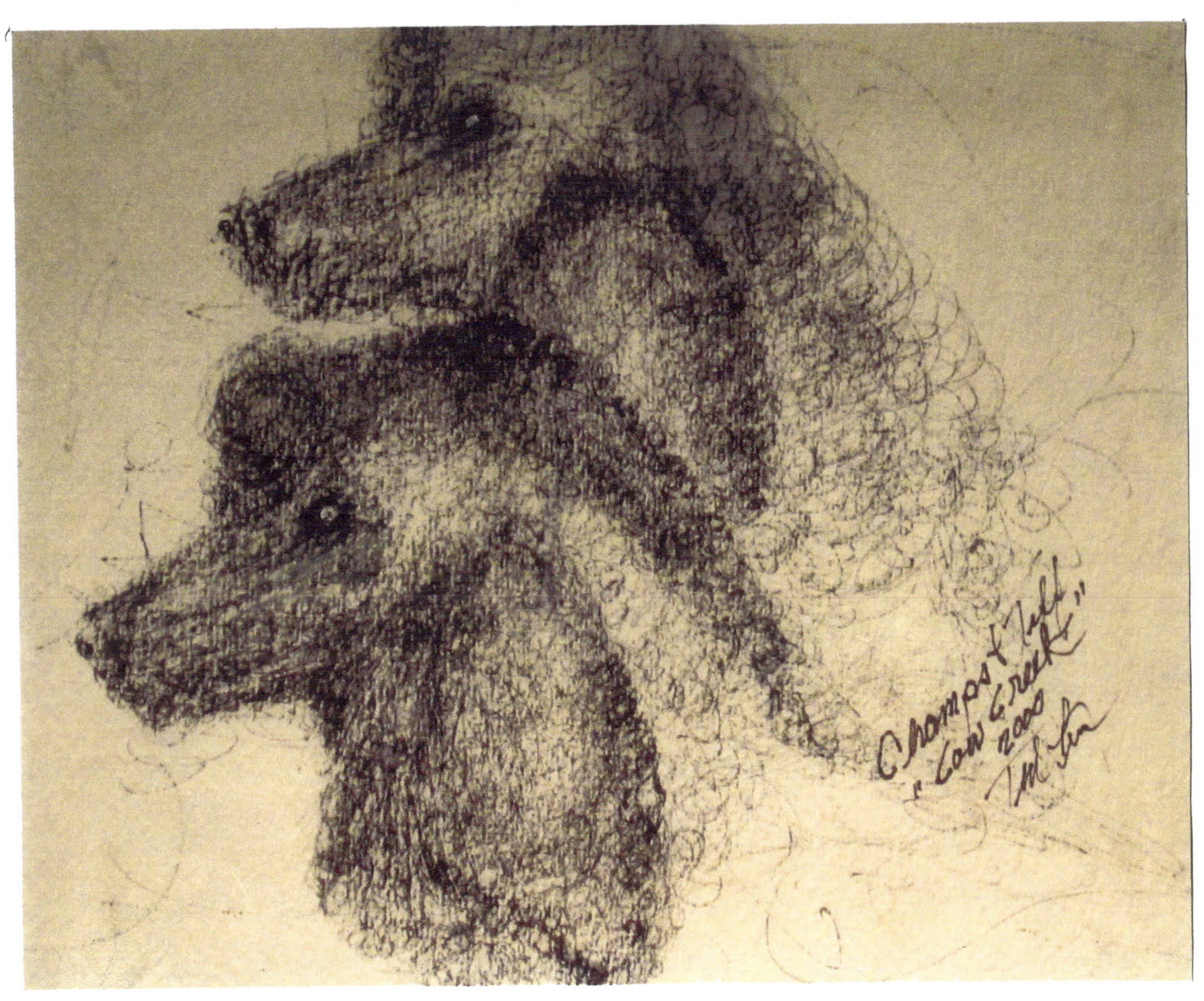

Champs + Tel
"Cow Greek"
2000

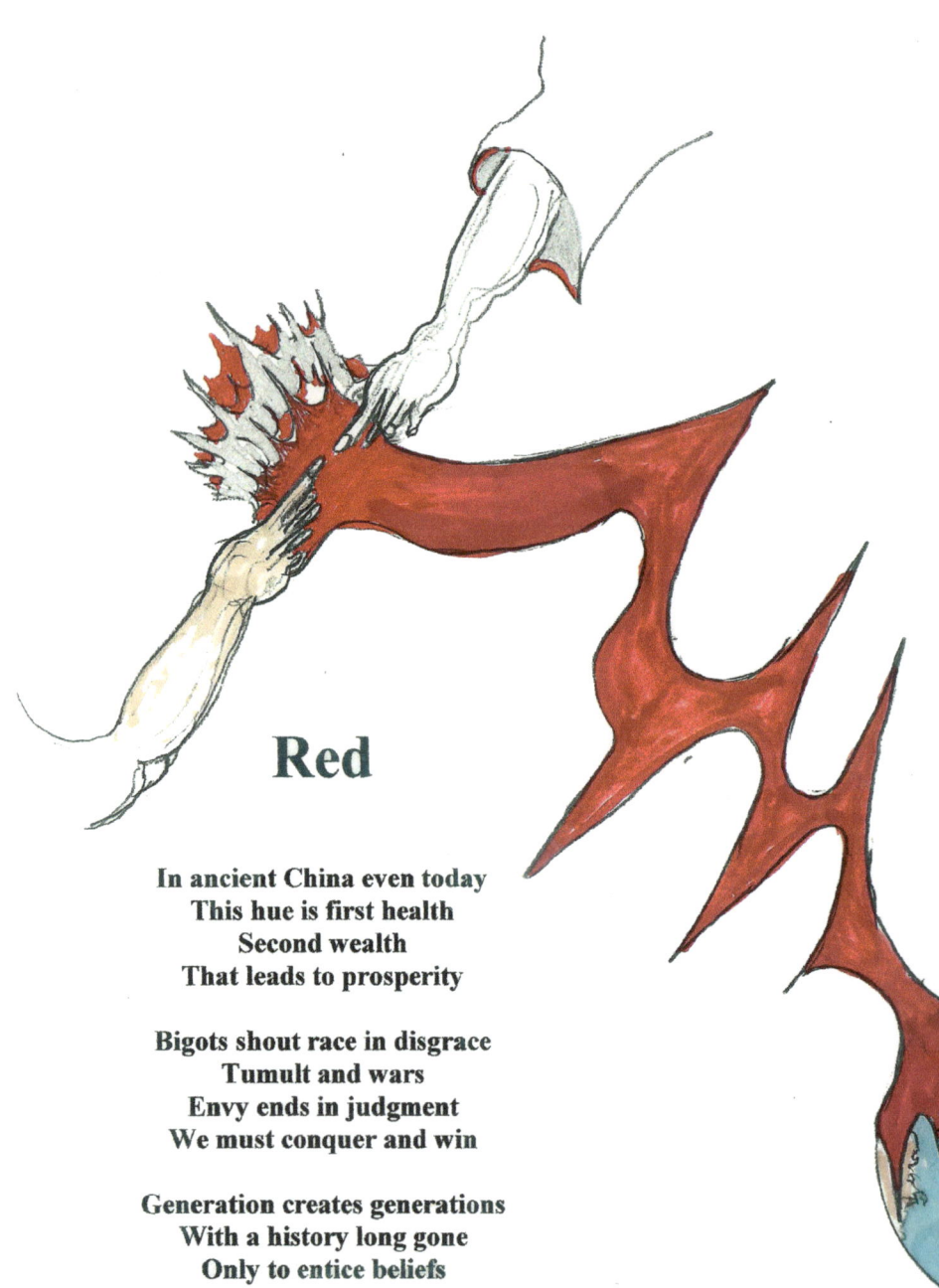

Red

In ancient China even today
This hue is first health
Second wealth
That leads to prosperity

Bigots shout race in disgrace
Tumult and wars
Envy ends in judgment
We must conquer and win

Generation creates generations
With a history long gone
Only to entice beliefs
That no longer belong

Boredom and wants
To take your land
Nations to expand
Or keep it safe

This the way the only one
I will convert you to know
My way of life
My beliefs are enhanced
Backward we go

All races of the globe
Books with different covers
Some thick some slim
Most to be read
We human that way

I give you a lifeline
The color is Red
By now your thinking
What does it mean

It flows in us all
Most creatures too
White black only skin
Or colors of the rainbow

The color that binds
For you and your world
When you can't understand
What is being said

Stop and contemplate
The smile on the human race
Dressed in glory in a different way
You have found a new friend

All nations are different
People and animals too
Fish in their kingdom
Creatures of the forest

Even your neighbors
Your community too
Your state and country
The oceans of the world

This is my tale
For you see
Blood is the color red
That is our lifeline
For peace on this
Earth

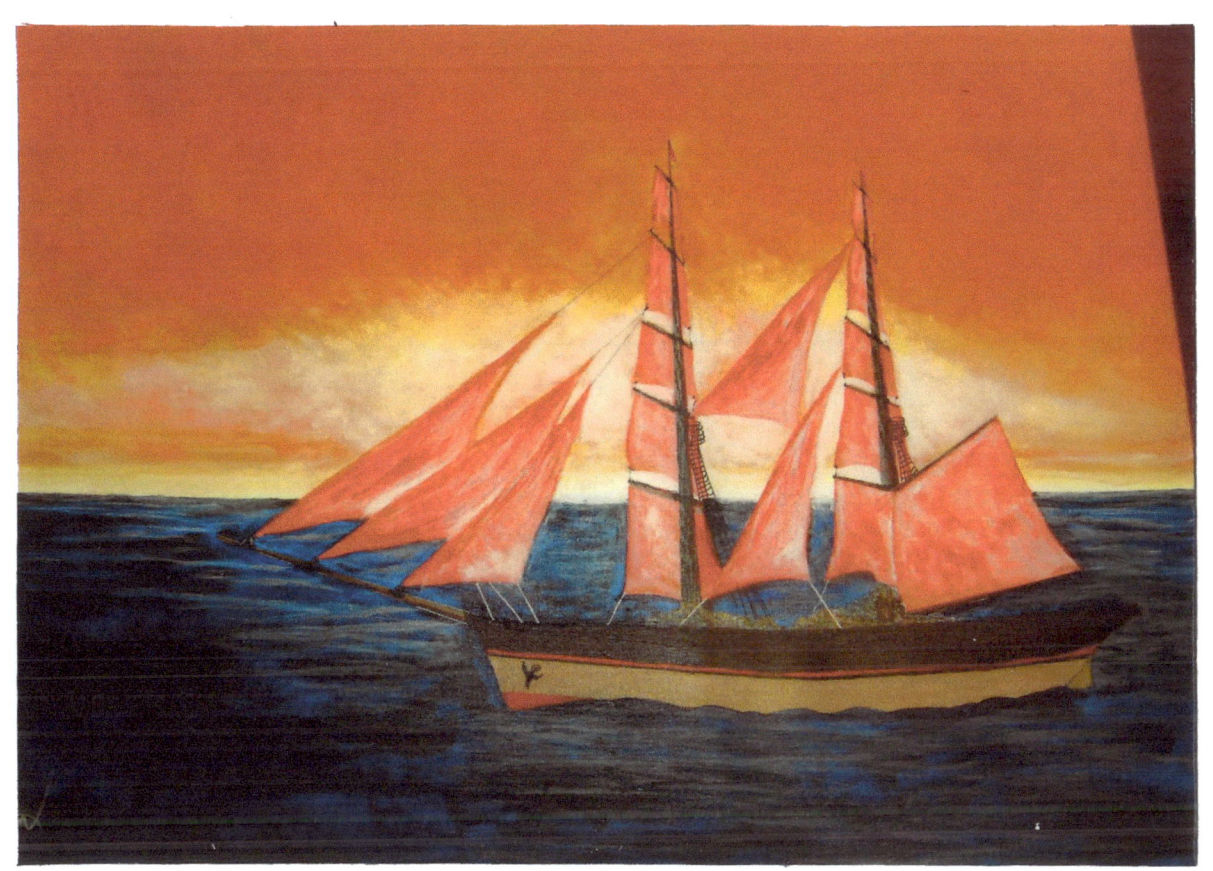

DEVINE LA FEMININ

Slick sailing ships
Beautiful brilliant and bright
Some are like "Man of Wars"
Sharks of the night
Others are like trade wind merchants
Benign quiet and nice
If you know the difference
Please tell me
All yearning to find a captain
To lead them to a
Safe harbor and port

short distance away
He committed for life
Till death do us part
The heavenly ship builders
Its time to build more ships
To send them down
To sail the sea of life
They mustered the angelic angels
And worked earthly day and night
By now you have discovered my plight
The committed captain did mingle

And to his surprise
Soon had a small armada
A captain no more
An admiral for his fleet
To lead them in the sea of life
Devinely La Feminin where can you be
I hope lost at sea
I am a captain of my soul
I am searching and if you find them
Don't tell me

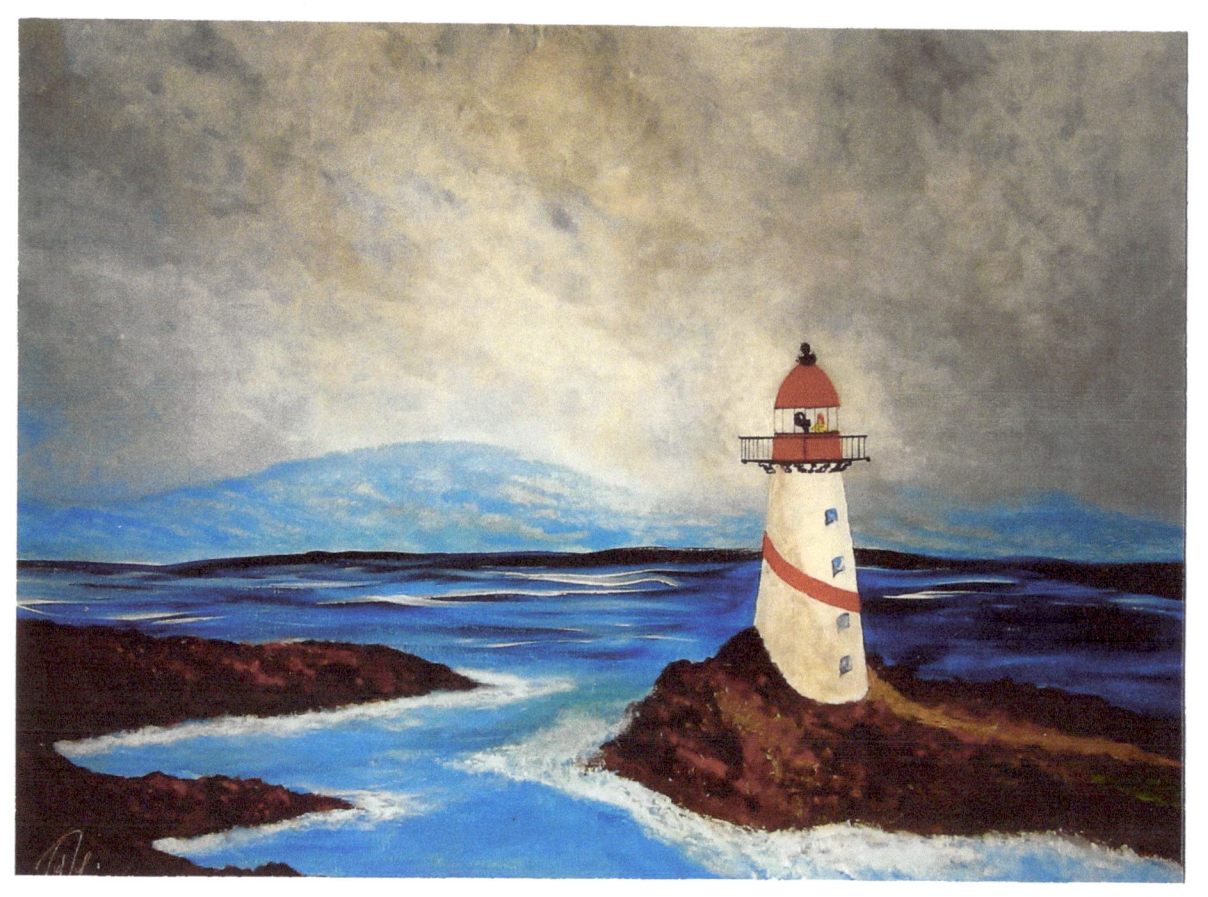

THE LIGHTHOUSE
ON BOARD A US NAVEL BATTLE SHIP SAILING AT FULL STEAM
THE CAPITAN WAS ON THE BRIDGE
WHEN A VOICE BROKE THE SILENCE
THIS IS RADAR AND WE ARE ON A COLISTION COURSE WITH ANOTHER VESSEL
RADIO THEM TO CHANGE THEIR COURSE
AYE AYE SIR
THIS IS RADAR AND THEY RECOMMEND YOU CHANGE YOUR COURSE.
WHY THE CAPTAIN ANSWERED
SIR THEY ARE A LIGHTHOUSE

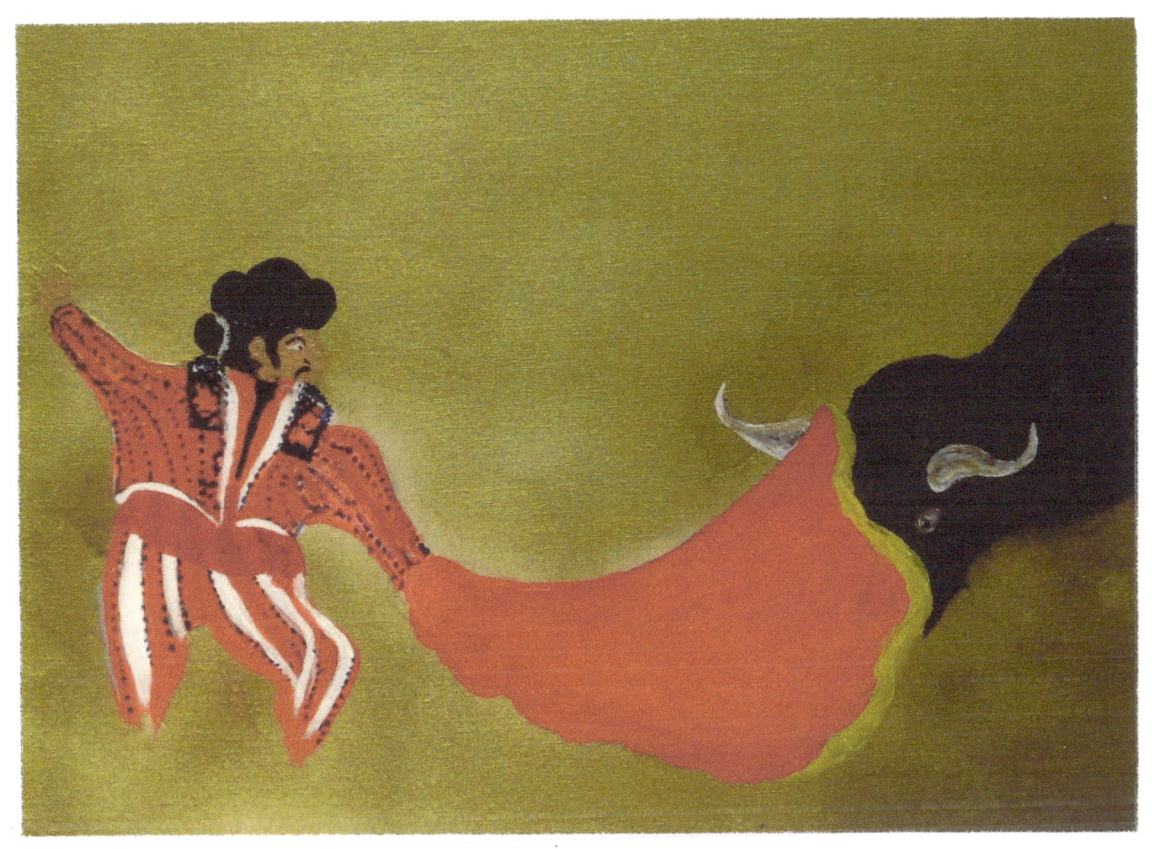

CORRIDA SPIRIT

WE WERE IN SEVILLA SPAIN CHECKING INTO A VERY ELEGANT HOTEL. EVERY ONE
THERE WAS VERY EXCITED. THEN WE SAW THE POSTER. THE ICON OF THE
MATADORS WAS RETIREING FROM THE CORRIDA AND TONIGHT WOULD BE HIS LAST
APPEARANCE. WE ASKED IF WE GET TICKETS THROGH THE HOTEL. THE DESK
CLERK REACHED IN HIS POCKET AND SCALPED US FOR THE TICKETS. OUR SEATS
WERE IN THE SHADE AND ALL THE PEOPLE WERE EXCITED. REMINDED ME OF A NFL
FOOTBALL GAME. WHAT A PERFORMANCE BY ICON MATADOR. I EXPERIENCED
A VERY DIFFERENT FEELING ABOUT BULL FIGHTING. MICHENER WAS RIGHT WHEN
HE DESCRIBED IT IN IBERIA. THE ICON MATADOR WAS AWARD EVERY TOKEN OF HIS
SUCCESS. HIS RECEPTION LATER WAS AT THE SAME HOTEL WE WERE AT. WE JOINED
THE PARTY AND DRANK CHAMPAGNE FREE. HE WAS A SMALL MAN BUT LOOKED
LIKE A GIANT IN THE RING. I WAS TALLER THEN HIM. THE LOVELY LADIES WERE
ALL OVER HIM. WHAT A WAY TO GO.

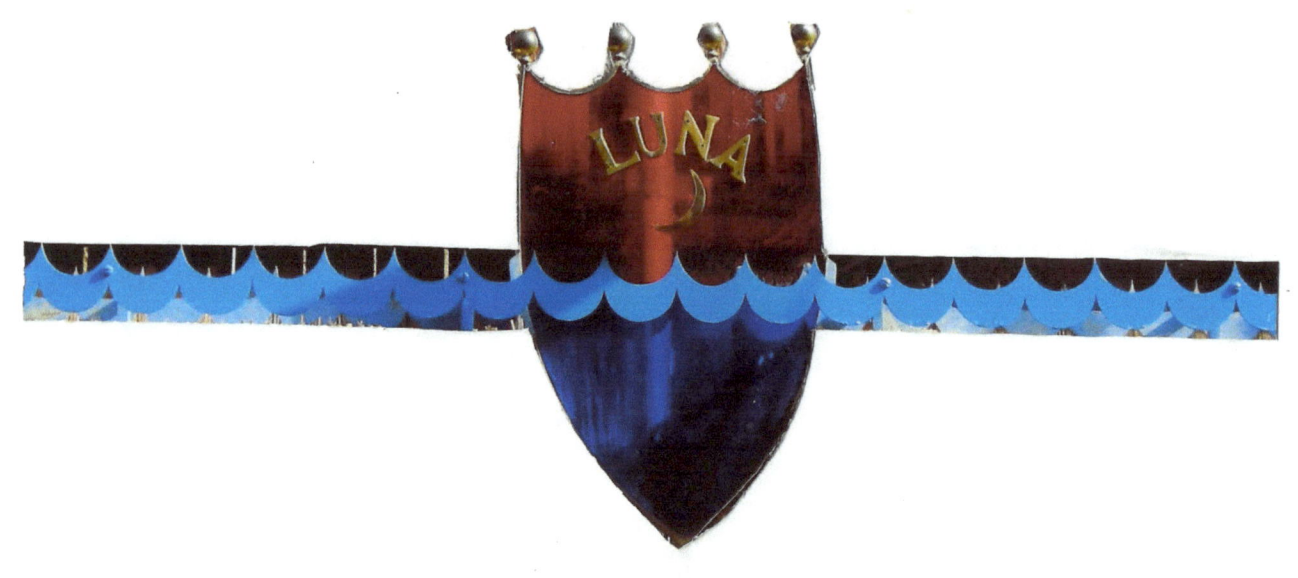

GENEALOGY

LUNA COAT OF ARMS MODIFIED BY ME. A SPANISH ADMIRAL WON A SEA BATTLE OVER THE MOORS HE WAS LATER GIVEN THE NAME DE LUNA. THE RED REPRSENTS THE BATTLE WITH THE CRESCENT MOON, THE BLUE IS THE MEDITERANEAN SEA. A WEALTHY CARDINAL IN SEVILLE SPAIN SENT HIS 3 SONS TO THE SPANISH LAND HOLDINGS WHICH IS NOW NEW MEXICO. ONE WENT TO TAOS, ONE WENT A FOUNDED LOS LUNAS, ONE WENT SOUTH EAST AND FOUNDED PEURTOS DE LUNA. JUST A FEW GENERATIONS AND INTER MARRIAGES GRAND FATHER SIRED SIX SONS. ONE WAS NAMED TIMOTHY LUNA (MY FATHER) LATER TO MARRY ALICE MONDRAGON. THEY LIVED IN SANTA FE ON GALISTEO STREET. WHERE PEGGY AND I WERE BORN. TIM WAS IN WW1 IN FRANCE AND HAD MUSTARD GAS BURNS ON HIS NECK. HE DIED AT 96 YEARS AND MOTHER DIED AT 92 YEARS.

I RETURNED TO SEVILLE SPAIN AND SPENT TIME AT THE CATHEDRAL AND THE LUNA CHAPEL. LOTS OF DE LUNAS ENTOMB THERE IN THE CHAPEL. I SOON MET THE HISTORIAN THAT HAD THE KEY TO THE ROOM OF RECORDS. WHEN WE ENTERED I WAS AMAZED AT THE PAINTINGS OF ALL OF THE POPES IN THEIR HISTORY. HE POINTED OUT THE PAINTING OF POPE DE LUNA. IT ALMOST MADE ME FAINT BECAUSE HE LOOKED LIKE ME. WHEN HE WAS A CARDINAL HE SENT HIS THREE SONS TO THE SPANISH LAND HOLDINGS NOW NM. MICHENER WROTE ABOUT HIM IN HIS BOOK IBERIA. HE STATED THAT THIS POPE WAS THE FIRST MECHANICAL MAN. EVEN DEAD THE CARDINALS MANIPULATED ARMS AND VOICE. THIS WENT ON UNTILL A NEW POPE WAS SELECTED. MY FAIR SKIN AND BLUE EYES ARE MY LINEAGE OF NOBILITY.

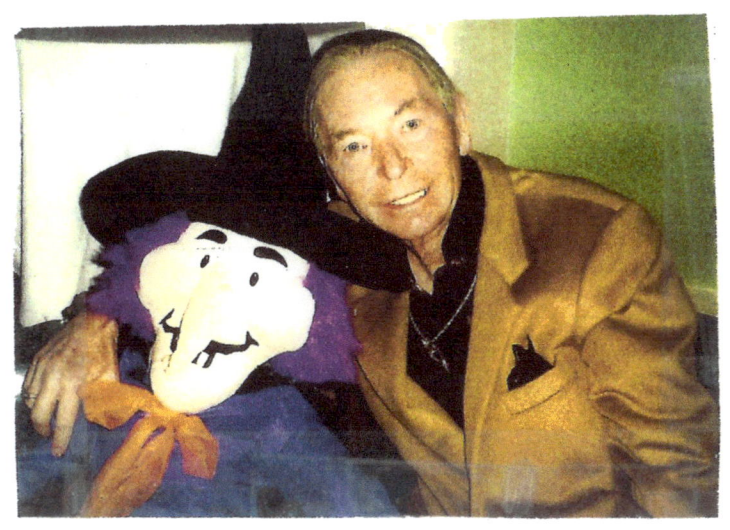

I have also served on many committees
Public and private. Traveled to many
Countries in the world. Not all, only
The ones I wanted to visit. My writings
Include both poetry and prose. Book
One "A View From the Moon" is
Finished and working on book two.
I realize that poetry can be frozen
In architecture as in the Vietnam
Veterans National Memorial at
Angel Fire which I conceived and
Designed. Of course there many
More throughout the South West.
Some of my paintings are in oil I
Did switch to acrylics and do just
As well.

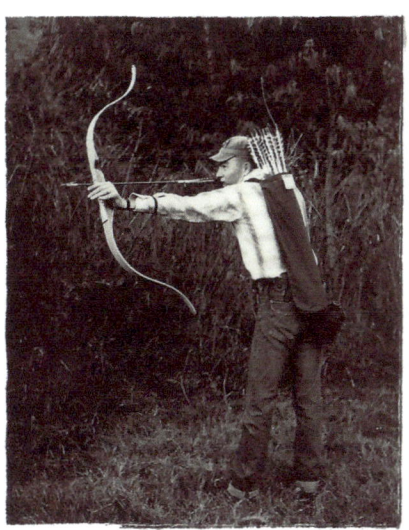

SYNOPTICAL CURRICULUM VITAE

My friends call me Ted and some say I am a
Renaissance man. Lost in time and space. Other
Say I should check into Painters, Writers, Golf,
Architecture, Photography, Art History, Travel,
Rehabilitation Centers. Of course I declined.
Way to much academic training. BFA in Arts,
BA Architecture at UNM. Raised in the wilds
Of Northern New Mexico in bygone old
Santa Fe. In the seventh grade the gift of art
Came to me because Jose Backos was teaching
Art at Harrington Junior High. He is one of
The original "5 Pintor's fathers of the arts".
I knew many of them, Will Shuster, etc. etc.
After a stint with US Naval Aviation I returned
To Santa Fe and started my love in the
Architectural profession but still doing my art
Work. I did work for many of the Architects
That are the grand fathers of the New Mexico
Architectural movement. I finally become one.
Starting at UNM I received many Academic
Awards as the years that followed many more
Honors and awards in architecture, professional
organizations, my buildings and paintings.

I DESIGNED THE FIRST BUILDINGS HERE IN THE STATE

THE NATIONAL MEMORIAL AT ANGLE FIRE
NO OTHER ARCHITECT HERE AS DONE
AN NATIONAL MEMORIAL

THE MANUAL LUJAN OFFICE BUILDING
84,000 SQUARE FEET
ONE HUNDRED % POURED IN PLACE CONCRETE
THE COST $2,000,1000.00 SHOULD HAVE BEEN
NAMED THE BRUCE KING BLDG.

THE FIRST PASSIVE SOLAR ELEMENTARY SCHOOL
EL DORADO ELEMENTARY

INTREGRATED USE OF SOLAR PANELS
IN RESIDENTIAL DESIGN
AND A FEW OTHERS
THROUGH OUT THE
SOUTHWEST

TED C. LUNA
ARCHITECT-PLANNER-ARTIST
1500 DONETTE PLACE, NE
ALBUQUERQUE, NEW MEXICO 87112
TEL: 505-299-2946
E-MAIL: T2011LUNA@GMAIL.COM

EDUCATION AND REGISTRATIONS
EXTENSIVE TRAINING U.S. NAVAL AVIATION
COLLEGE OF SANTA FE, 1960
UNIVERSITY OF NEW MEXICO, BACHELOR OF FINE ARTS, PAINTING, 1965
UNIVERSITY OF NEW MEXICO, BACHELOR OF ARCHITECTURE, ARCHITECTURE AND PLANNING, 1966
CORPORATE MEMBER, AMERICAN INSTITUTE OF ARCHITECTS, 1968
STATE OF NEW MEXICO, REGISTRATION NUMBER 412, 1967
STATE OF COLORADO, REGISTRATION NUMBER C-1013, 1972
STATE OF ARIZONA, REGISTRATION NUMBER 20183, 1986
STATE OF CALIFORNIA, REGISTRATION NUMBER C-18618, 1985
NATIONAL COUNCIL OF ARCHITECTURAL, REGISTRATION BOARDS NUMBER 30394, 1984

EXPERIENCE
UNITED STATES NAVAL AVIATION, 1958
W.C. KRUGER, ARCHITECTS-ENGINEERS, 1959
WOLGAMOOD AND MILLINGTON, ARCHITECTS, 1961
E.S. BRANDON, STRUCTURAL ENGINEERING, 1961
LOUIS WALKER, ARCHITECT, 1962
W.W. ELLISON, ARCHITECT, 1962
NEUNER AND CABINESS, ARCHITECTS-ENGINEERS, 1964
GEORGE WRIGHT, ARCHITECTS-ENGINEERS, 1965
ROWLAND AND ASSOCIATES, ARCHITECTS, 1966
URBAN WEIDNER, ARCHITECTS, 1967
TED LUNA ASSOCIATES, ARCHITECTS, 1967
LUNA-ROSS AND ASSOCIATES, ARCHITECTS, 1975
LUNA ASSOCIATES, ARCHITECTS, 1985
ARCH-CADIAN GROUP, ARCHITECT-PLANNERS, 1988
SEVERAL ARIZONA AND CALIFORNIA DESIGN FIRMS AS SPECIAL DESIGN CONSULTANT
SAN DIEGO, LA JOLLA, PHOENIX, SCOTTSDALE, THROUGH 1989
TED "C" LUNA, ARCHITECT-PLANNER, NCARB CERTIFIED THROUGH 1999
ANGEL FIRE ARCHITECTS & PLANNERS 2000 –
TED "C" LUNA, AIA ARCHITECT –PLANNER 2002

ACADEMIC AWARDS
1963 OUTSTANDING ART AND PAINTING DISPLAY
1964 UNM ARCHITECTURAL OUTSTANDING DESIGN STUDENT
1965 NATIONAL AWARD REYNOLDS DESIGN COMPETITION
1965 URBAN DEVELOPMENT PLANNING DESIGN COMPETION
1965 OUSTANDING ARTS DISPLAY OLD TOWN ALBUQUERQUE

TRAVEL
UNITED STATES, ALASKA, HAWAII MIDWAY ISLAND, BAHAMAS
MEXICO, WEST INDIES, CARIBBEAN ISLANDS, ENGLAND, BELGIUM,
GERMANY, FRANCE, AUSTRIA, ITALY, FRANCE, GREECE, CHINA, JAPAN
THAILAND

PROFESSIONAL • COMMUNITY • BUSINESS
TED C. LUNA, AIA, ARCHITECT-PLANNER
THE ARCH-CADAIN GROUP PRESIDENT, LUNA ASSOCIATES PRESIDENT
LMT CORPORATION PRESIDENT, AIA SANTA FE CHAPTER, PAST PRESIDENT
N.M. SOCIETY OF ARCHITECTS, PAST DIRECTOR, SANTA FE JAYCEES, PAST DIRECTOR
CITIZENS ADVISORY BOARD, CITY OF SANTA FE, KIWANIS INTERNATIONAL
CHAMBER OF COMMERCE SANTA FE, CHAMBER OF COMMERCE SCOTTSDALE
LA TIERRA ASSOCIATION, PAST CHAIRMAN, MUSEUM OF NEW MEXICO CONSULTANT
SANTA FE COUNTRY CLUB, PAST DIRECTOR, SOCIETY FOR THE ARTS, PAST CHAIRMAN
SCOTTSDALE SYMPHONY, PAST CHAIRMAN, CANCER SOCIETY SCOTTSDALE MEMBER
LISTED IN WHO'S WHO, LISTED PERSONALITIES OF THE WEST
CHAMBER OF COMMERCE ANGEL FIRE, ROTARY INTERNATIONAL ANGEL FIRE, CHARTER MEMBER
EOC DAVID WESTPHALL VETERANS FOUNDATION, ANGEL FIRE
CHAIRMAN STATE OF NEVADA AIA DESIGN AWARDS

HONORS AND AWARDS
N.M. SOCIETY OF ARCHITECTS, JEMEZ STATE MONUMENT, HISTORICAL DOCUMENTATION, 1979
(HIGHEST HONOR), U.N.M. STUDENT AWARD PROGRAM, RESIDENTIAL, LUNA HOME LA TIERRA, 1979
N.M. SOCIETY OF ARCHITECTS, EL DORADO ELEMENTARY SCHOOL, 1980
NATIONAL HONOR AWARD, AMERICAN ASSOCIATION OF SCHOOL ADMINISTRATORS,
EL DORADO ELEMENTARY, HIGHEST AWARD, 1980
RESEARCH GRANT AWARD, N.M. STATE UNIVERSITY FOR SOLAR ENERGY, 1980
HONORARIUM, UNIVERSITY OF NEW MEXICO, GRADUATE STUDENT STUDIES, 1981
NATIONAL COUNCIL OF ARCHITECTURAL REGISTRATION, PROFESSIONAL JURY SELECTION, 1981
NATIONAL COUNCIL OF ARCHITECTURAL REGISTRATION, PROFESSIONAL JURY SELECTION, 1984
ARIZONA STATE SOCIETY OF ARCHITECTS, AWARDS PROGRAM, JURY MEMBER, 1982
DAV VIETNAM VETERANS NATIONAL AWARD, 1991

INTERESTS
GOLF, TENNIS, HORSES, SAILING, SKIING, FISHING
CAMPING, ART, WRITING, PHOTOGRAPHY

ART
RECOGNIZED PAINTER WORKS IN PRIVATE COLLECTIONS
THROUGHOUT THE UNITED STATES
CITI CORP, PHOENIX ARIZONA CORPORATE
LIFE TIME PHOTOGRAPHY OF NORTHERN NEW MEXICO
TIN ROOF STRUCTURES

Curriculum Vitae

RELIGION

MY VIEW

I STUDIED THE WORLDS RECORDED RELIGIONS AT THE UNIVERSITY. ALL RELIGIONS ARE MAN MADE. THERE ARE GOOD, BAD AND EVIL AND INBETWEEN. IT IS A SOURCE OF POWER TO A FEW LEADERS THAT WANT MONEY. THEY CONTROL THE MASSES. THE TOOLS ARE SIMPLE. YOU CAN GO TO HEAVEN OR HELL UNLESS YOU BELIEVE IN THIS RELIGION AND ITS TEACHINGS. YES THERE IS A HEAVEN AND HELL. WE LIVE IT IN OUR DAILY LIVES, MOST OF THE TIME WE ARE NEVER THERE. THESE TWO PLACES EXIST ONLY IN OUR WORLD, NO WHERE ELSE. DUST TO DUST, ITS MORE LIKE LUST TO DUST. IF YOU CONSIDER YOUR BODY AS A CAR. WHEN IT GETS TOTALED ITS SENT TO THE WRECKING WITH ALL OF THE OTHERS. I CALL THEM CEMETERYS. YOU RETURN TO DUST WHEN YOU ARE CREMATED. STEPHANIE DESCRIBES US BEST " WE ARE STAR DUST MIXED WITH THE WATER AND SALT OF THE OCEAN." IF THE SOUL EXISTS IT MUST COME FROM THE OCEAN. I THINK THE SPIRIT DOES EXIST AND IT'S A GIFT FROM THE UNIVERSE. AND IF YOU LOOK YOU CAN SEE IT DAILY IN ALL BEINGS.

LEGACY

THERE ARE MANY FORMS OF LEGACY. FROM MONEY TO HEIRS. BUSINESSES, ACTORS AND ACTRESS AND AUTHORS. THE LIST NEVER ENDS. MY GRANDFATHER GRAVE WAS JUST STONE IN A PILE AND WE NEVER FOUND MY GRANDMOTHERS GRAVE. NO WRITTEN LEGACY OF THEIR LIFES. THEY DID PASS THEIR GENES ONTO ME. I HAVE DOCUEMENTED MY LIFE IN THIS BOOK SO THAT FAMILY AND FRIENDS AND MOST OF ALL THE FUTURE GENERATIONS WOULD HAVE KNOWLEDGE OF THEIR GREAT AND GREAT AND GREAT GRANDFATHER. I AM STILL TRYING TO HAVE AN INTERESTING LIFE.

SET TO MUSIC
FARE THEE WELL
FOR I MUST LEAVE THEE
DO NOT LEFT THE PARTING GREIVE THEE
REMEMBER THAT THE
BEST OF FRIENDS MUST PART

SOME OF THE PAINTINGS ARE AVAILABLE
CONTACT ME

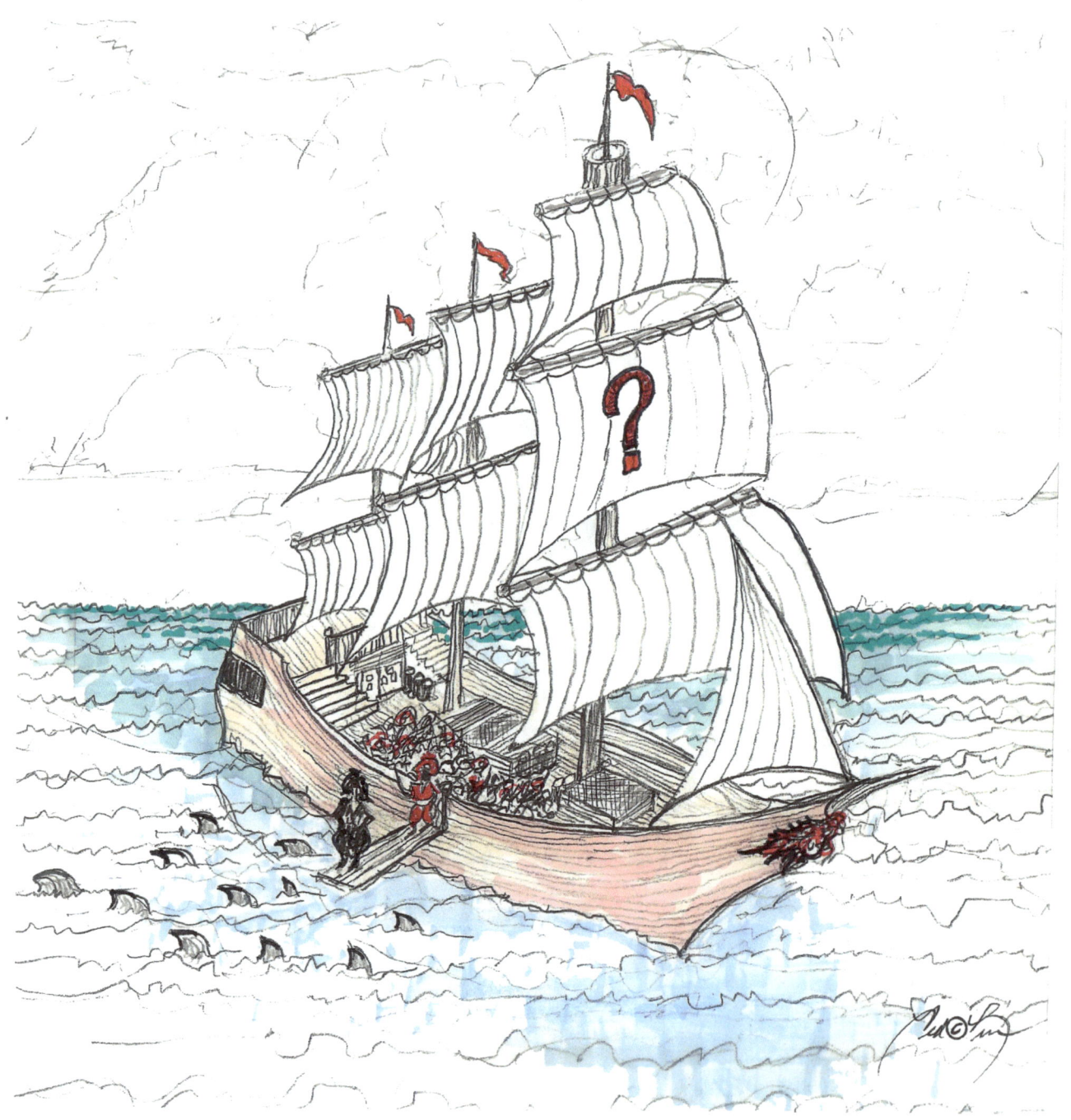

FARE THEE WELL

Ancient mariners wish
A parting thought
Of good will
Never ending till
We meet again
May the wind fill your sails
And the gentle waves be kind
For a fair voyage
For you and your ship
Till you rest in your port
This journey done
Rest not sailor
For the sea becomes
Me

Good Bye or Bye
Final as an English lance
As it goes through your pants
Not till we meet again
Nor a wish to see you
Never to wish you love
Or have a great life
Well used on the departed
Just for the living to hear
Passage to the universe
Is a silent trip you see

But what can we say
That will convey our thoughts
And hope you well
And I will see you again someday
For I love you
As you love me
We will meet again
A sincere hug gentle kiss
Now you have the secret
Of the ancient wish
"Fair Thee Well"